Complete MathSmart

Revised and Updated!

Grade
1

ISBN: 978-1-897164-11-2

 Contents

ISBN: 978-1-897164-11-2

Section IV

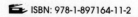 ISBN: 978-1-897164-11-2

Overview

In this section, Grade 1 students are provided with practice in comparing, sorting and ordering objects according to one attribute such as size, height, width and weight.

They will be colouring and copying objects as well as copying or choosing between words that describe objects, such as heavier/lighter and biggest/smallest. Minimal reading and writing skills are required.

Parents can enrich children's learning by providing them with real objects or drawings for comparing, sorting and ordering, to help arouse and sustain their interest in exploring and learning mathematics.

Comparing Heights and Lengths

1

Colour the longer sausage.

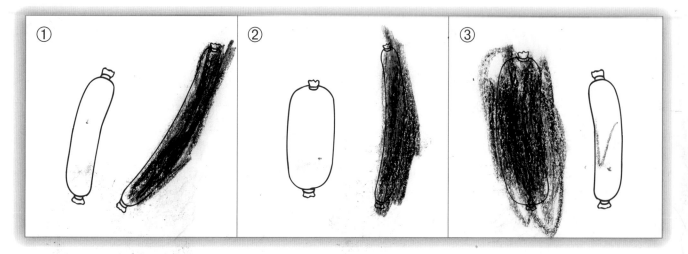

Colour the shortest pencil.

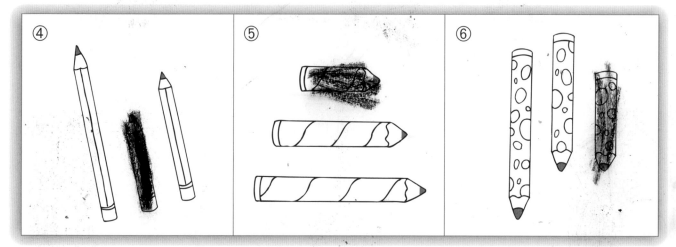

Draw a similar object which is longer than the one shown.

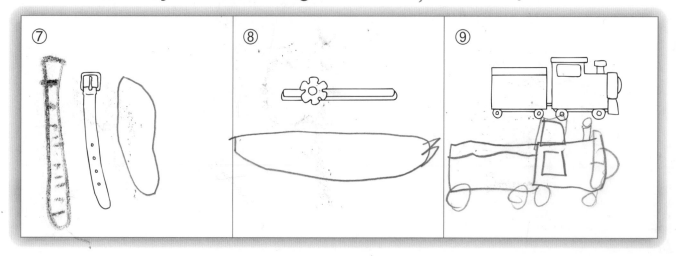

ISBN: 978-1-897164-11-2

Draw a line which is as long as the one given.

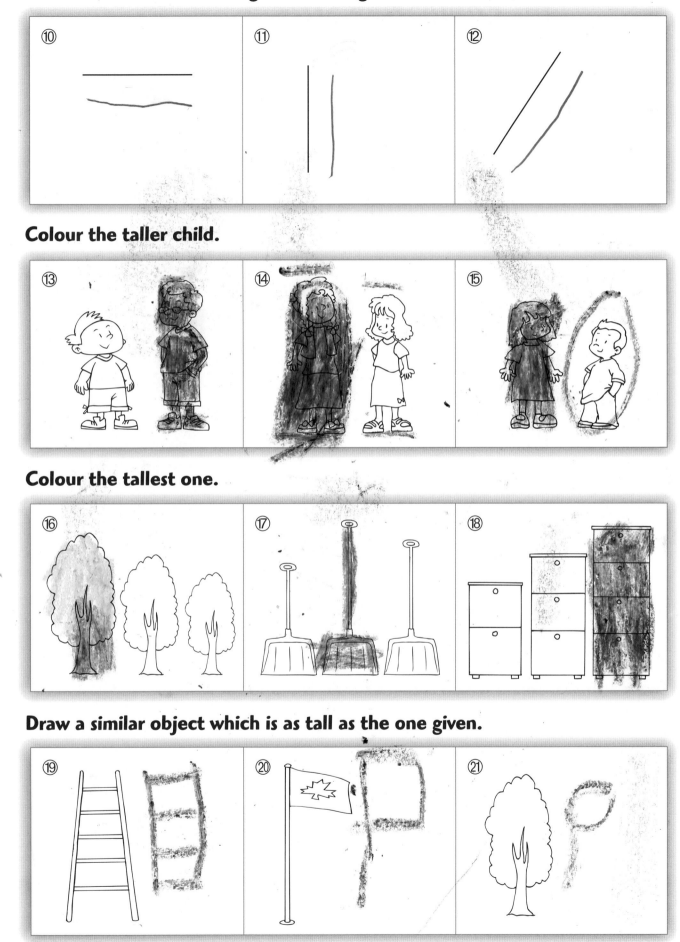

Colour the taller child.

Colour the tallest one.

Draw a similar object which is as tall as the one given.

ISBN: 978-1-897164-11-2

Comparing Sizes

Circle the smaller object.

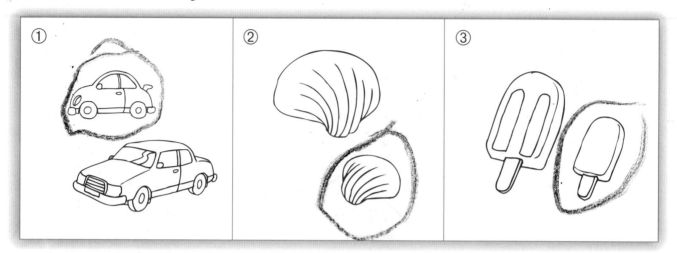

Circle the bigger animal.

Draw a similar shape which is bigger than the one shown.

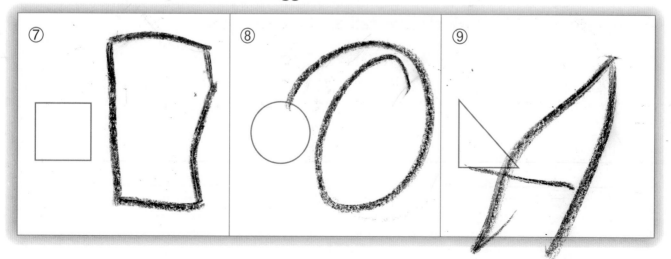

   ISBN: 978-1-897164-11-2

Colour the container which holds more juice.

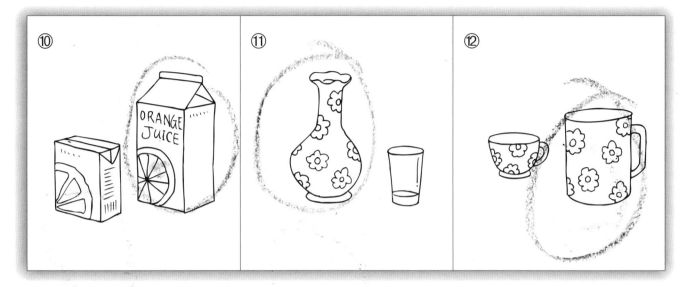

Draw a similar snack which is smaller than the one shown.

Colour the biggest fruit.

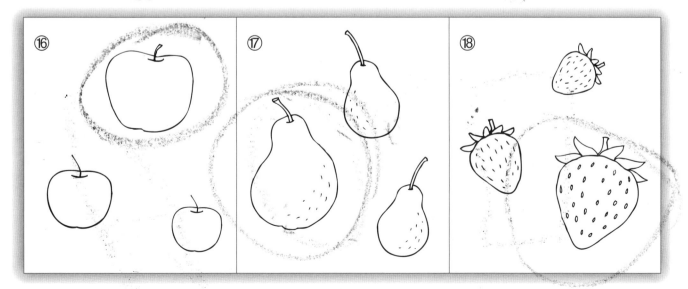

ISBN: 978-1-897164-11-2

COMPLETE MATHSMART (GRADE 1)

Colour the smallest animal.

Colour the container with the least water.

Draw lines to join the bears to their chairs.

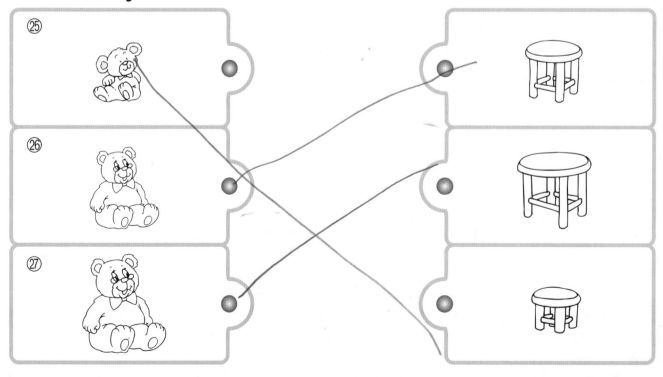

ISBN: 978-1-897164-11-2

Circle the correct word in each sentence.

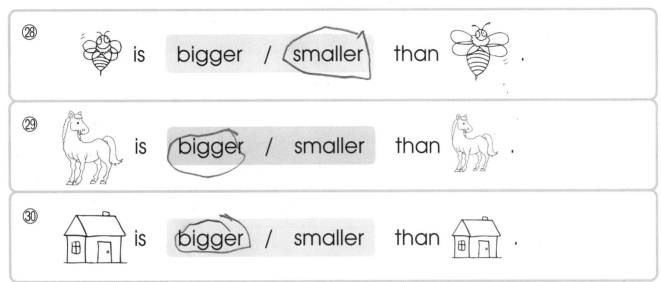

㉘ 🐝 is **bigger** / (smaller) than 🐝 .

㉙ 🐴 is (bigger) / **smaller** than 🐴 .

㉚ 🏠 is (bigger) / **smaller** than 🏠 .

Look at the gift boxes. Circle the correct word in each sentence.

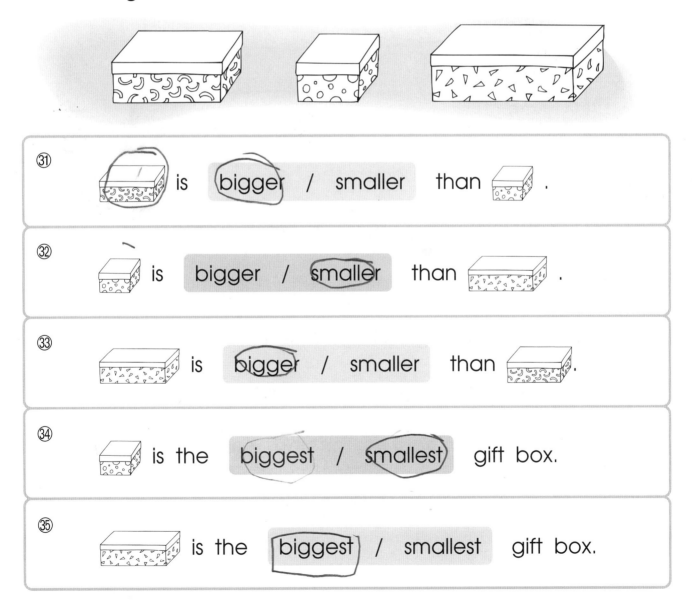

㉛ is (bigger) / smaller than .

㉜ is bigger / (smaller) than .

㉝ is (bigger) / smaller than .

㉞ is the biggest / (smallest) gift box.

㉟ is the (biggest) / smallest gift box.

ISBN: 978-1-897164-11-2

Comparing Positions

Circle the correct words.

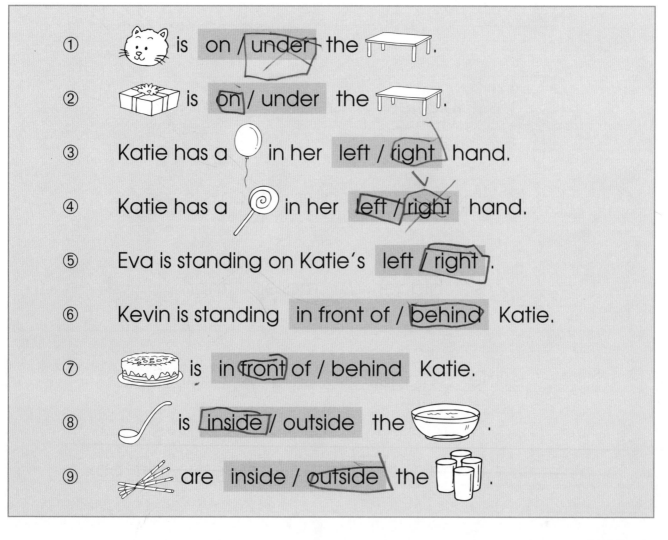

① is on /(under) the ⬜.

② is (on)/ under the ⬜.

③ Katie has a 🎈 in her left /(right) hand.

④ Katie has a 🍭 in her (left)/ right hand.

⑤ Eva is standing on Katie's left /(right).

⑥ Kevin is standing in front of /(behind) Katie.

⑦ 🎂 is in (front) of / behind Katie.

⑧ is (inside)/ outside the 🥣.

⑨ are inside /(outside) the 🥤.

ISBN: 978-1-897164-11-2

Write 'left' or 'right' to complete each sentence.

⑩  holds the  with her right hand.

⑪ 's leash is in 's left hand.

⑫ The  are on 's right.

⑬  is on 's right.

Write 'in front of' or 'behind' to complete each sentence.

⑭ There is a  standing ________ the .

⑮ There are some  standing ________ the .

⑯ The  is standing ________ the .

Write 'over' or 'under' to complete each sentence.

⑰ The  is jumping ________ the 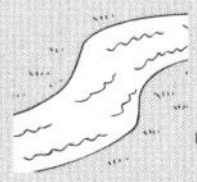.

⑱ The  is standing ________ the .

⑲ The  is flying ________ the .

⑳ Two  are ________ the .

ISBN: 978-1-897164-11-2

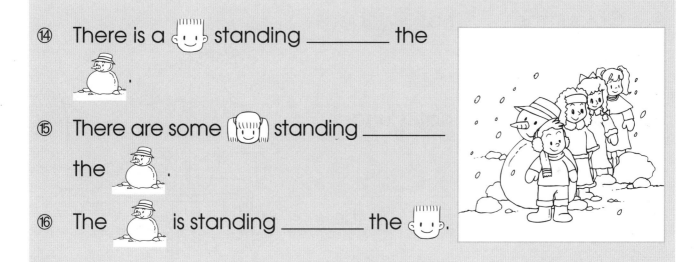

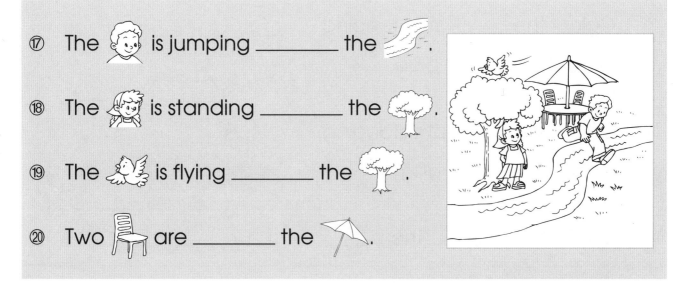

Colour the pictures. Then write the correct words.

㉑ Colour the 🧸 that is inside the 📦 brown.

㉒ Colour the 🪆 that is outside the 📦 green.

㉓ 🤖 is _____ the box.

㉔ Colour the 👦 that is under the ☂ yellow.

㉕ Colour the 🧰 that is under the 🪑 red.

㉖ The 🐦 is flying _____ the ☂.

㉗ Colour the 👦 that is standing in front of the 🌳 blue.

㉘ Colour the 👧 that is standing behind the 🌳 orange.

㉙ The 🐶 is _____ the 🐱.

ISBN: 978-1-897164-11-2

Draw the pictures.

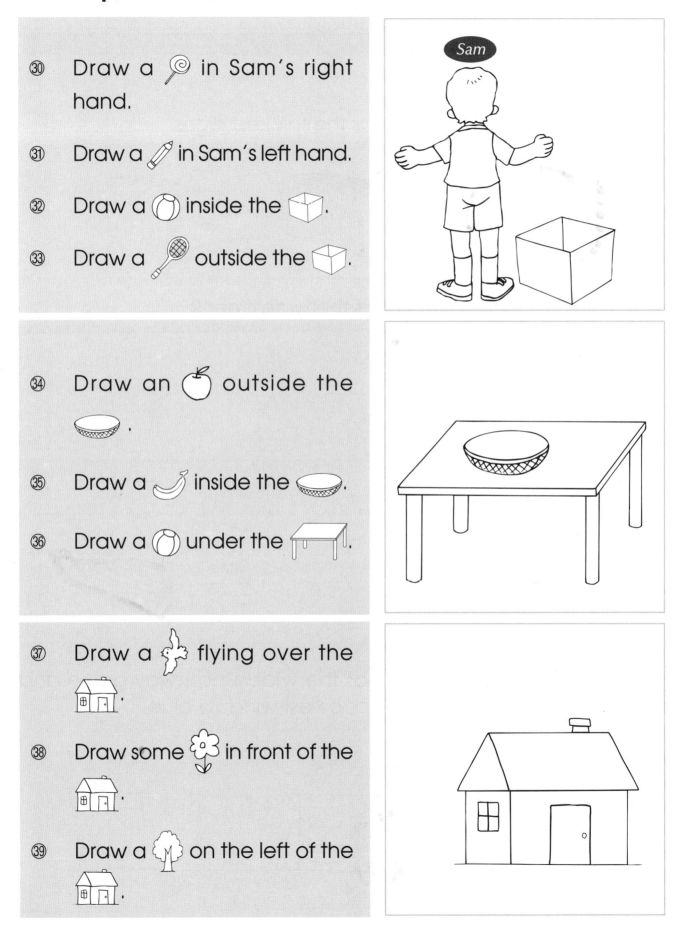

30 Draw a 🍭 in Sam's right hand.

31 Draw a ✏️ in Sam's left hand.

32 Draw a ⚾ inside the ☐.

33 Draw a 🏸 outside the ☐.

34 Draw an 🍎 outside the ◡.

35 Draw a 🍌 inside the ◡.

36 Draw a ⚾ under the 🪑.

37 Draw a 🕊️ flying over the 🏠.

38 Draw some 🌸 in front of the 🏠.

39 Draw a 🌳 on the left of the 🏠.

ISBN: 978-1-897164-11-2

4 Comparing Shapes and Weights

Colour the correct answers.

① Colour the bread which has the thickest slices.

② Colour the bottle which has the widest neck.

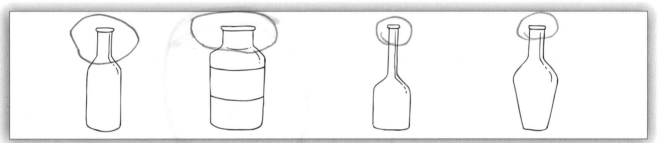

③ Colour the sharpest pencil.

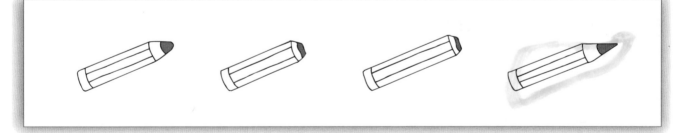

④ Colour the house which has the widest pathway green and the house which has the narrowest window blue.

ISBN: 978-1-897164-11-2

⑤ Colour the thing which is flat.

⑥ Colour the thing which is hollow.

⑦ Colour the thinnest book.

⑧ Colour the widest shape.

⑨ Colour the heaviest fruit.

⑩ Colour the lightest stationery.

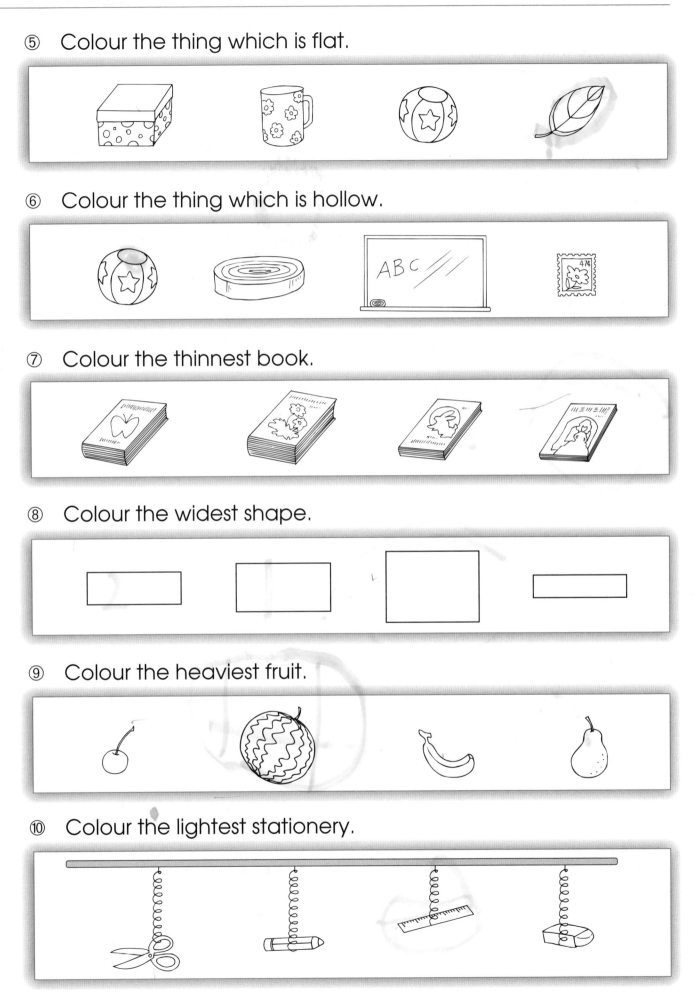

ISBN: 978-1-897164-11-2

Colour the heavier box.

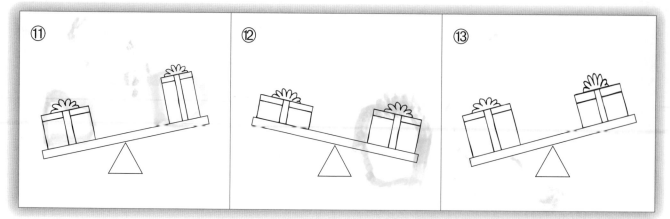

Check ✔ the correct balances.

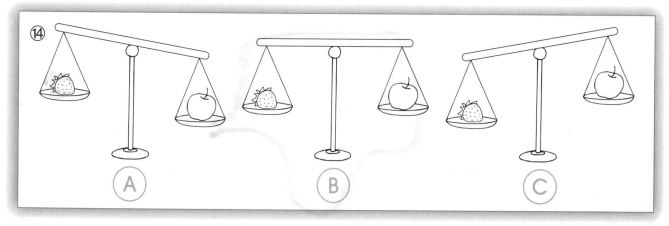

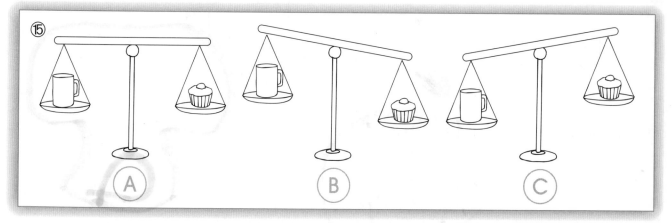

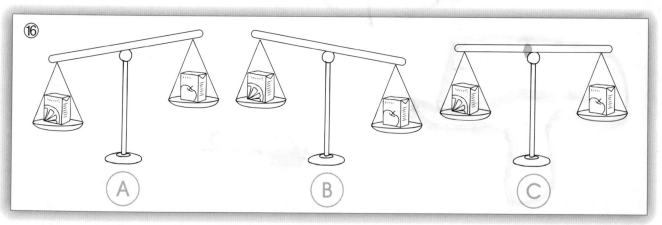

ISBN: 978-1-897164-11-2

Look at the balances. Draw a picture to complete each sentence.

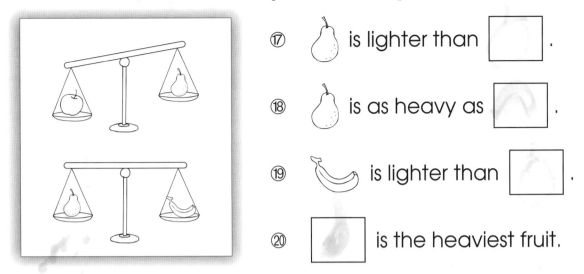

⑰ 🍐 is lighter than ☐ .

⑱ 🍐 is as heavy as ☐ .

⑲ 🍌 is lighter than ☐ .

⑳ ☐ is the heaviest fruit.

Look at the pictures. Circle the correct word in each sentence.

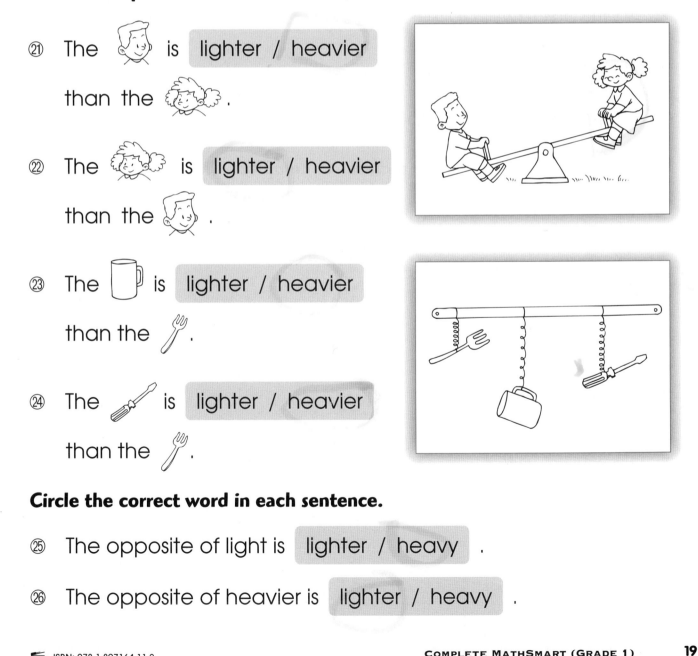

㉑ The 👦 is lighter / heavier than the 👧 .

㉒ The 👧 is lighter / heavier than the 👦 .

㉓ The 🍵 is lighter / heavier than the 🍴 .

㉔ The 🔧 is lighter / heavier than the 🍴 .

Circle the correct word in each sentence.

㉕ The opposite of light is lighter / heavy .

㉖ The opposite of heavier is lighter / heavy .

ISBN: 978-1-897164-11-2

5 Matching and Arranging Objects

Write the correct word to complete each sentence.

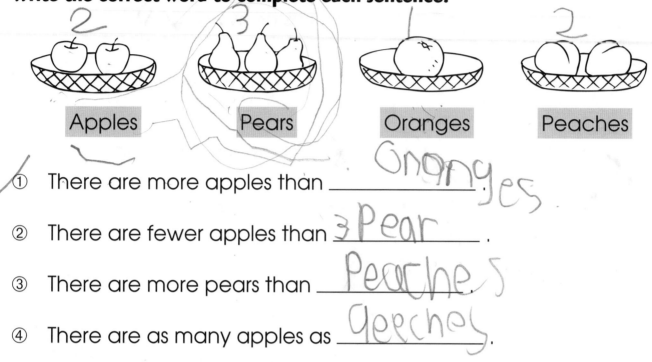

Apples   Pears   Oranges   Peaches

① There are more apples than ___Oranges___

② There are fewer apples than ___3 Pear___ .

③ There are more pears than ___Peaches___ .

④ There are as many apples as ___qeeches___ .

Look at the stickers. Draw the pictures to complete the sentences.

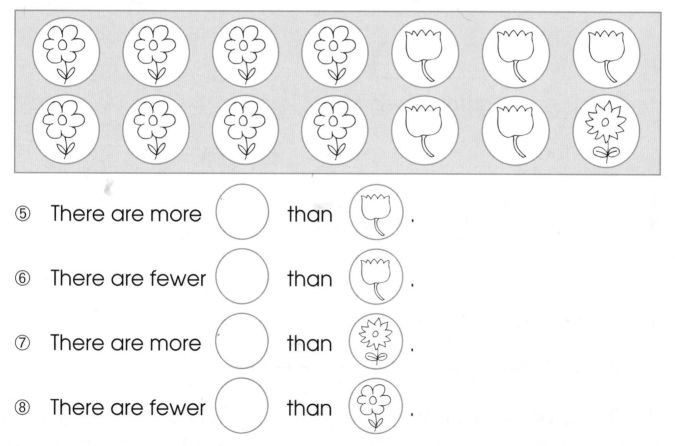

⑤ There are more ◯ than 🌷 .

⑥ There are fewer ◯ than 🌷 .

⑦ There are more ◯ than 🌼 .

⑧ There are fewer ◯ than 🌸 .

ISBN: 978-1-897164-11-2

Look at the pictures. Put a check mark ✔ in the correct circle to complete each sentence.

⑨ There are more 🔨 than ◯ ⭐   ◯ 🪣   ◯ 🐚 .

⑩ There are fewer 🪣 than ◯ ⭐   ◯ 🔨   ◯ 🐚 .

⑪ If Joe takes 1 🔨 away, there are as many 🔨 as

◯ ⭐   ◯ 🔨   ◯ 🐚 .

Look at Joe's balloons. Circle the correct word to complete each sentence.

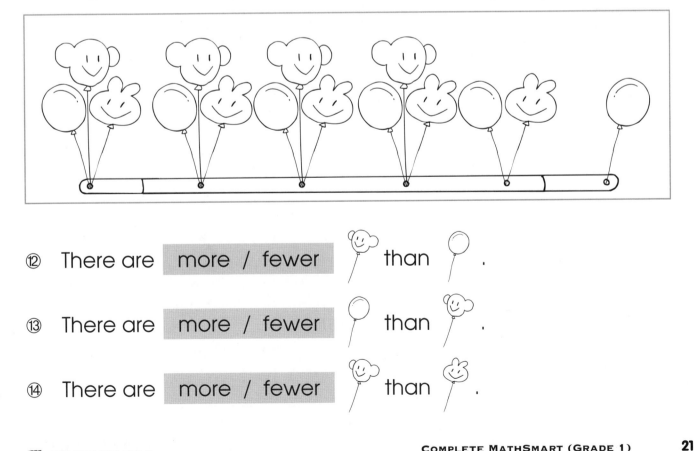

⑫ There are   more / fewer   🎈 than 🎈 .

⑬ There are   more / fewer   🎈 than 🎈 .

⑭ There are   more / fewer   🎈 than 🎈 .

Put each group in order. Write the letters only.

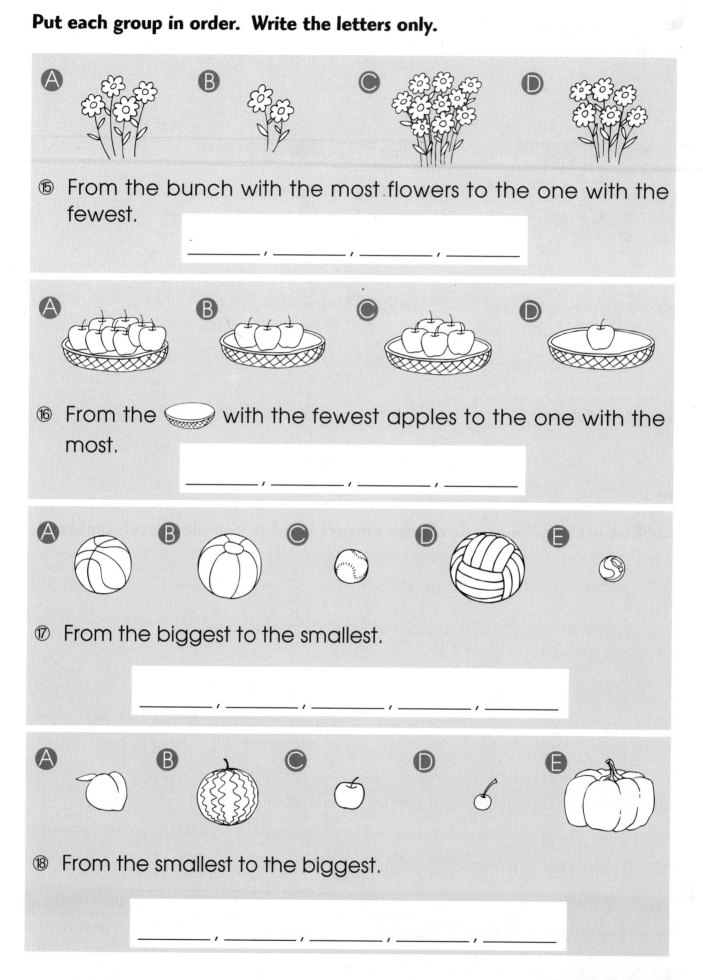

⑮ From the bunch with the most flowers to the one with the fewest.

_____ , _____ , _____ , _____

⑯ From the 🥣 with the fewest apples to the one with the most.

_____ , _____ , _____ , _____

⑰ From the biggest to the smallest.

_____ , _____ , _____ , _____ , _____

⑱ From the smallest to the biggest.

_____ , _____ , _____ , _____ , _____

ISBN: 978-1-897164-11-2

Look at Jill's cookies. Circle the correct word or letter to complete each sentence. Then draw the pictures.

Ⓐ   Ⓑ   Ⓒ

⑲ Cookie A is   smaller / **bigger**   than cookie C.

⑳ Cookie B is   smaller / bigger   than cookie A.

㉑ Cookie   A / **B** / C   is the biggest.

㉒ Cookie   A / B / **C**   is the smallest.

㉓ Put the cookies in order from the biggest to the smallest.

_____ , _____ , _____

㉔ Draw a cookie that is bigger than cookie B and with more chocolate chips on top.

㉕ Draw a cookie that is smaller than cookie A and with fewer chocolate chips on top.

ISBN: 978-1-897164-11-2

Colour the things. Then write the letters to put them in order.

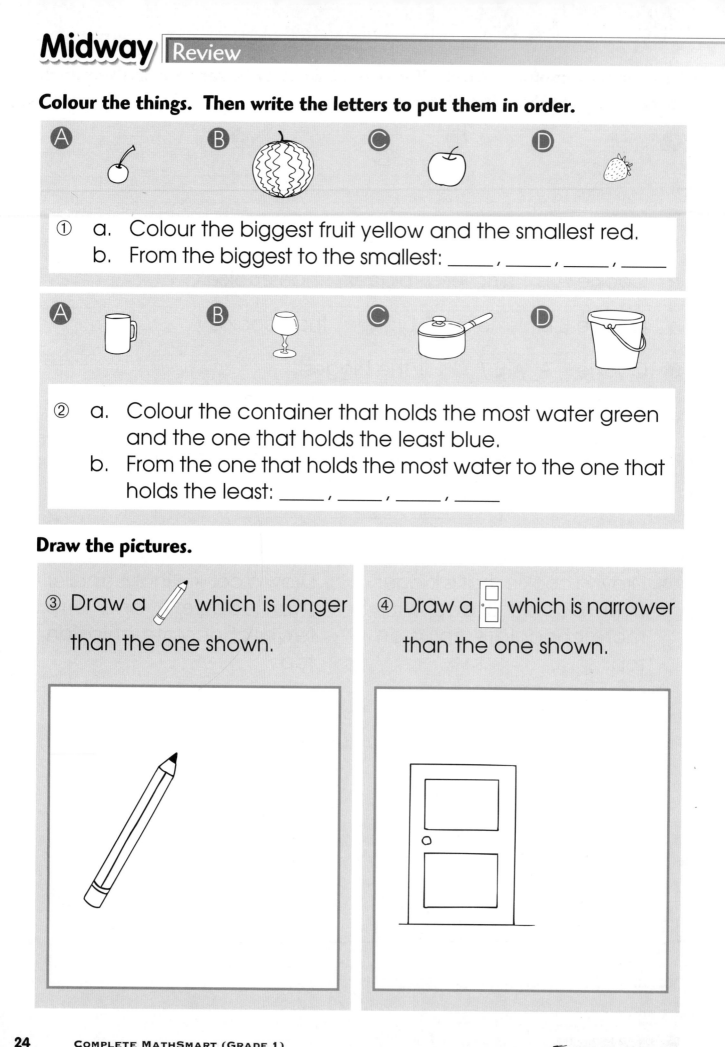

Ⓐ   Ⓑ   Ⓒ   Ⓓ

① a. Colour the biggest fruit yellow and the smallest red.

b. From the biggest to the smallest: _____ , _____ , _____ , _____

Ⓐ   Ⓑ   Ⓒ   Ⓓ

② a. Colour the container that holds the most water green and the one that holds the least blue.

b. From the one that holds the most water to the one that holds the least: _____ , _____ , _____ , _____

Draw the pictures.

③ Draw a ✏ which is longer than the one shown.

④ Draw a 🚪 which is narrower than the one shown.

⑤ Draw a  which is taller than the one shown.

⑥ Draw a which is thinner than the one shown.

Circle the correct words.

⑦ Jack is standing   in front of / behind   Lucy.

⑧ Katie is standing on Lucy's   left / right .

⑨ Jack is holding a towel with his   left / right   hand.

⑩ The carpet is   over / under   the box.

⑪ The dolls are   inside / outside   the box.

⑫ The robot is   bigger / smaller   than the doll.

⑬ There are   more / fewer   dolls than robots.

Check ✔ the heavier object.

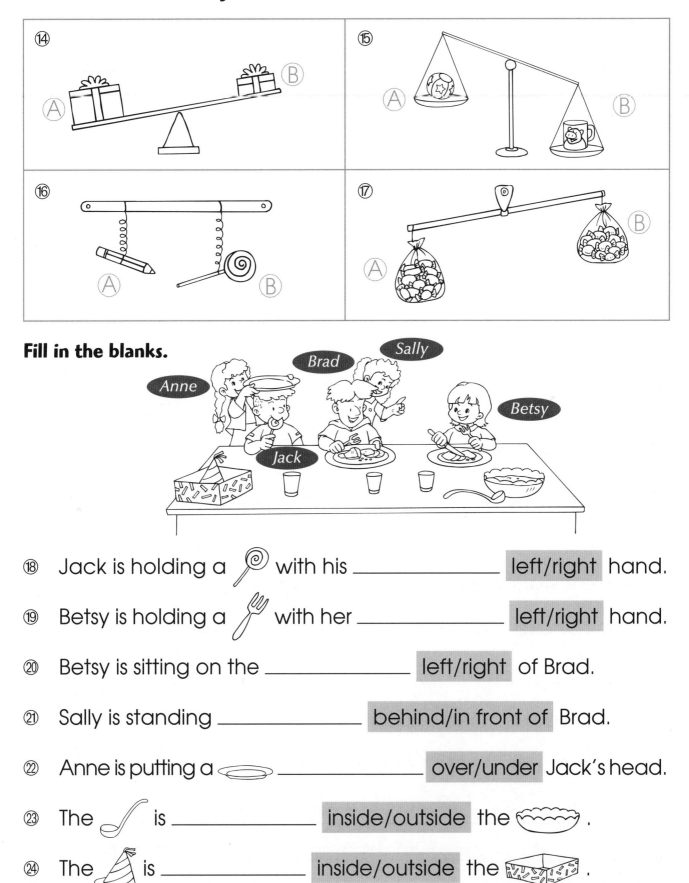

Fill in the blanks.

⑱ Jack is holding a 🍭 with his _____ left/right hand.

⑲ Betsy is holding a 🍴 with her _____ left/right hand.

⑳ Betsy is sitting on the _____ left/right of Brad.

㉑ Sally is standing _____ behind/in front of Brad.

㉒ Anne is putting a 🍽 _____ over/under Jack's head.

㉓ The 🥄 is _____ inside/outside the 🥧 .

㉔ The 🎉 is _____ inside/outside the 📦 .

ISBN: 978-1-897164-11-2

Check ✔ the group which has more.

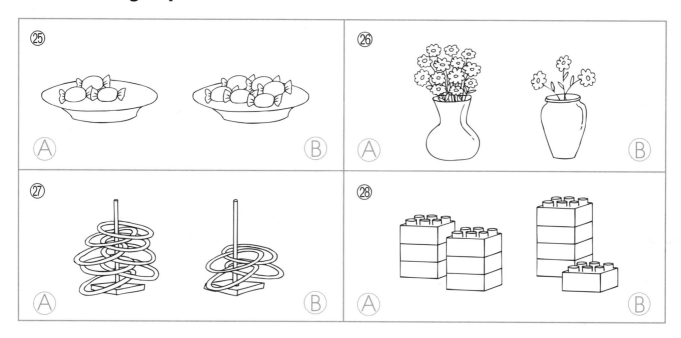

Match the muffins with the boxes. Then fill in the blanks with the correct letters.

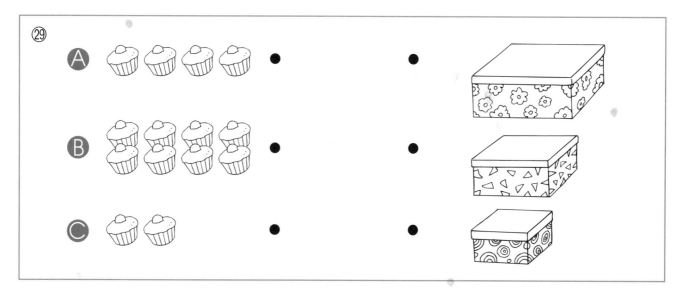

㉚ Group _____ has the most 🧁 .

㉛ Group _____ has the fewest 🧁 .

㉜ Put the groups in order from the one which has the most 🧁 to the one which has the least.

_____ , _____ , _____

ISBN: 978-1-897164-11-2

Sorting Objects (1)

Cross out X the one that does not belong.

ISBN: 978-1-897164-11-2

⑦

⑧

⑨

⑩

⑪

⑫

Cross out **X** the objects which are in the wrong place.

ISBN: 978-1-897164-11-2

Draw lines to join the toys to the box and the clothing to the basket.

㉑

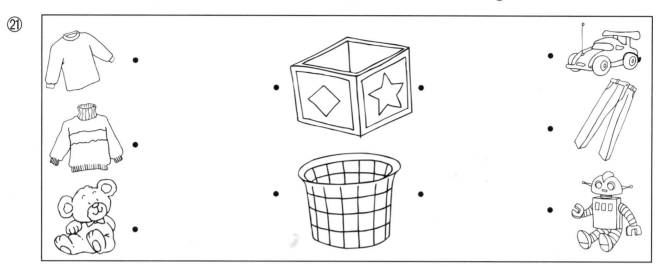

Draw lines to join the letters to the letter box and the numbers to the number box.

㉒

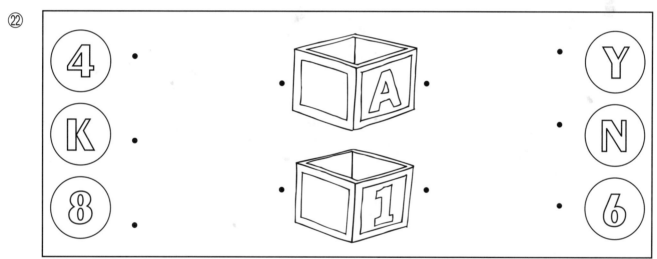

Draw lines to join the tools to the tool box and the cooking utensils to the tray.

㉓

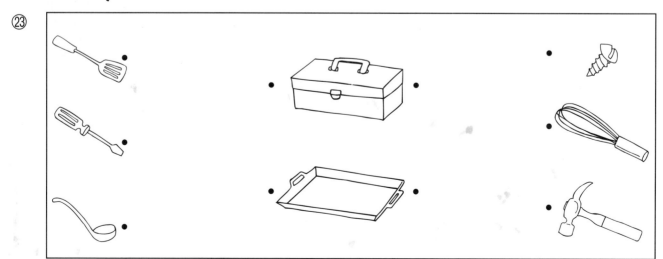

ISBN: 978-1-897164-11-2

Sorting Objects (2)

Colour the correct pictures.

① Colour the things you might find at a birthday party.

② Colour the animals you would find in water.

③ Colour the things you might find on the beach.

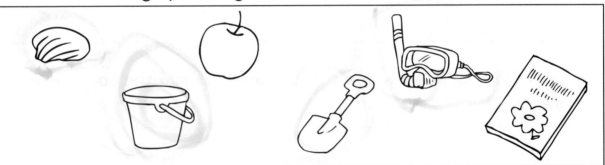

④ Colour the food you would put in the refrigerator.

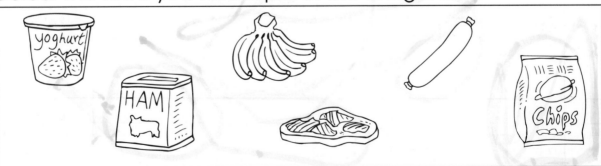

ISBN: 978-1-897164-11-2

⑤ Colour the things you would put in the closet.

⑥ Colour the things you would find in a grocery store.

⑦ Colour the things you would find on a farm.

⑧ Colour the things you would drink.

ISBN: 978-1-897164-11-2

Sort the things. Write the letters in the boxes.

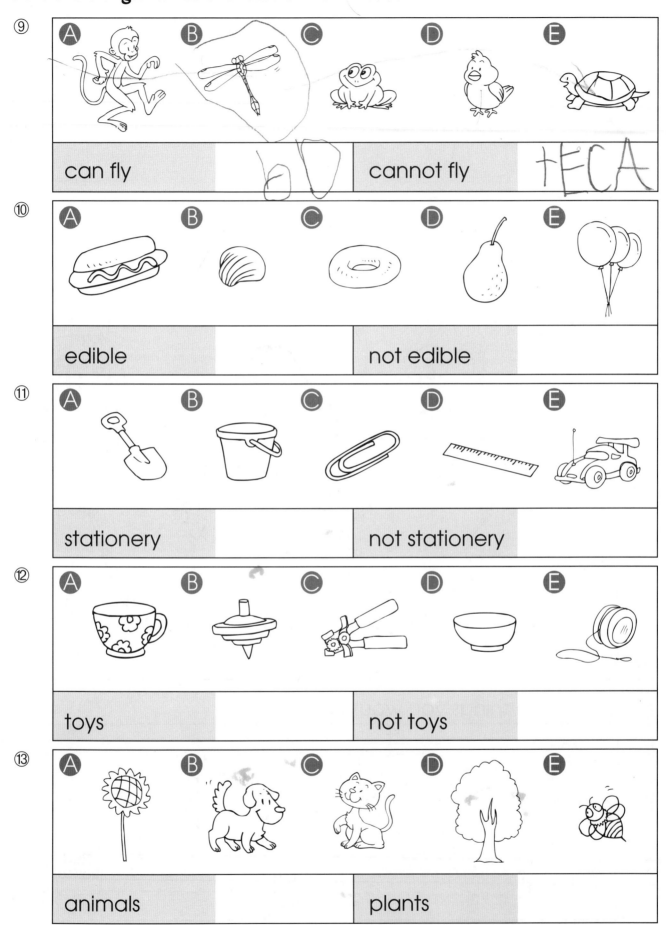

⑨

| A | B | C | D | E |

can fly ‎ ‎ ‎ ‎ ‎ ‎ **cannot fly** ‎ ‎ TECA

⑩

| A | B | C | D | E |

edible ‎ ‎ ‎ ‎ **not edible**

⑪

| A | B | C | D | E |

stationery ‎ ‎ ‎ ‎ **not stationery**

⑫

| A | B | C | D | E |

toys ‎ ‎ ‎ ‎ **not toys**

⑬

| A | B | C | D | E |

animals ‎ ‎ ‎ ‎ **plants**

ISBN: 978-1-897164-11-2

Divide the clothing into 3 different groups. Colour each group with the same colour.

⑭

Divide the animals into 2 groups. Colour each group of animals with the same colour.

⑮

Divide the toys into 2 groups. Colour each group of toys with the same colour.

⑯

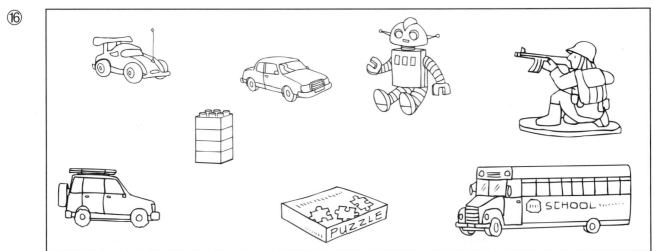

8 Ordering Objects (1)

Cross out X the thing in each group which is in the wrong order.

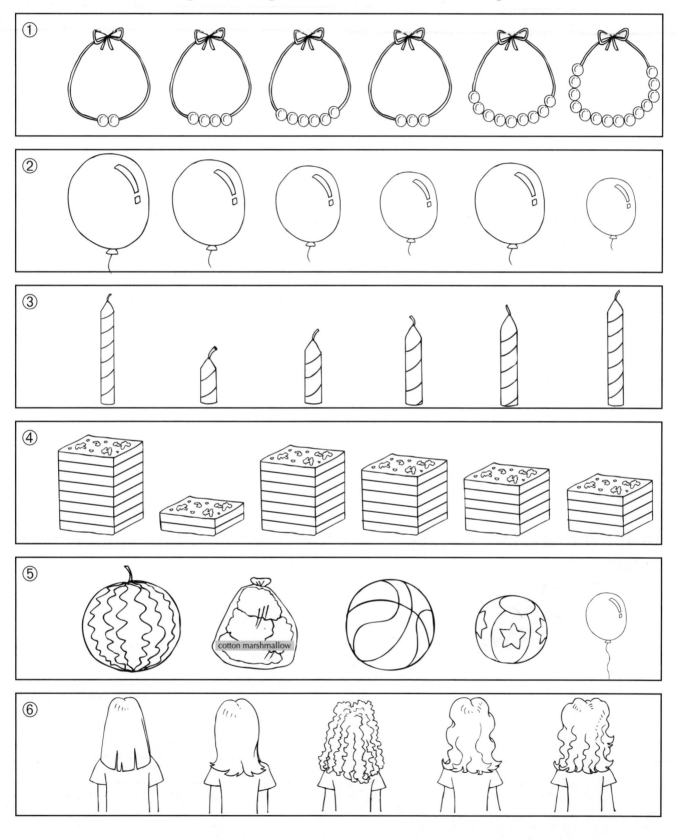

cotton marshmallow

ISBN: 978-1-897164-11-2

Draw lines to match the animals with their food by size.

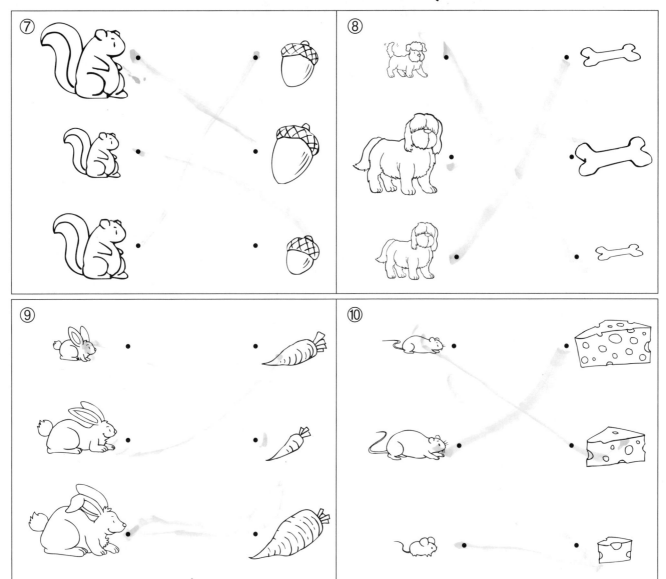

Match the things with the correct boxes. Write the letters in the circles.

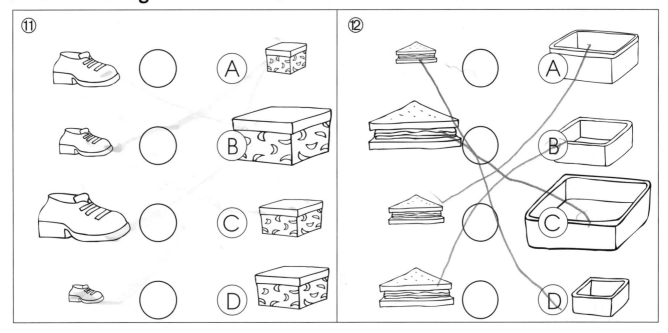

ISBN: 978-1-897164-11-2

Ordering Objects (2)

Put each group of things in order. Write the letters only.

①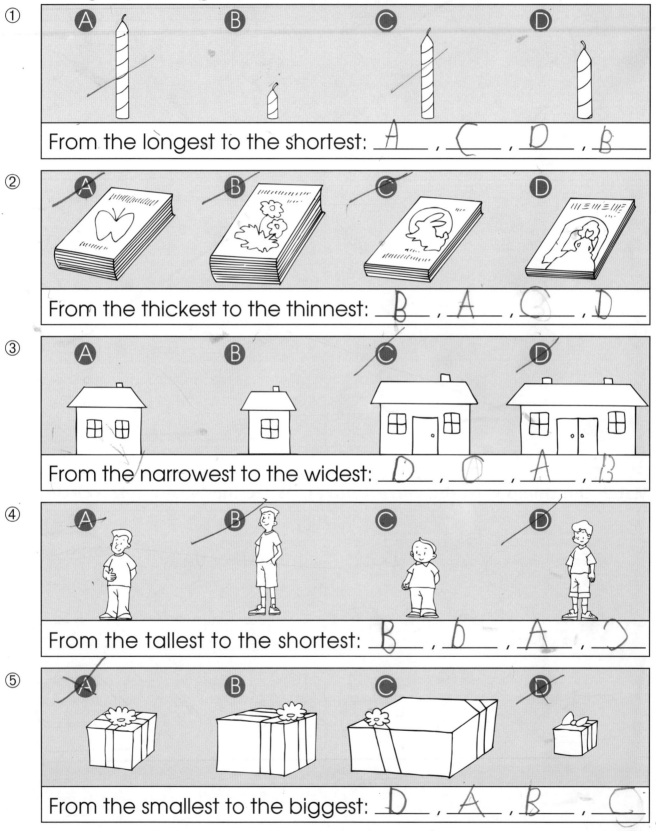

From the longest to the shortest: _A_ , _C_ , _D_ , _B_

② From the thickest to the thinnest: _B_ , _A_ , _C_ , _D_

③ From the narrowest to the widest: _D_ , _C_ , _A_ , _B_

④ From the tallest to the shortest: _B_ , _D_ , _A_ , _C_

⑤ From the smallest to the biggest: _D_ , _A_ , _B_ , _C_

ISBN: 978-1-897164-11-2

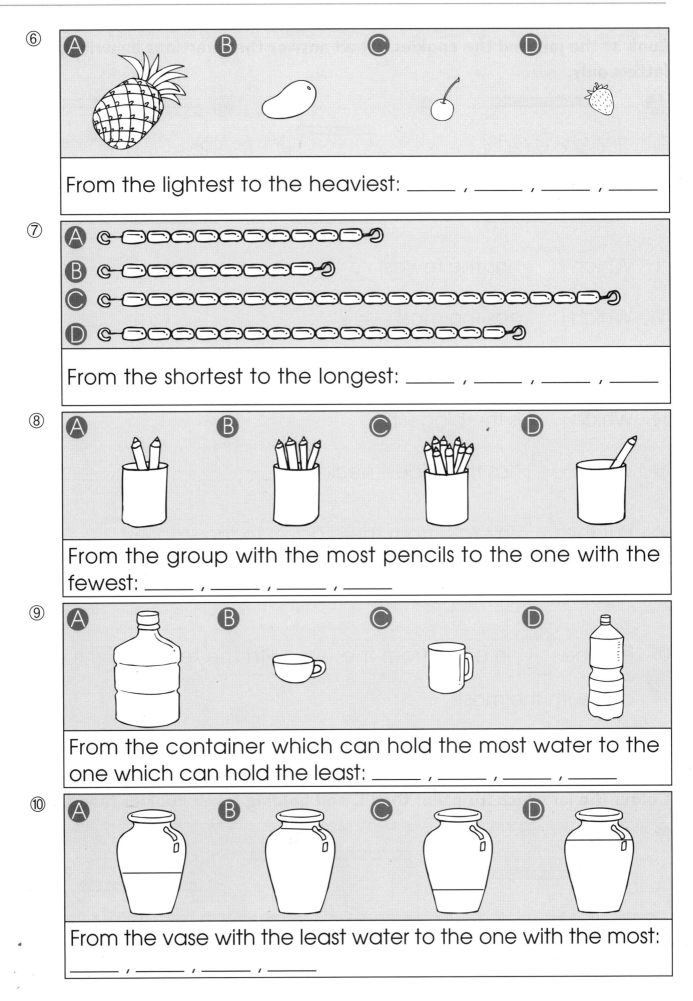

⑥

| Ⓐ | Ⓑ | Ⓒ | Ⓓ |

From the lightest to the heaviest: _____ , _____ , _____ , _____

⑦

Ⓐ
Ⓑ
Ⓒ
Ⓓ

From the shortest to the longest: _____ , _____ , _____ , _____

⑧

| Ⓐ | Ⓑ | Ⓒ | Ⓓ |

From the group with the most pencils to the one with the fewest: _____ , _____ , _____ , _____

⑨

| Ⓐ | Ⓑ | Ⓒ | Ⓓ |

From the container which can hold the most water to the one which can hold the least: _____ , _____ , _____ , _____

⑩

| Ⓐ | Ⓑ | Ⓒ | Ⓓ |

From the vase with the least water to the one with the most: _____ , _____ , _____ , _____

ISBN: 978-1-897164-11-2

Look at the jars and the cookies. Then answer the questions by writing the letters only.

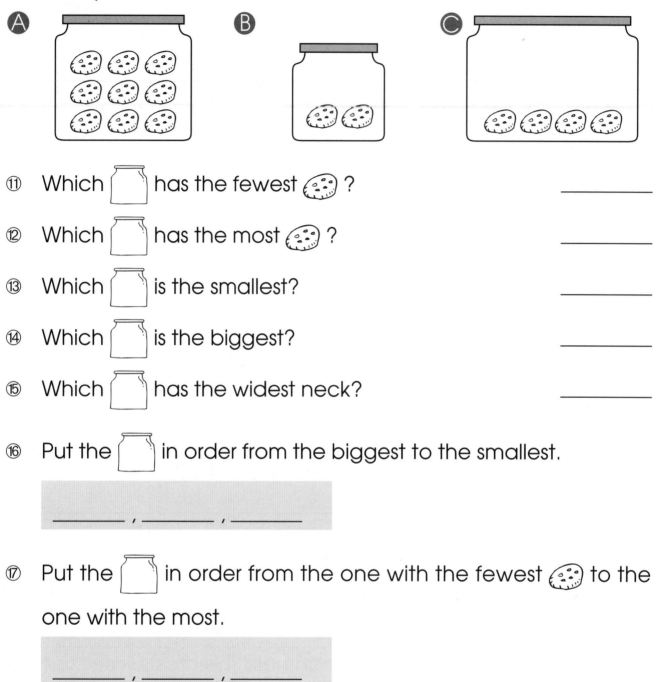

⑪ Which ⬚ has the fewest 🍪 ? _____

⑫ Which ⬚ has the most 🍪 ? _____

⑬ Which ⬚ is the smallest? _____

⑭ Which ⬚ is the biggest? _____

⑮ Which ⬚ has the widest neck? _____

⑯ Put the ⬚ in order from the biggest to the smallest.

_____ , _____ , _____

⑰ Put the ⬚ in order from the one with the fewest 🍪 to the one with the most.

_____ , _____ , _____

Colour the jar which is smaller than C and holding fewer cookies than C.

⑱

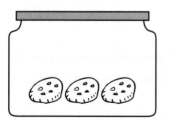

ISBN: 978-1-897164-11-2

Look at the baskets of apples. Fill in the blanks and put the baskets in order.

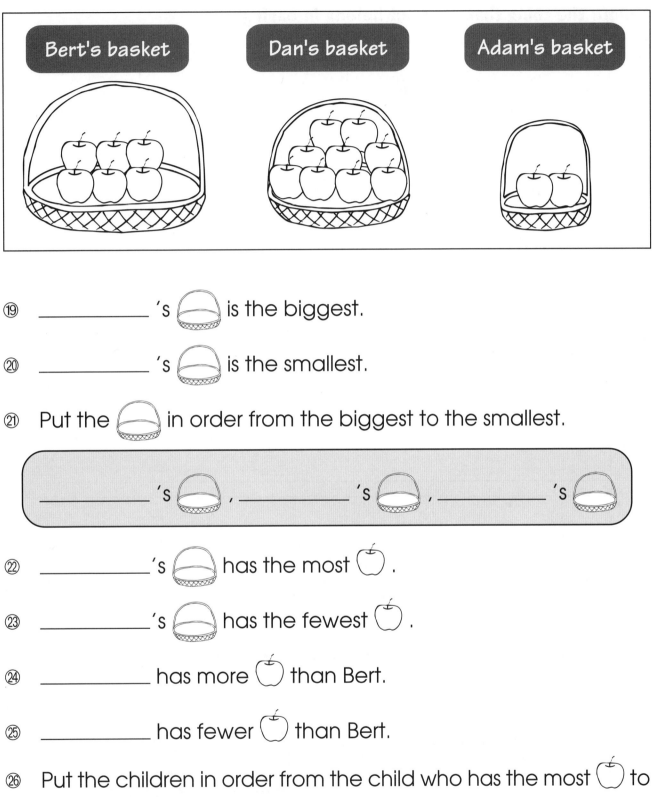

Bert's basket   Dan's basket   Adam's basket

⑲ _____ 's 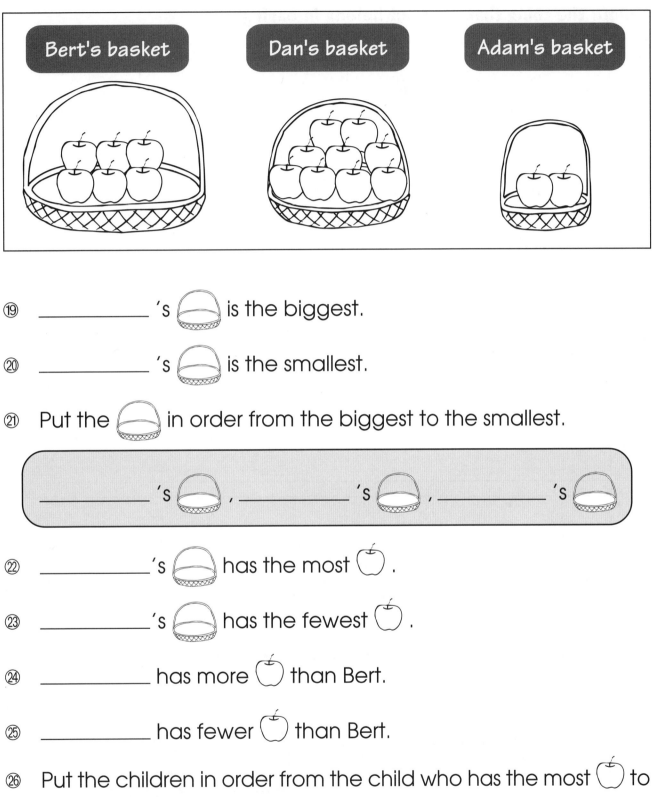 is the biggest.

⑳ _____ 's is the smallest.

㉑ Put the in order from the biggest to the smallest.

_____ 's , _____ 's , _____ 's

㉒ _____ 's has the most .

㉓ _____ 's has the fewest .

㉔ _____ has more than Bert.

㉕ _____ has fewer than Bert.

㉖ Put the children in order from the child who has the most to the one who has the least.

_____ , _____ , _____

ISBN: 978-1-897164-11-2

Colour the thing that does not belong in each group.

①

②

③

④

Cross out X the things that are put in the wrong place.

⑤

⑥

ISBN: 978-1-897164-11-2

Colour the ribbons and put them in order.

⑦

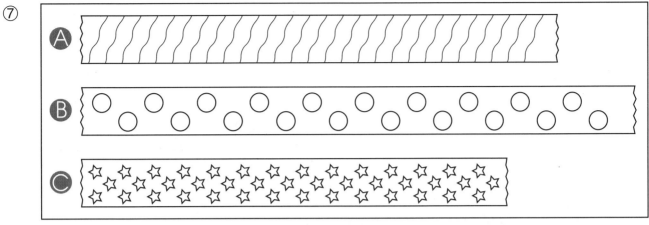

a. Colour the longest ribbon blue and the shortest yellow.

b. Put the ribbons in order from the longest to the shortest.

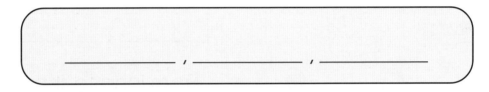

_____ , _____ , _____

Cross out ✗ the thing which is in the wrong order.

⑧

⑨

⑩

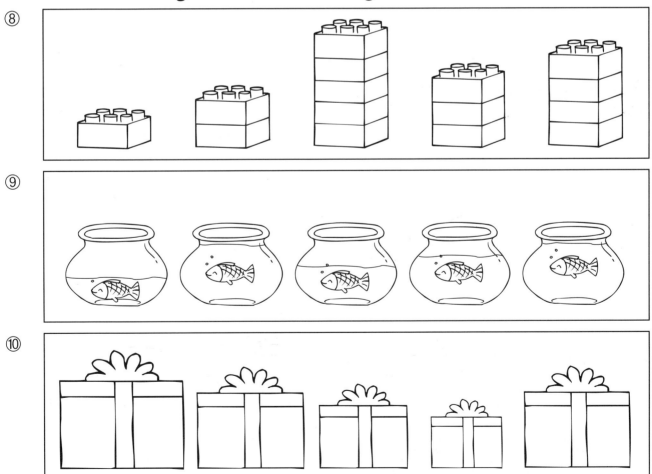

ISBN: 978-1-897164-11-2

Put the things in order. Write the letters.

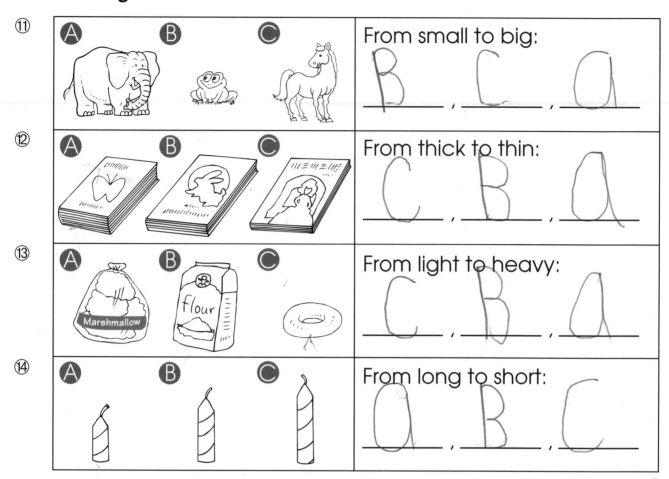

11) From small to big:

B , C , a

12) From thick to thin:

C , B , a

13) From light to heavy:

C , B , a

14) From long to short:

a , B , C

Draw lines to join the stationery to the pencil case and the toys to the toy box.

15)

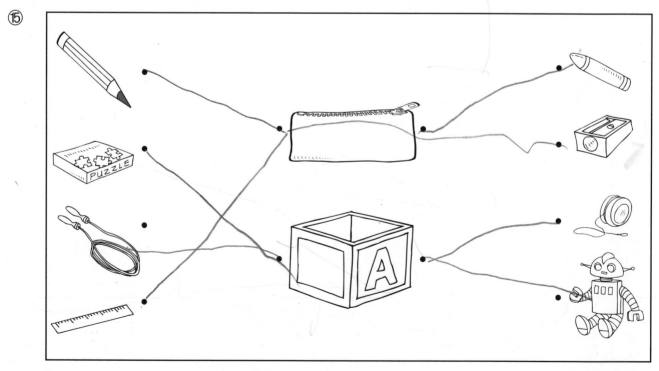

ISBN: 978-1-897164-11-2

Draw lines to join the things to the correct stores.

⑯

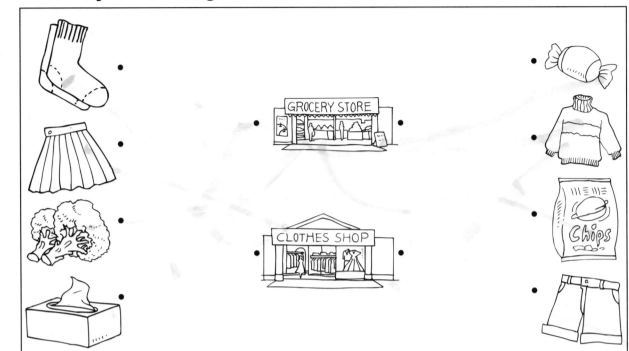

Divide the things into two groups. Colour each group with the same colour.

⑰

⑱

ISBN: 978-1-897164-11-2

Help the bee reach the flowers by colouring the animals that have wings.

⑲

Which comes next? Circle the correct picture.

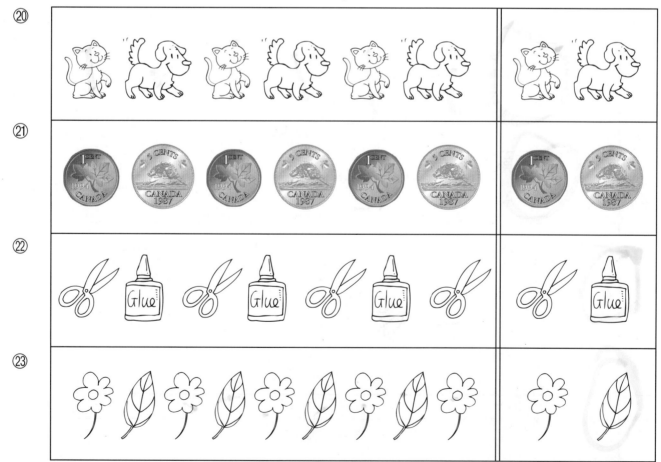

ISBN: 978-1-897164-11-2

Overview

In Section I, children practised preschool skills such as comparing, sorting and ordering objects according to a single attribute such as size, height and weight. They also matched objects by one-to-one correspondence and practised counting to identify sets with more, fewer, or the same number of objects. These skills are now built upon in Section II.

In this section, children are given exercises to develop and practise the basic arithmetic skills of addition and subtraction.

Addition involves putting two groups together whereas subtraction involves taking one group from another.

Through drawing or using concrete materials, the concept of addition and subtraction is reinforced. Children learn such mathematical terms as sum, difference, total and equal, and also the signs (+, –, =) that represent these terms.

Before children make any number sentences, they must understand the quantities the numbers represent, and what happens when quantities are combined or when two groups are compared.

These skills are applied in everyday situations, using whole numbers up to 20.

Addition and Subtraction of 1

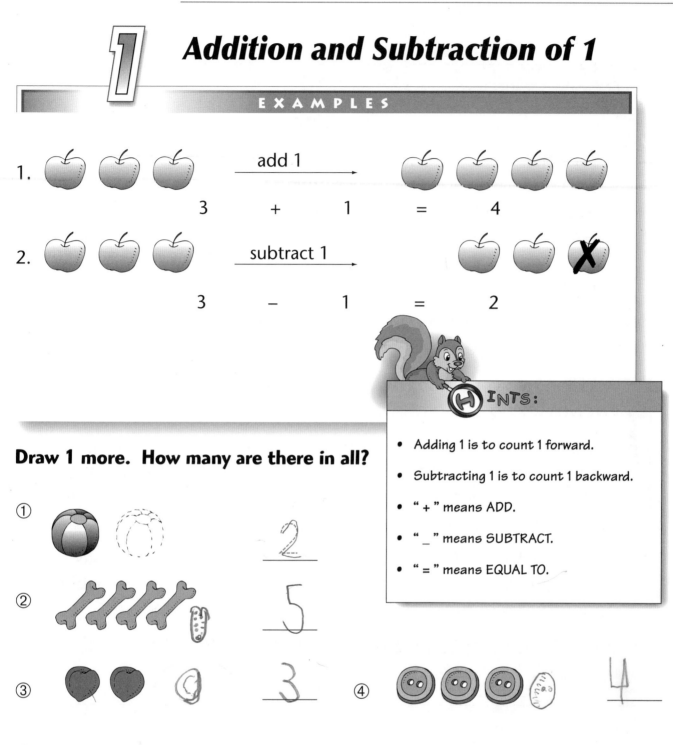

1.   add 1

3 + 1 = 4

2.   subtract 1

3 – 1 = 2

HINTS:

- Adding 1 is to count 1 forward.
- Subtracting 1 is to count 1 backward.
- " + " means ADD.
- " _ " means SUBTRACT.
- " = " means EQUAL TO.

Draw 1 more. How many are there in all?

① 2

② 5

③ 3

④ 4

Cross 1 out. How many are left?

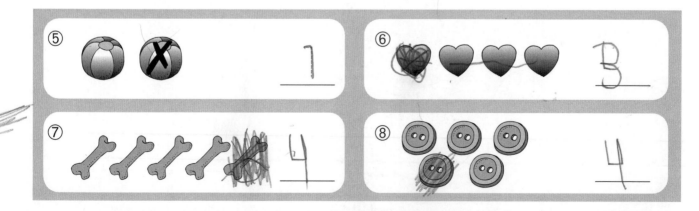

⑤ 1

⑥ 3

⑦ 4

⑧ 4

ISBN: 978-1-897164-11-2

How many are there?

⑨

$3 + 1 =$ 4

$$\begin{array}{r} 3 \\ +\ 1 \\ \hline \boxed{4} \end{array}$$

⑩

$4 + 1 =$ 5

$$\begin{array}{r} 4 \\ +\ 1 \\ \hline \boxed{5} \end{array}$$

⑪

$4 - 1 =$ 3

$$\begin{array}{r} 4 \\ -\ 1 \\ \hline \boxed{3} \end{array}$$

⑫

$6 + 1 =$ 7

$$\begin{array}{r} 6 \\ +\ 1 \\ \hline \boxed{7} \end{array}$$

⑬

$2 + 1 =$ 3

$$\begin{array}{r} 2 \\ +\ 1 \\ \hline \boxed{3} \end{array}$$

⑭

$5 - 1 =$ 4

$$\begin{array}{r} 5 \\ -\ 1 \\ \hline \boxed{4} \end{array}$$

⑮

$7 - 1 =$ 6

$$\begin{array}{r} 7 \\ -\ 1 \\ \hline \boxed{6} \end{array}$$

⑯

$3 - 1 =$ 2

$$\begin{array}{r} 3 \\ -\ 1 \\ \hline \boxed{2} \end{array}$$

⑰

$8 + 1 =$ 9

$$\begin{array}{r} 8 \\ +\ 1 \\ \hline \boxed{9} \end{array}$$

⑱

$8 - 1 =$ 7

$$\begin{array}{r} 8 \\ -\ 1 \\ \hline \boxed{7} \end{array}$$

ISBN: 978-1-897164-11-2

Add or subtract.

⑲ $1 + 1 =$ ☐　　⑳ $2 - 1 =$ ☐

㉑ $2 + 1 =$ ☐　　㉒ $3 - 1 =$ ☐

㉓ $3 + 1 =$ ☐　　㉔ $4 - 1 =$ ☐

㉕ $4 + 1 =$ ☐　　㉖ $5 - 1 =$ ☐

㉗ $5 + 1 =$ ☐　　㉘ $6 - 1 =$ ☐

㉙ $6 + 1 =$ ☐　　㉚ $7 - 1 =$ ☐

㉛ $7 + 1 =$ ☐　　㉜ $8 - 1 =$ ☐

㉝
$$\begin{array}{r} 8 \\ + \ 1 \\ \hline \end{array}$$
☐

㉞
$$\begin{array}{r} 9 \\ + \ 1 \\ \hline \end{array}$$
☐

㉟
$$\begin{array}{r} 10 \\ - \ 1 \\ \hline \end{array}$$
☐

㊱
$$\begin{array}{r} 2 \\ + \ 1 \\ \hline \end{array}$$
☐

㊲
$$\begin{array}{r} 5 \\ + \ 1 \\ \hline \end{array}$$
☐

㊳
$$\begin{array}{r} 9 \\ - \ 1 \\ \hline \end{array}$$
☐

㊴
$$\begin{array}{r} 4 \\ + \ 1 \\ \hline \end{array}$$
☐

㊵
$$\begin{array}{r} 5 \\ - \ 1 \\ \hline \end{array}$$
☐

㊶
$$\begin{array}{r} 4 \\ - \ 1 \\ \hline \end{array}$$
☐

㊷
$$\begin{array}{r} 3 \\ + \ 1 \\ \hline \end{array}$$
☐

㊸
$$\begin{array}{r} 7 \\ - \ 1 \\ \hline \end{array}$$
☐

㊹
$$\begin{array}{r} 8 \\ - \ 1 \\ \hline \end{array}$$
☐

ISBN: 978-1-897164-11-2

Complete. Write + or – in ◯ .

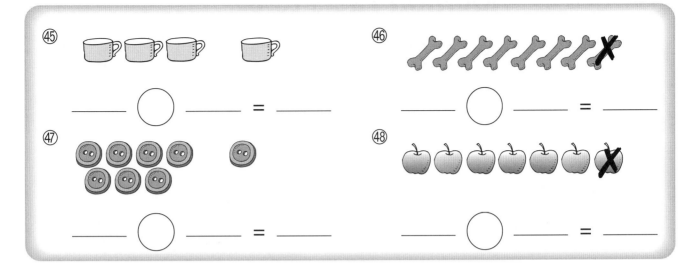

④⑤ _____ ◯ _____ = _____

④⑥ _____ ◯ _____ = _____

④⑦ _____ ◯ _____ = _____

④⑧ _____ ◯ _____ = _____

Complete each number sentence. Write + or − in ◯ .

④⑨ There are 8 ✎ . Buy 1 ✎ more . How many ✎ are there in all?

_____ ◯ _____ = _____   _____ ✎ in all.

㊿ There are 7 🍊 . 1 🍊 is eaten. How many 🍊 are left?

_____ ◯ _____ = _____   _____ 🍊 left.

⑤① There are 6 🦜 . 1 🦜 flies away. How many 🦜 are left?

_____ ◯ _____ = _____   _____ 🦜 left.

Just for Fun

Write the missing numbers.

1   2   5   9   14

ISBN: 978-1-897164-11-2

2 Addition Facts to 6

4 and 2; 6 in all

4 + 2 = 6

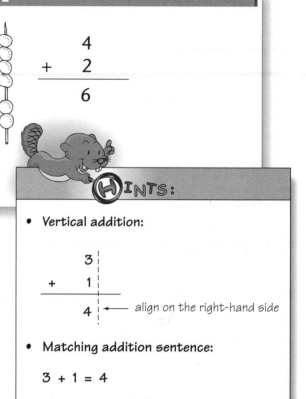

$$\begin{array}{r} 4 \\ +\ 2 \\ \hline 6 \end{array}$$

HINTS:

- Vertical addition:

$$\begin{array}{r} 3 \\ +\ 1 \\ \hline 4 \end{array}$$ ← align on the right-hand side

- Matching addition sentence:

3 + 1 = 4

Complete each addition sentence.

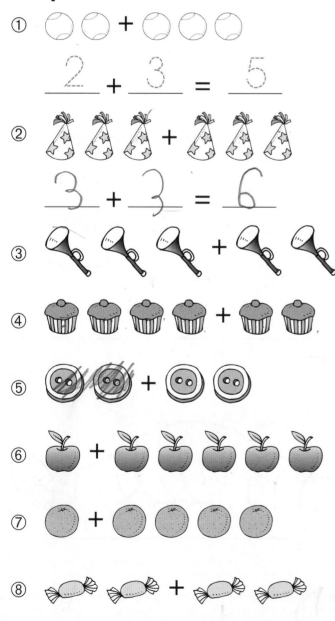

① ⚾⚾ + ⚾⚾⚾

__2__ + __3__ = __5__

② 🎉🎉🎉 + 🎉🎉🎉

__3__ + __3__ = __6__

③ 🎺🎺🎺 + 🎺🎺

④ 🧁🧁🧁🧁 + 🧁🧁

⑤ 🔘🔘 + 🔘🔘

⑥ 🍎 + 🍎🍎🍎🍎🍎

⑦ 🍊 + 🍊🍊🍊🍊

⑧ 🍬🍬 + 🍬🍬

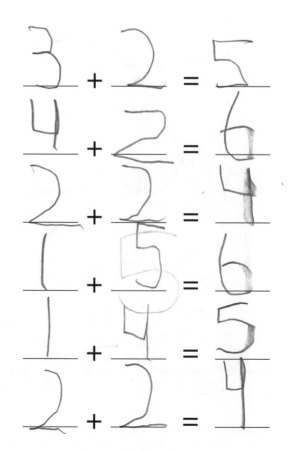

__3__ + __2__ = __5__

__4__ + __2__ = __6__

__2__ + __2__ = ____

__1__ + __5__ = ____

__1__ + __1__ = __5__

__2__ + __2__ = ____

ISBN: 978-1-897164-11-2

Add.

⑨ $3 + 3 = \boxed{}$

⑩ $3 + 2 = \boxed{}$

⑪ $1 + 4 = \boxed{}$

⑫ $1 + 2 = \boxed{}$

⑬ $4 + 2 = \boxed{}$

⑭ $2 + 2 = \boxed{}$

⑮ $2 + 3 = \boxed{}$

⑯ $5 + 1 = \boxed{}$

⑰ $2 + 4 = \boxed{}$

⑱ $1 + 1 = \boxed{}$

⑲ $3 + 1 = \boxed{}$

⑳ $4 + 1 = \boxed{}$

㉑ $1 + 5 = \boxed{}$

㉒ $1 + 3 = \boxed{}$

㉓ $\begin{array}{r} 3 \\ + 3 \\ \hline \boxed{} \end{array}$

㉔ $\begin{array}{r} 2 \\ + 4 \\ \hline \boxed{} \end{array}$

㉕ $\begin{array}{r} 2 \\ + 2 \\ \hline \boxed{} \end{array}$

㉖ $\begin{array}{r} 2 \\ + 1 \\ \hline \boxed{} \end{array}$

㉗ $\begin{array}{r} 3 \\ + 2 \\ \hline \boxed{} \end{array}$

㉘ $\begin{array}{r} 1 \\ + 5 \\ \hline \boxed{} \end{array}$

㉙ $\begin{array}{r} 2 \\ + 3 \\ \hline \boxed{} \end{array}$

㉚ $\begin{array}{r} 1 \\ + 4 \\ \hline \boxed{} \end{array}$

㉛ $\begin{array}{r} 1 \\ + 2 \\ \hline \boxed{} \end{array}$

㉜ $\begin{array}{r} 4 \\ + 2 \\ \hline \boxed{} \end{array}$

㉝ $\begin{array}{r} 5 \\ + 1 \\ \hline \boxed{} \end{array}$

㉞ $\begin{array}{r} 1 \\ + 3 \\ \hline \boxed{} \end{array}$

ISBN: 978-1-897164-11-2

Match.

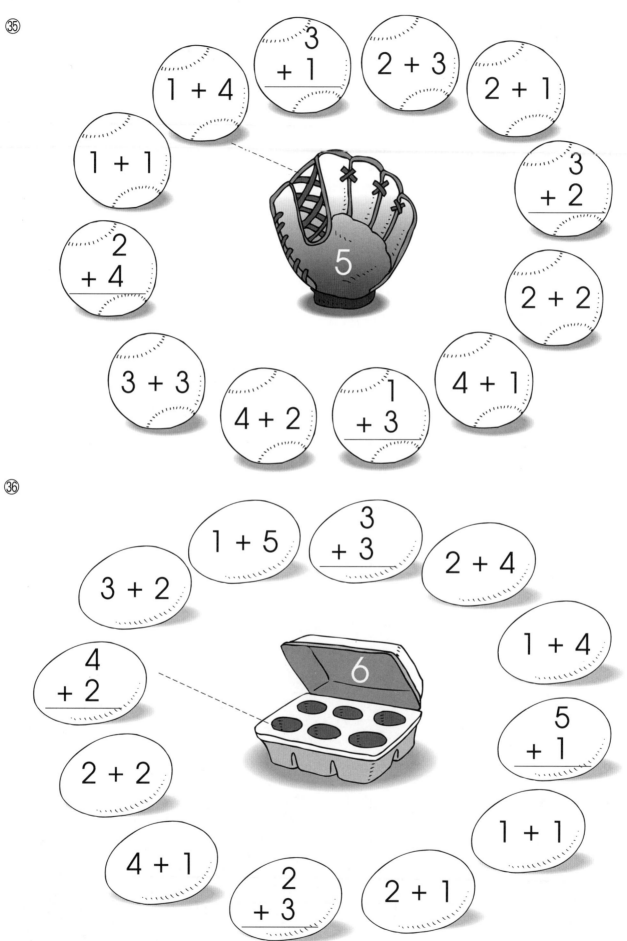

㉟

1 + 4   3 +1   2 + 3   2 + 1

1 + 1

3 + 2

2 + 4   **5**   2 + 2

3 + 3   4 + 2   1 + 3   4 + 1

㊱

3 + 2   1 + 5   3 + 3   2 + 4

4 + 2   **6**   1 + 4

2 + 2   5 + 1

4 + 1   2 + 3   2 + 1   1 + 1

ISBN: 978-1-897164-11-2

Colour the two sets of beads that make each bracelet. Write addition sentences to match.

㊲ —OO— —OOO— —OOOO— ⟹

_____ + _____ = _____

㊳ —OO— —OOO— —OOOO— ⟹

_____ + _____ = _____

Complete each addition sentence.

㊴ There are 3 🍎 and 2 🍎 . How many 🍎 🍎 are there?

_____ + _____ = _____   There are _____ 🍎 🍎 .

㊵ There are 4 🐿 and 2 🐿 . How many 🐿 🐿 are there?

_____ + _____ = _____   There are _____ 🐿 🐿 .

㊶ There are 3 👒 and 3 👒 . How many 👒 👒 are there?

_____ + _____ = _____   There are _____ 👒 👒 .

Just for Fun

Match.

| 2 + 3 | 1 + 3 | 2 + 4 | 2 + 1 |

• • • •

• • • •

| 2 + 2 | 4 + 1 | 1 + 2 | 3 + 3 |

ISBN: 978-1-897164-11-2

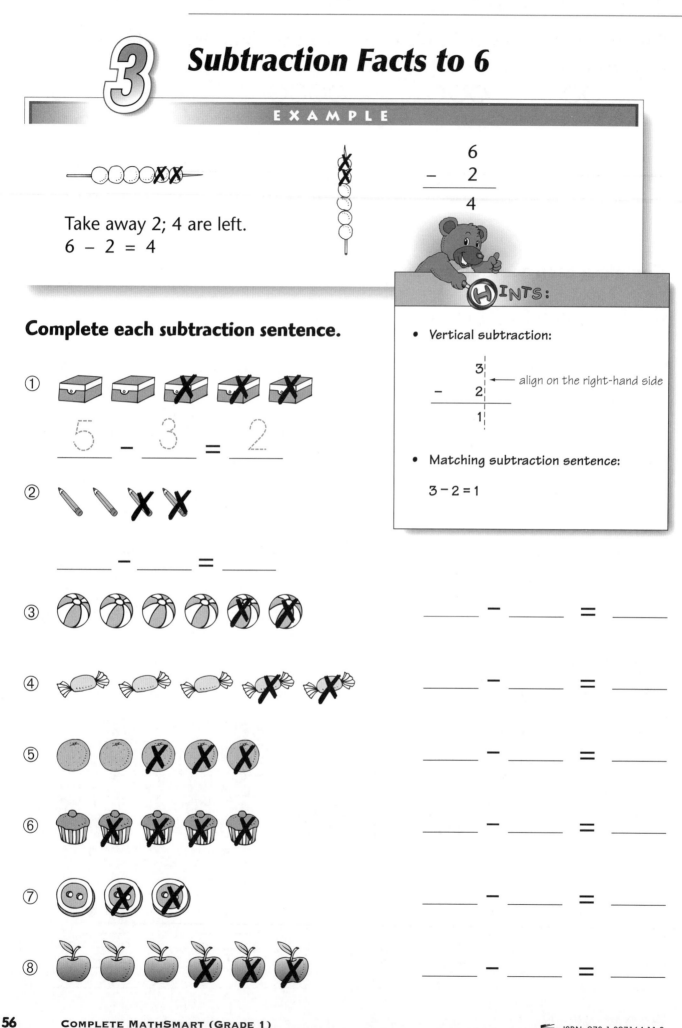

3 Subtraction Facts to 6

EXAMPLE

Take away 2; 4 are left.
6 − 2 = 4

$$\begin{array}{r} 6 \\ -\ 2 \\ \hline 4 \end{array}$$

HINTS:

- Vertical subtraction:

$$\begin{array}{r} 3 \\ -\ 2 \\ \hline 1 \end{array}$$ ← align on the right-hand side

- Matching subtraction sentence:

  3 − 2 = 1

Complete each subtraction sentence.

① 5 − 3 = 2

② ____ − ____ = ____

③ ____ − ____ = ____

④ ____ − ____ = ____

⑤ ____ − ____ = ____

⑥ ____ − ____ = ____

⑦ ____ − ____ = ____

⑧ ____ − ____ = ____

COMPLETE MATHSMART (GRADE 1)   ISBN: 978-1-897164-11-2

Subtract.

⑨ $4 - 2 = \boxed{}$

⑩ $6 - 1 = \boxed{}$

⑪ $6 - 5 = \boxed{}$

⑫ $5 - 4 = \boxed{}$

⑬ $5 - 3 = \boxed{}$

⑭ $4 - 3 = \boxed{}$

⑮ $6 - 2 = \boxed{}$

⑯ $5 - 2 = \boxed{}$

⑰ $3 - 2 = \boxed{}$

⑱ $6 - 4 = \boxed{}$

⑲ $6 - 3 = \boxed{}$

⑳ $4 - 1 = \boxed{}$

㉑ $5 - 1 = \boxed{}$

㉒ $3 - 1 = \boxed{}$

㉓
$$\begin{array}{r} 5 \\ -\ 4 \\ \hline \end{array}$$

㉔
$$\begin{array}{r} 4 \\ -\ 2 \\ \hline \end{array}$$

㉕
$$\begin{array}{r} 6 \\ -\ 2 \\ \hline \end{array}$$

㉖
$$\begin{array}{r} 3 \\ -\ 1 \\ \hline \end{array}$$

㉗
$$\begin{array}{r} 6 \\ -\ 4 \\ \hline \end{array}$$

㉘
$$\begin{array}{r} 5 \\ -\ 3 \\ \hline \end{array}$$

㉙
$$\begin{array}{r} 4 \\ -\ 3 \\ \hline \end{array}$$

㉚
$$\begin{array}{r} 5 \\ -\ 2 \\ \hline \end{array}$$

㉛
$$\begin{array}{r} 3 \\ -\ 2 \\ \hline \end{array}$$

㉜
$$\begin{array}{r} 6 \\ -\ 3 \\ \hline \end{array}$$

㉝
$$\begin{array}{r} 5 \\ -\ 1 \\ \hline \end{array}$$

㉞
$$\begin{array}{r} 6 \\ -\ 5 \\ \hline \end{array}$$

ISBN: 978-1-897164-11-2

Match.

㉟

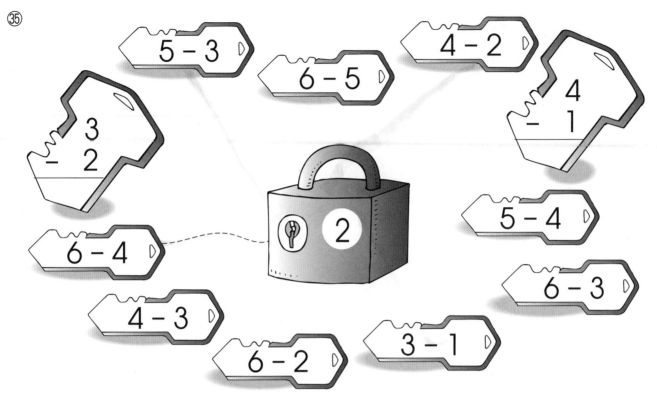

㊱

ISBN: 978-1-897164-11-2

Which bunches are the fruit on the plates cut from? Colour the right bunches and complete the subtraction sentences.

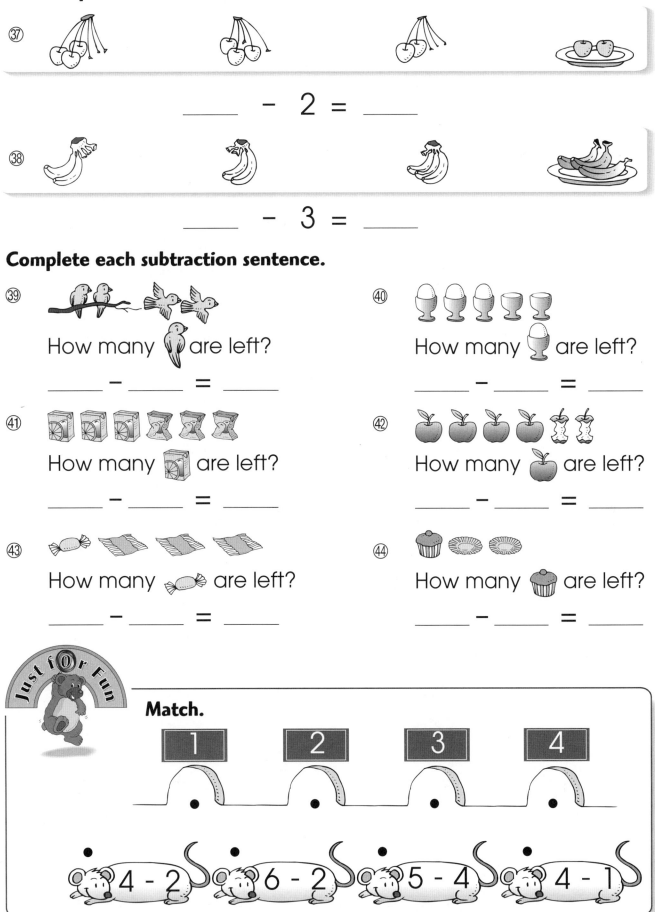

㊲ 

____ − 2 = ____

㊳ 

____ − 3 = ____

Complete each subtraction sentence.

㊴ 

How many are left?

____ − ____ = ____

㊵ 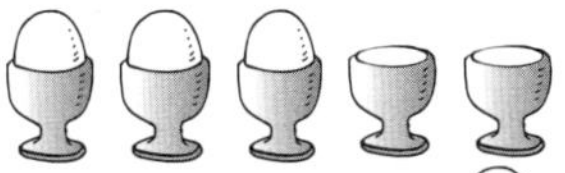

How many are left?

____ − ____ = ____

㊶ 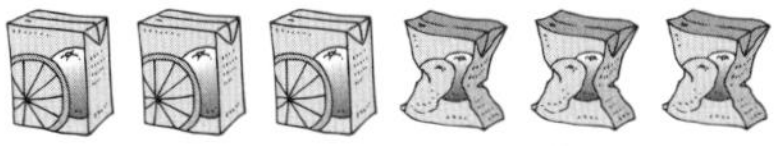

How many are left?

____ − ____ = ____

㊷ 

How many are left?

____ − ____ = ____

㊸ 

How many are left?

____ − ____ = ____

㊹ 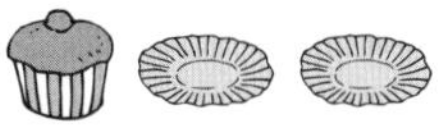

How many are left?

____ − ____ = ____

Just for Fun

Match.

1
2
3
4
4 - 2
6 - 2
5 - 4
4 - 1

ISBN: 978-1-897164-11-2

4 Addition and Subtraction of 0

None goes. 5 − 0 = 5

None comes. 5 + 0 = 5

HINTS:

- " 0 " means NONE.
- Any number plus 0 equals itself.
- Any number minus 0 equals itself.

How many are there?

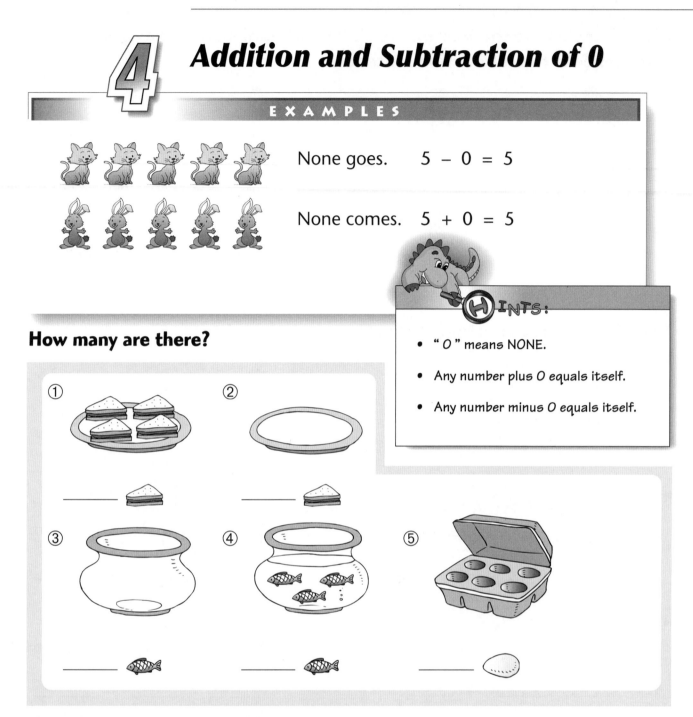

① _____

② _____

③ _____

④ _____

⑤ _____

Complete each number sentence.

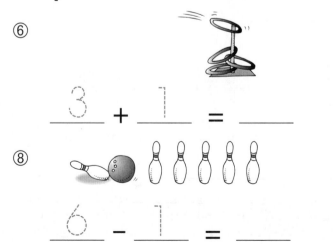

⑥ ____ 3 ____ + ____ 1 ____ = ____

⑧ ____ 6 ____ − ____ 1 ____ = ____

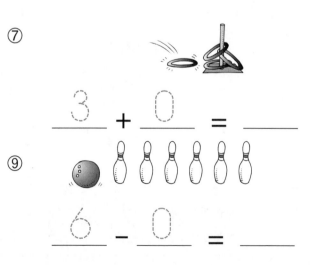

⑦ ____ 3 ____ + ____ 0 ____ = ____

⑨ ____ 6 ____ − ____ 0 ____ = ____

ISBN: 978-1-897164-11-2

Add or subtract.

⑩ $6 + 0 = \boxed{6}$ ⑪ $6 - 0 = \boxed{}$

⑫ $5 + 0 = \boxed{}$ ⑬ $5 - 0 = \boxed{}$

⑭ $4 + 0 = \boxed{}$ ⑮ $4 - 0 = \boxed{}$

⑯ $3 + 0 = \boxed{}$ ⑰ $3 - 0 = \boxed{}$

⑱ $2 + 0 = \boxed{}$ ⑲ $2 - 0 = \boxed{}$

⑳ $1 + 0 = \boxed{}$ ㉑ $1 - 0 = \boxed{}$

㉒ $0 + 0 = \boxed{}$ ㉓ $0 - 0 = \boxed{}$

㉔
$$\begin{array}{r} 5 \\ +\ 0 \\ \hline \end{array}$$

㉕
$$\begin{array}{r} 0 \\ +\ 4 \\ \hline \end{array}$$

㉖
$$\begin{array}{r} 3 \\ -\ 0 \\ \hline \end{array}$$

㉗
$$\begin{array}{r} 0 \\ +\ 1 \\ \hline \end{array}$$

㉘
$$\begin{array}{r} 0 \\ +\ 6 \\ \hline \end{array}$$

㉙
$$\begin{array}{r} 3 \\ +\ 0 \\ \hline \end{array}$$

㉚
$$\begin{array}{r} 0 \\ +\ 5 \\ \hline \end{array}$$

㉛
$$\begin{array}{r} 6 \\ -\ 0 \\ \hline \end{array}$$

㉜
$$\begin{array}{r} 4 \\ -\ 0 \\ \hline \end{array}$$

㉝
$$\begin{array}{r} 0 \\ +\ 2 \\ \hline \end{array}$$

㉞
$$\begin{array}{r} 4 \\ +\ 0 \\ \hline \end{array}$$

㉟
$$\begin{array}{r} 2 \\ -\ 0 \\ \hline \end{array}$$

ISBN: 978-1-897164-11-2

Match.

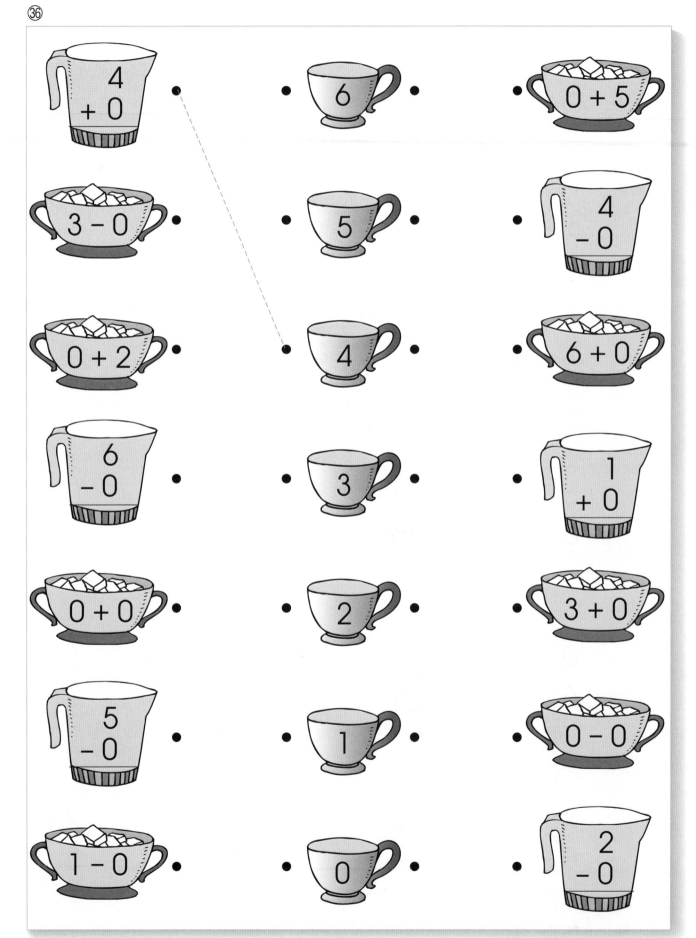

COMPLETE MATHSMART (GRADE 1)

ISBN: 978-1-897164-11-2

Add or subtract 0.

㊲ Add 0		㊳ Subtract 0		㊴ Add 0		㊵ Subtract 0	
4	*4*	5		1		6	
2		3		3		2	
6		1		5		4	

Complete.

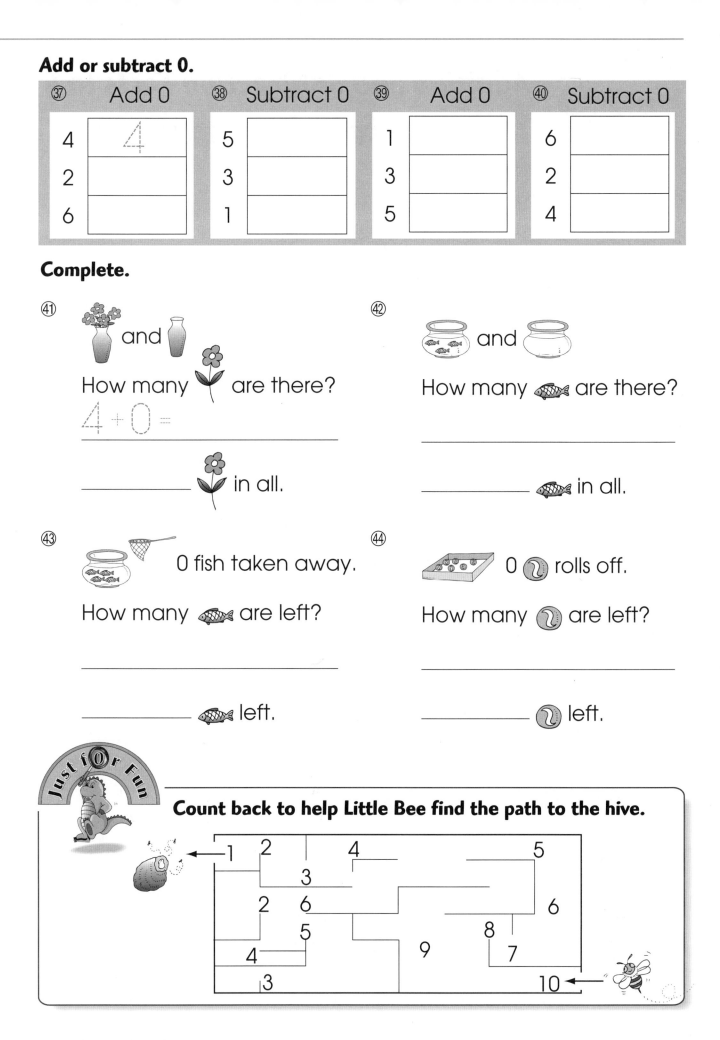

㊶ and

How many 🌷 are there?

4 + 0 =

_____ 🌸 in all.

㊷ and

How many 🐟 are there?

_____

_____ 🐟 in all.

㊸ 0 fish taken away.

How many 🐟 are left?

_____

_____ 🐟 left.

㊹ 0 🎾 rolls off.

How many 🎾 are left?

_____

_____ 🎾 left.

Just for Fun

Count back to help Little Bee find the path to the hive.

5 Addition and Subtraction Facts to 6

1. The sum of 3 and 2 is 5.

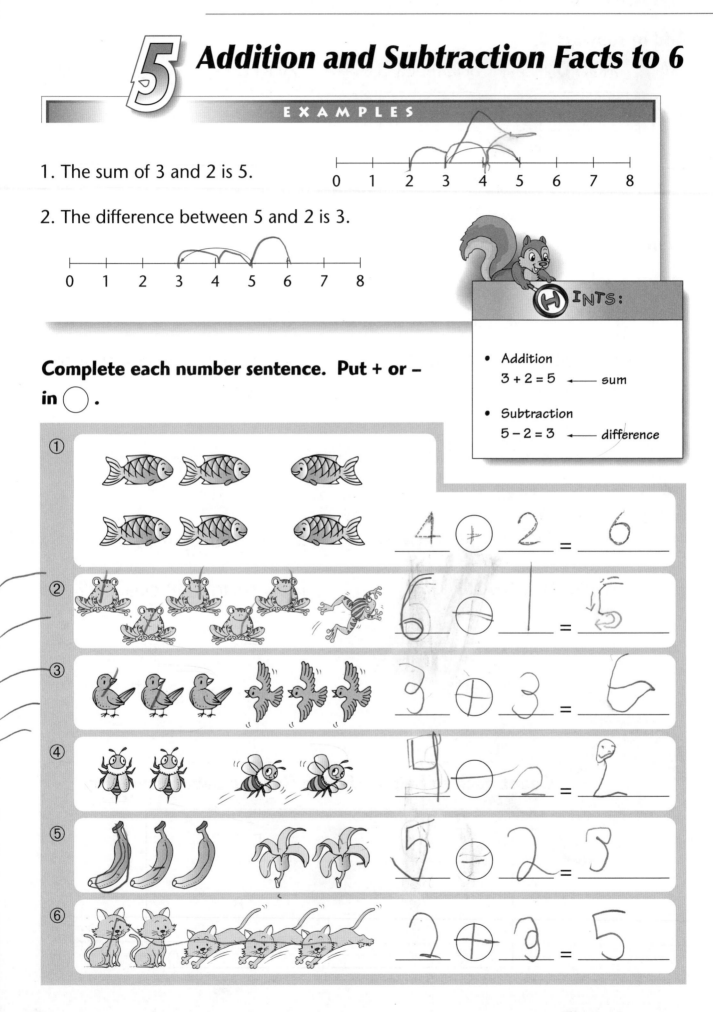

2. The difference between 5 and 2 is 3.

Complete each number sentence. Put + or – in ◯ .

HINTS:

- Addition
  3 + 2 = 5 ⟵ sum

- Subtraction
  5 – 2 = 3 ⟵ difference

① 4 ⊕ 2 = 6

② 6 ⊖ 1 = 5

③ 3 ⊕ 3 = 6

④ 4 ⊖ 2 = 2

⑤ 5 ⊖ 2 = 3

⑥ 2 ⊕ 3 = 5

ISBN: 978-1-897164-11-2

Add or subtract.

⑦ 4 − 3 = ☐   ⑧ 2 + 2 = ☐

⑨ 3 + 1 = ☐   ⑩ 5 − 2 = ☐

⑪ 4 + 2 = ☐   ⑫ 6 − 3 = ☐

⑬ 3 + 3 = ☐   ⑭ 3 + 0 = ☐

⑮ 1 − 1 = ☐   ⑯ 4 − 2 = ☐

⑰ 5 − 3 = ☐   ⑱ 2 + 1 = ☐

⑲ 6 − 2 = ☐   ⑳ 2 + 3 = ☐

㉑
$$5 + 0 = \boxed{}$$
㉒
$$6 - 5 = \boxed{}$$
㉓
$$4 - 0 = \boxed{}$$
㉔
$$2 - 1 = \boxed{}$$

㉕
$$4 + 1 = \boxed{}$$
㉖
$$5 - 4 = \boxed{}$$
㉗
$$3 - 2 = \boxed{}$$
㉘
$$6 + 0 = \boxed{}$$

㉙
$$2 - 0 = \boxed{}$$
㉚
$$6 - 4 = \boxed{}$$
㉛
$$1 + 1 = \boxed{}$$
㉜
$$4 - 0 = \boxed{}$$

Find the sums or differences. Help the snake get back to the hole.

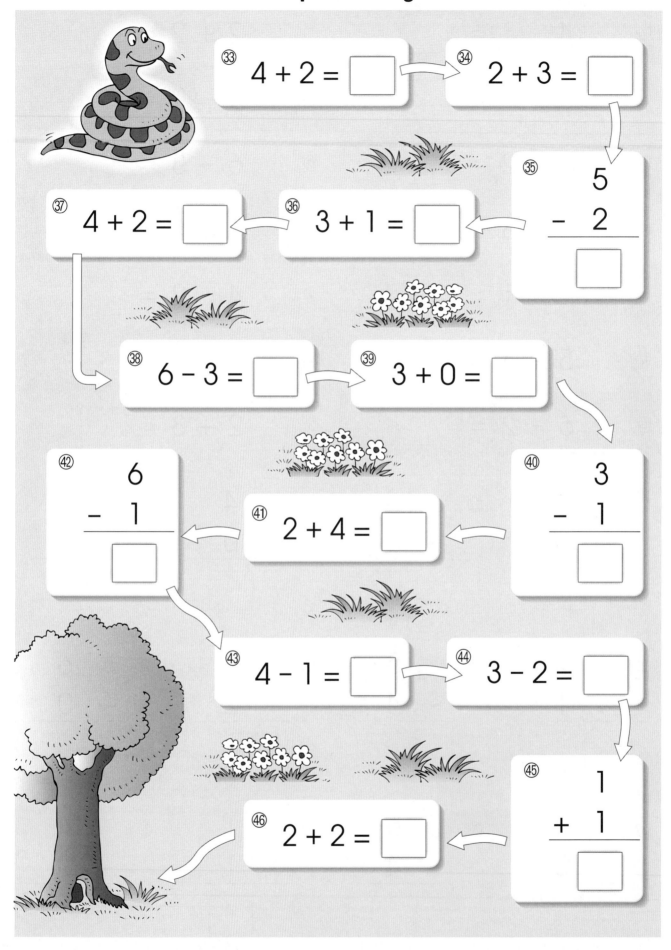

㉝ 4 + 2 = ☐

㉞ 2 + 3 = ☐

㉟ 5 − 2 = ☐

㊱ 3 + 1 = ☐

㊲ 4 + 2 = ☐

㊳ 6 − 3 = ☐

㊴ 3 + 0 = ☐

㊵ 3 − 1 = ☐

㊶ 2 + 4 = ☐

㊷ 6 − 1 = ☐

㊸ 4 − 1 = ☐

㊹ 3 − 2 = ☐

㊺ 1 + 1 = ☐

㊻ 2 + 2 = ☐

ISBN: 978-1-897164-11-2

Complete.

(47) There are 4 ; 2 are eaten.

How many are left?

4 − 2 =

______

______ left.

(48) There are 4 and 2 .

How many are there in all?

______

______ in all.

(49) There are 3 and 3 .

How many are there in all?

______

______ in all.

(50) There are 6 ; 4 are broken.

How many are left?

______

______ left.

(51) There are 5 ; 2 burst.

How many are left?

______

______ left.

(52) Sue has 5 ; 1 is eaten.

How many are left?

______

______ left.

Just for Fun

Add or Subtract. Match the answers with the words.

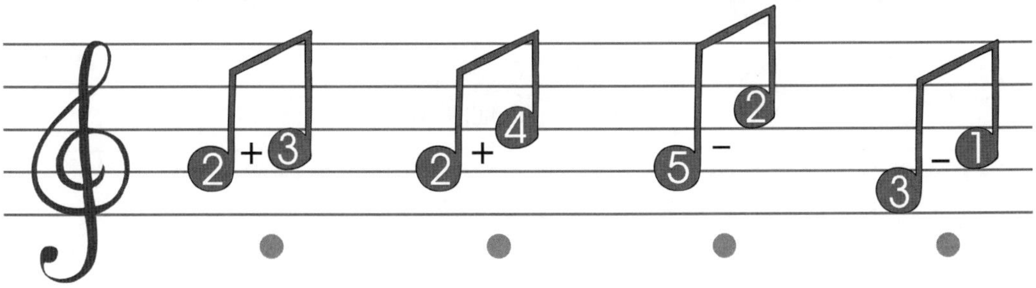

Six Two Five Three

ISBN: 978-1-897164-11-2

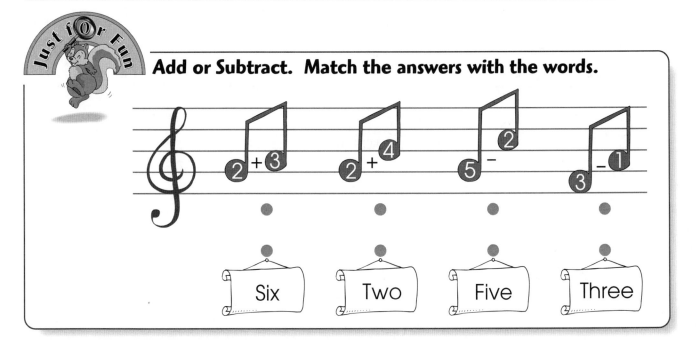

6 Addition Facts to 10

EXAMPLES

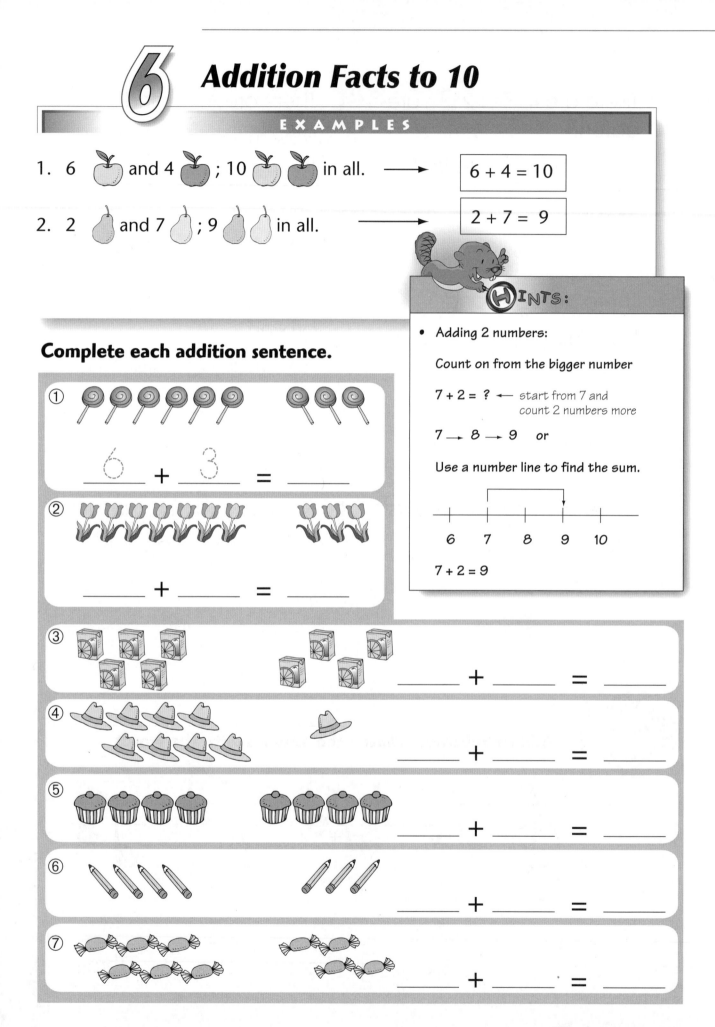

1. 6 🍎 and 4 🍎 ; 10 🍎 🍎 in all. → $6 + 4 = 10$

2. 2 🍐 and 7 🍐 ; 9 🍐 🍐 in all. → $2 + 7 = 9$

HINTS:

- Adding 2 numbers:

  Count on from the bigger number

  $7 + 2 = ?$ ← start from 7 and count 2 numbers more

  $7 \rightarrow 8 \rightarrow 9$ or

  Use a number line to find the sum.

  $7 + 2 = 9$

Complete each addition sentence.

① ____6____ + ____3____ = _____

② _____ + _____ = _____

③ _____ + _____ = _____

④ _____ + _____ = _____

⑤ _____ + _____ = _____

⑥ _____ + _____ = _____

⑦ _____ + _____ = _____

ISBN: 978-1-897164-11-2

Add.

⑧ 5 + 4 = ☐   ⑨ 7 + 3 = ☐

⑩ 9 + 1 = ☐   ⑪ 6 + 3 = ☐

⑫ 7 + 2 = ☐   ⑬ 8 + 2 = ☐

⑭ 8 + 1 = ☐   ⑮ 6 + 4 = ☐

⑯ 6 + 2 = ☐   ⑰ 5 + 3 = ☐

⑱ 5 + 2 = ☐   ⑲ 3 + 4 = ☐

⑳ 10 + 0 = ☐   ㉑ 4 + 4 = ☐

㉒ 3
  + 6
  ☐

㉓ 2
  + 8
  ☐

㉔ 3
  + 5
  ☐

㉕ 2
  + 7
  ☐

㉖ 8
  + 0
  ☐

㉗ 6
  + 2
  ☐

㉘ 9
  + 0
  ☐

㉙ 7
  + 3
  ☐

㉚ 3
  + 4
  ☐

㉛ 4
  + 5
  ☐

㉜ 7
  + 0
  ☐

㉝ 4
  + 3
  ☐

ISBN: 978-1-897164-11-2

Complete the addition sentences for each number family. Draw the correct number of items.

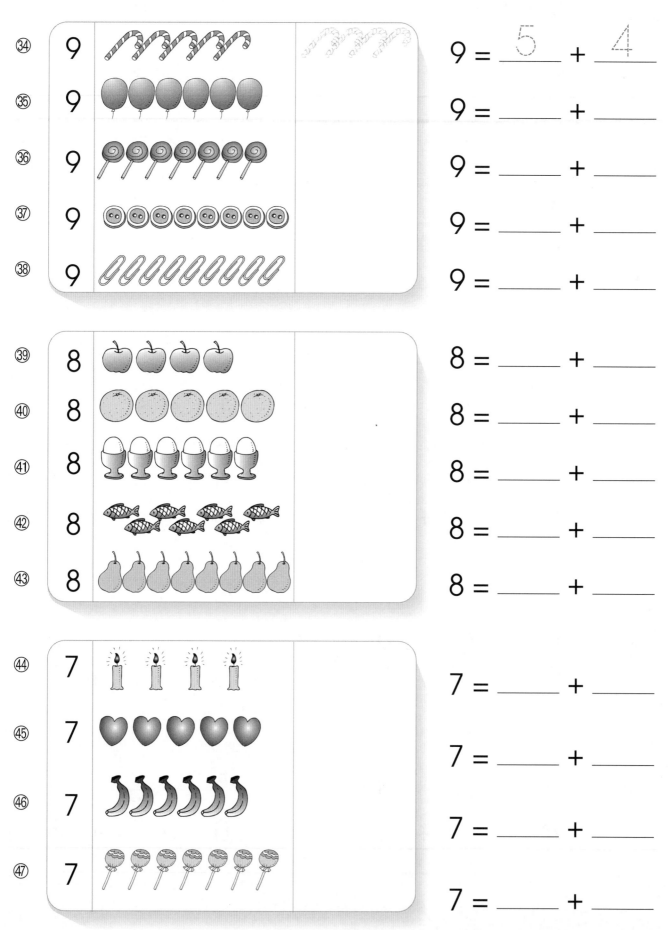

③④ 9

9 = _5_ + _4_

③⑤ 9

9 = ____ + ____

③⑥ 9

9 = ____ + ____

③⑦ 9

9 = ____ + ____

③⑧ 9

9 = ____ + ____

③⑨ 8

8 = ____ + ____

④⓪ 8

8 = ____ + ____

④① 8

8 = ____ + ____

④② 8

8 = ____ + ____

④③ 8

8 = ____ + ____

④④ 7

7 = ____ + ____

④⑤ 7

7 = ____ + ____

④⑥ 7

7 = ____ + ____

④⑦ 7

7 = ____ + ____

ISBN: 978-1-897164-11-2

Add.

⑱

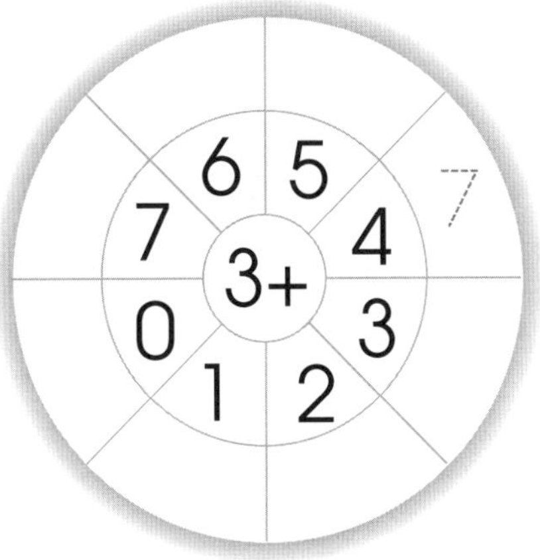

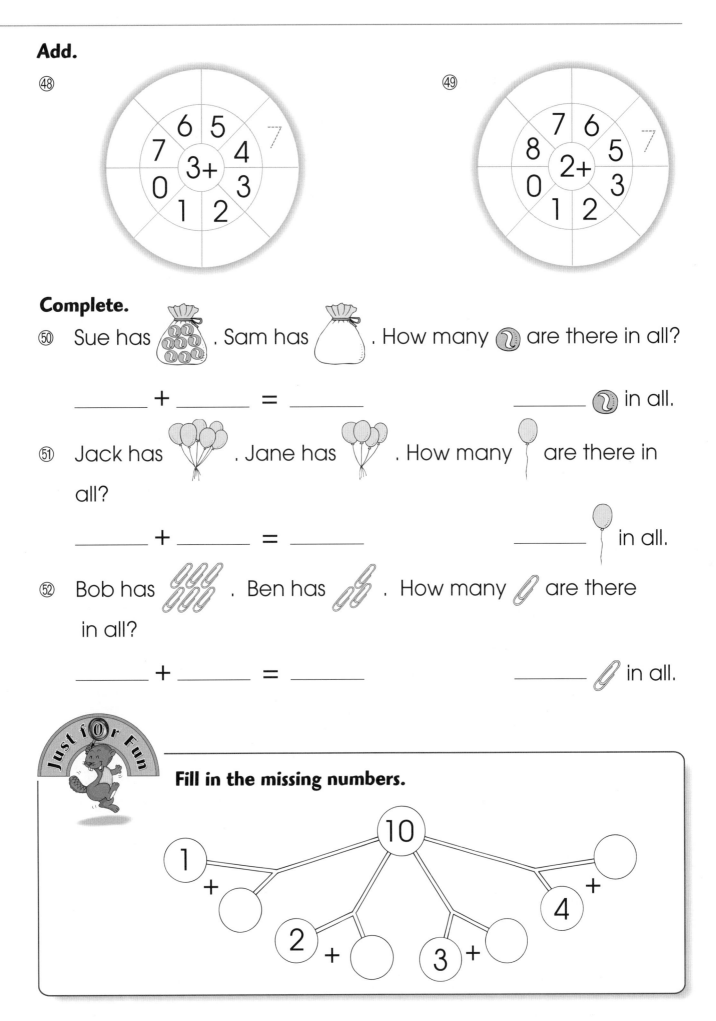

⑲

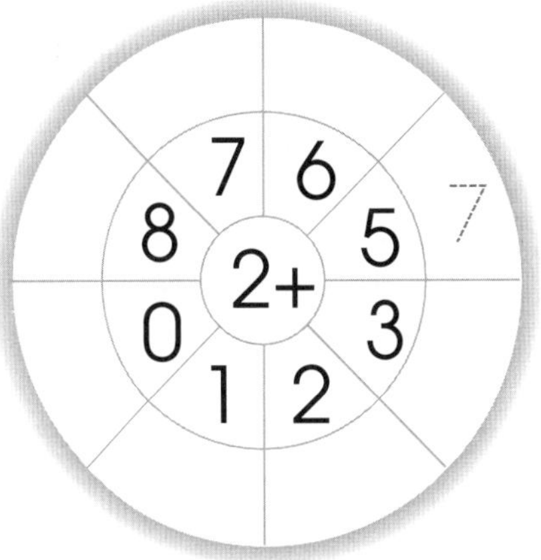

Complete.

(50) Sue has 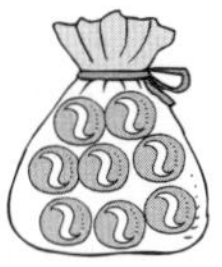 . Sam has  . How many  are there in all?

______ + ______ = ______ ______  in all.

(51) Jack has  . Jane has  . How many  are there in all?

______ + ______ = ______ ______  in all.

(52) Bob has 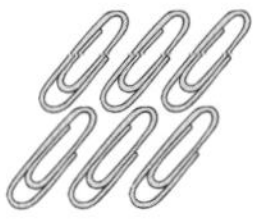 . Ben has  . How many  are there in all?

______ + ______ = ______ ______  in all.

Fill in the missing numbers.

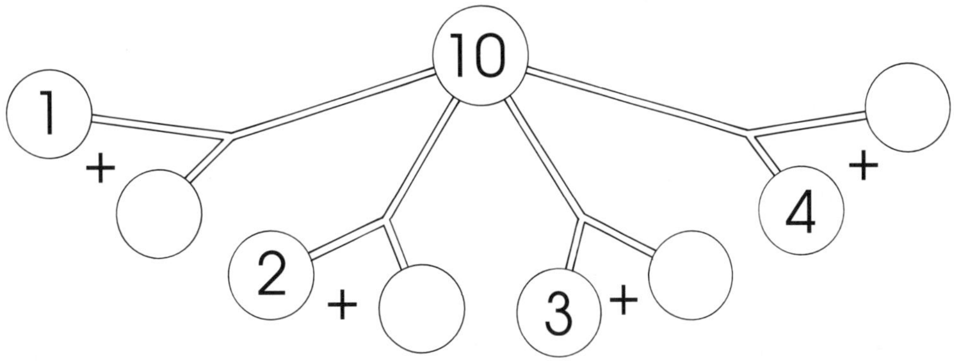

ISBN: 978-1-897164-11-2

7 Subtraction Facts to 10

1. 8 🐟 ; 2 🐟 were taken away ; 6 🐟 were left. $8 - 2 = 6$

2. 9 🦋 ; 4 🦋 flew away ; 5 🦋 were left. $9 - 4 = 5$

Complete each subtraction sentence.

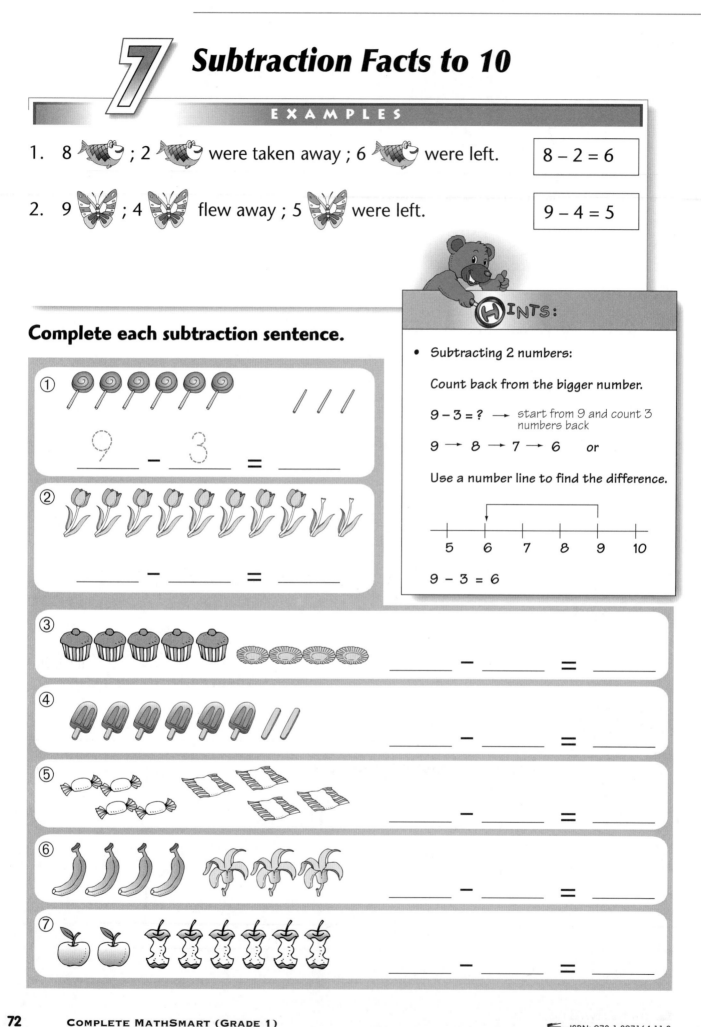

HINTS:

- Subtracting 2 numbers:

  Count back from the bigger number.

  $9 - 3 = ?$ → start from 9 and count 3 numbers back

  $9 \rightarrow 8 \rightarrow 7 \rightarrow 6$ or

  Use a number line to find the difference.

  $9 - 3 = 6$

① _____ – _____ = _____

② _____ – _____ = _____

③ _____ – _____ = _____

④ _____ – _____ = _____

⑤ _____ – _____ = _____

⑥ _____ – _____ = _____

⑦ _____ – _____ = _____

ISBN: 978-1-897164-11-2

Subtract.

⑧ $9 - 3 = \boxed{}$ ⑨ $8 - 2 = \boxed{}$

⑩ $10 - 4 = \boxed{}$ ⑪ $7 - 5 = \boxed{}$

⑫ $8 - 3 = \boxed{}$ ⑬ $10 - 5 = \boxed{}$

⑭ $9 - 4 = \boxed{}$ ⑮ $8 - 7 = \boxed{}$

⑯ $7 - 6 = \boxed{}$ ⑰ $10 - 8 = \boxed{}$

⑱ $9 - 7 = \boxed{}$ ⑲ $7 - 3 = \boxed{}$

⑳ $10 - 6 = \boxed{}$ ㉑ $9 - 6 = \boxed{}$

㉒ $\begin{array}{r} 7 \\ -\ 4 \\ \hline \end{array}$ $\boxed{}$
㉓ $\begin{array}{r} 10 \\ -\ 9 \\ \hline \end{array}$ $\boxed{}$
㉔ $\begin{array}{r} 8 \\ -\ 6 \\ \hline \end{array}$ $\boxed{}$
㉕ $\begin{array}{r} 9 \\ -\ 5 \\ \hline \end{array}$ $\boxed{}$

㉖ $\begin{array}{r} 9 \\ -\ 8 \\ \hline \end{array}$ $\boxed{}$
㉗ $\begin{array}{r} 8 \\ -\ 6 \\ \hline \end{array}$ $\boxed{}$
㉘ $\begin{array}{r} 10 \\ -\ 7 \\ \hline \end{array}$ $\boxed{}$
㉙ $\begin{array}{r} 7 \\ -\ 2 \\ \hline \end{array}$ $\boxed{}$

㉚ $\begin{array}{r} 10 \\ -\ 2 \\ \hline \end{array}$ $\boxed{}$
㉛ $\begin{array}{r} 8 \\ -\ 4 \\ \hline \end{array}$ $\boxed{}$
㉜ $\begin{array}{r} 10 \\ -\ 0 \\ \hline \end{array}$ $\boxed{}$
㉝ $\begin{array}{r} 9 \\ -\ 1 \\ \hline \end{array}$ $\boxed{}$

ISBN: 978-1-897164-11-2

Match and complete. Write the letters in ⑤ to solve the riddle.

③④ 10 − 5 = [5]

③⑤ 8 − 4 = [ ]

③⑥ 10 − 2 = [ ]

③⑦ 10 − 0 = [ ]

③⑧ 7 − 6 = [ ]

③⑨ 8 − 8 = [ ]

④⓪ 9 − 6 = [ ]

④① 10 − 1 = [ ]

④② 7 − 5 = [ ]

④③ 6 − 0 = [ ]

④④ 9 − 2 = [ ]

10 − 0 = [ ] (H)

8 − 0 = [ ] (U)

9 − 4 = [5] (I)

7 − 3 = [ ] (A)

8 − 5 = [ ] (S)

9 − 0 = [ ] (R)

8 − 7 = [ ] (L)

7 − 7 = [ ] (B)

8 − 2 = [ ] (T)

10 − 3 = [ ] (M)

10 − 8 = [ ] (O)

Riddle: Which is the westernmost province in Canada?

⑤

0	9	5	6	5	3	10		2	1	8	7	0	5	4
								C						

ISBN: 978-1-897164-11-2

Subtract.

㊻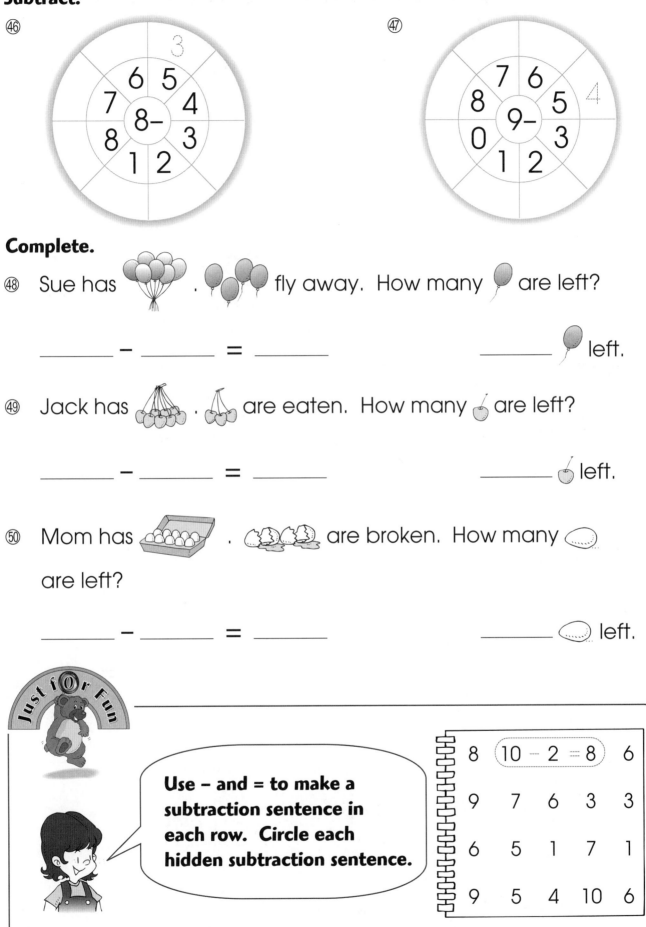

㊼

Complete.

㊽ Sue has [balloons] . [balloons] fly away. How many [balloon] are left?

_____ – _____ = _____   _____ [balloon] left.

㊾ Jack has [cherries] . [cherries] are eaten. How many [cherry] are left?

_____ – _____ = _____   _____ [cherry] left.

㊿ Mom has [eggs] . [broken eggs] are broken. How many [egg] are left?

_____ – _____ = _____   _____ [egg] left.

Just for Fun

Use – and = to make a subtraction sentence in each row. Circle each hidden subtraction sentence.

8	(10	– 2	= 8)	6
9	7	6	3	3
6	5	1	7	1
9	5	4	10	6

ISBN: 978-1-897164-11-2

8 Addition and Subtraction Facts to 10

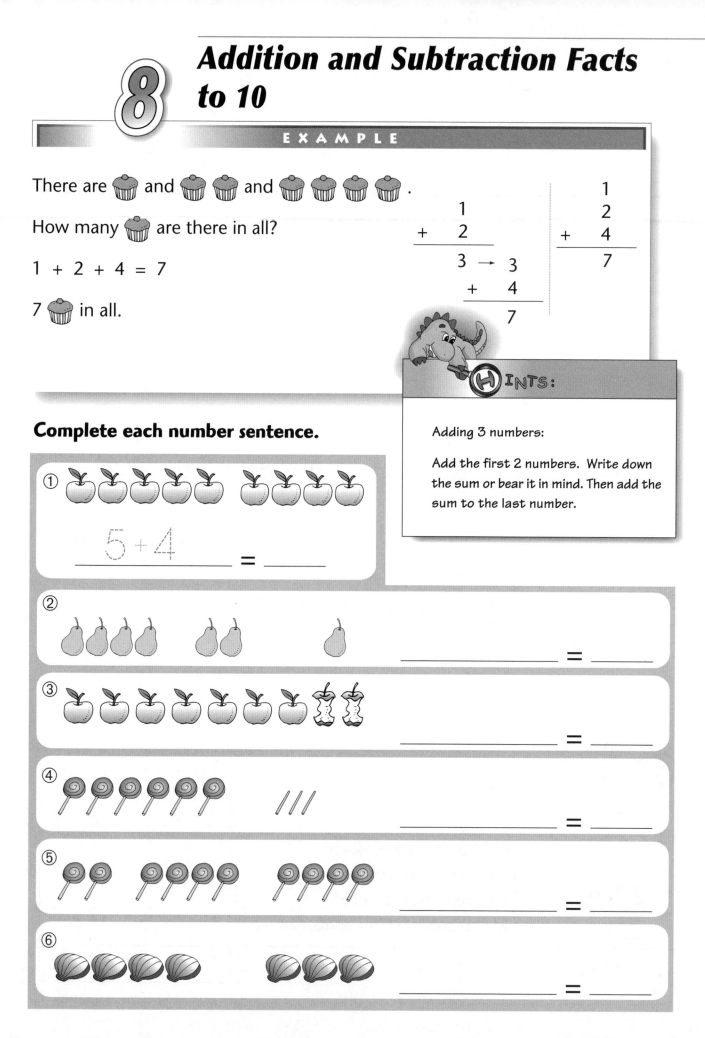

There are and   and   .

How many are there in all?

$1 + 2 + 4 = 7$

7 in all.

$$\begin{array}{r} 1 \\ + \quad 2 \\ \hline 3 \end{array} \rightarrow \begin{array}{r} 3 \\ + \quad 4 \\ \hline 7 \end{array}$$

$$\begin{array}{r} 1 \\ 2 \\ + \quad 4 \\ \hline 7 \end{array}$$

HINTS:

Adding 3 numbers:

Add the first 2 numbers. Write down the sum or bear it in mind. Then add the sum to the last number.

Complete each number sentence.

① $5 + 4$ ____ = ____

② _____ = ____

③ _____ = ____

④ _____ = ____

⑤ _____ = ____

⑥ _____ = ____

ISBN: 978-1-897164-11-2

Add or subtract.

⑦ 2 + 2 + 3 = ☐   ⑧ 8 – 6 = ☐

⑨ 10 – 4 = ☐   ⑩ 6 + 4 = ☐

⑪ 7 + 2 = ☐   ⑫ 9 – 6 = ☐

⑬ 7 – 5 = ☐   ⑭ 1 + 0 + 6 = ☐

⑮ 8 + 2 = ☐   ⑯ 7 – 6 = ☐

⑰ 1 + 1 + 5 = ☐   ⑱ 9 – 2 = ☐

⑲ 6 + 3 = ☐   ⑳ 5 + 5 = ☐

<table>
<tr><td>㉑   8
+ 0
☐</td><td>㉒   4
+ 5
☐</td><td>㉓   2
+ 7
☐</td><td>㉔   4
+ 4
☐</td></tr>
<tr><td>㉕   9
– 8
☐</td><td>㉖   10
– 7
☐</td><td>㉗   7
– 5
☐</td><td>㉘   8
– 3
☐</td></tr>
<tr><td>㉙   2
0
+ 5
☐</td><td>㉚   3
1
+ 4
☐</td><td>㉛   5
2
+ 3
☐</td><td>㉜   6
1
+ 2
☐</td></tr>
</table>

ISBN: 978-1-897164-11-2

Add or subtract. Help the cat find the path to the milk.

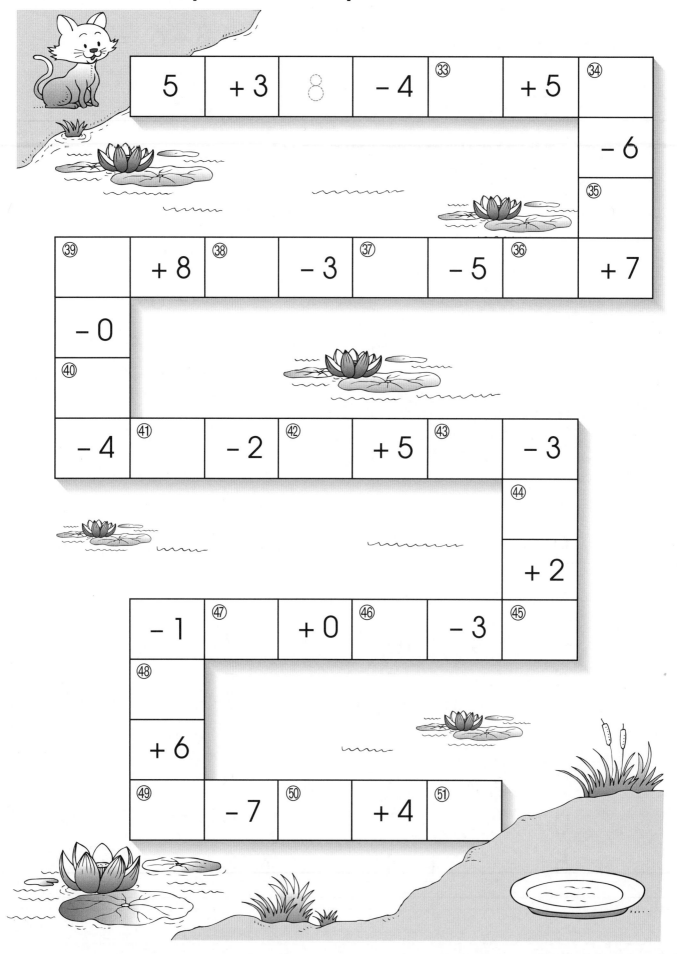

| 5 | + 3 | 8 | − 4 | ㉝ | + 5 | ㉞ |

- 6

㉟

| ㊴ | + 8 | ㊳ | − 3 | ㊲ | − 5 | ㊱ | + 7 |

− 0

㊵

| − 4 | ㊶ | − 2 | ㊷ | + 5 | ㊸ | − 3 |

㊹

+ 2

| − 1 | ㊼ | + 0 | ㊻ | − 3 | ㊺ |

㊽

+ 6

| ㊾ | − 7 | ㊿ | + 4 | 51 |

ISBN: 978-1-897164-11-2

Complete.

(52) 8 were in a tree. 2 flew away. How many were left in the tree? ________ left.	8 − 2
(53) 6 were on a rock. 4 more came. How many were on the rock? ________ were on the rock.	
(54) Sam has 5 . Sue has 4 . How many do they have altogether? ________ altogether.	
(55) 9 were in a tree. 6 jumped down. How many were left in the tree? ________ left.	
(56) Sue has 2 . Sam has 4 . Ann has 1 . How many do they have altogether? ________ altogether.	

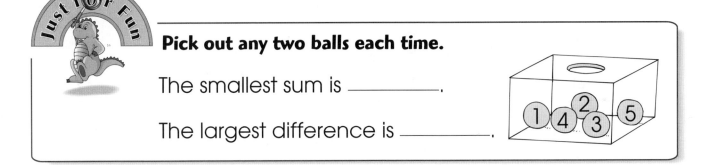

Pick out any two balls each time.

The smallest sum is ________.

The largest difference is ________.

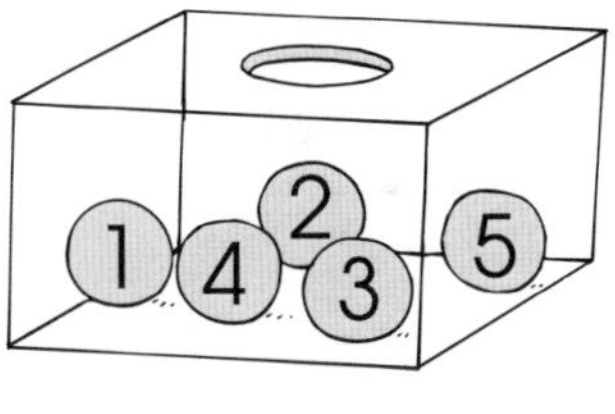

ISBN: 978-1-897164-11-2

Complete each number sentence.

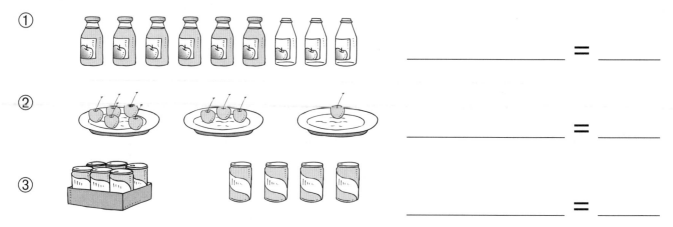

① _____ = _____

② _____ = _____

③ _____ = _____

Find the sums or differences.

④ 10 − 5 = ☐   ⑤ 4 + 2 = ☐

⑥ 9 − 7 = ☐   ⑦ 8 − 6 = ☐

⑧ 2 + 5 = ☐   ⑨ 6 − 5 = ☐

⑩ 3 + 3 = ☐   ⑪ 7 + 0 = ☐

⑫ 6 + 0 + 3 = ☐   ⑬ 4 + 1 + 2 = ☐

⑭
```
   0
 + 9
─────
  ☐
```
⑮
```
   5
 − 4
─────
  ☐
```
⑯
```
  10
 − 7
─────
  ☐
```
⑰
```
   3
 + 5
─────
  ☐
```

⑱
```
   6
 − 4
─────
  ☐
```
⑲
```
   3
 + 4
─────
  ☐
```
⑳
```
   8
 − 4
─────
  ☐
```
㉑
```
   1
 + 7
─────
  ☐
```

   ISBN: 978-1-897164-11-2

In each group, colour the pieces that match the number.

 ㉒ 8   5 + 3   10 − 2   3 + 6   9 − 1

 ㉓ 6   4 + 1   9 − 3   8 − 2   3 + 3

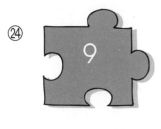 ㉔ 9   1 + 8   10 − 2   5 + 4   9 − 0

 ㉕ 5   10 − 5   3 + 2   8 − 2   4 + 1

 ㉖ 7   4 + 3   9 − 2   10 − 3   2 + 6

Complete the tables. Write + or − in ◯ .

㉗

+ 3	
2	5
7	
5	

㉘

− 4	
8	
4	
6	

㉙

◯	2
9	7
5	3
6	4

㉚

◯	4
2	6
6	10
5	9

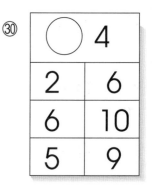

ISBN: 978-1-897164-11-2

Write the numbers.

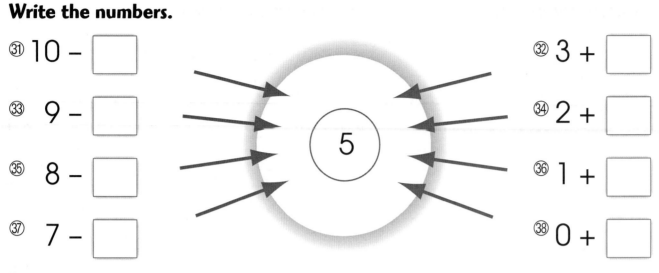

③¹ 10 − ☐

③³ 9 − ☐

③⁵ 8 − ☐

③⁷ 7 − ☐

5

³² 3 + ☐

³⁴ 2 + ☐

³⁶ 1 + ☐

³⁸ 0 + ☐

Put + or − in each box.

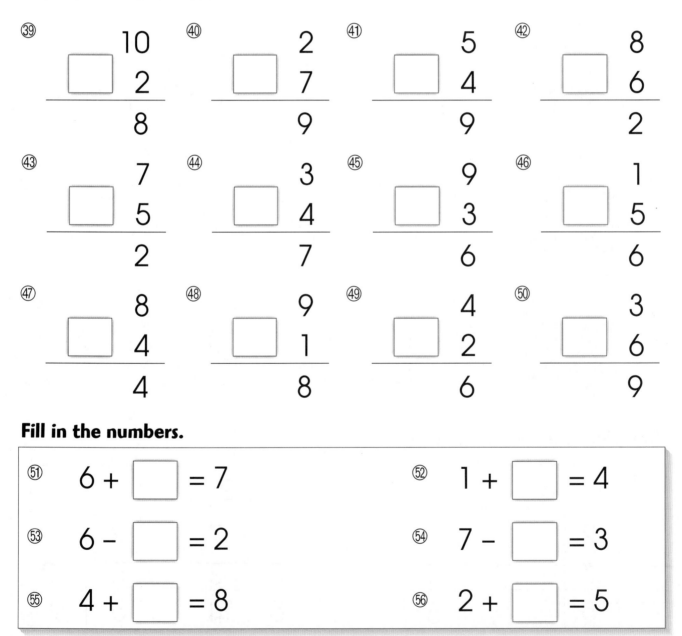

③⁹
```
    10
☐    2
─────
     8
```

⁴⁰
```
     2
☐    7
─────
     9
```

⁴¹
```
     5
☐    4
─────
     9
```

⁴²
```
     8
☐    6
─────
     2
```

⁴³
```
     7
☐    5
─────
     2
```

⁴⁴
```
     3
☐    4
─────
     7
```

⁴⁵
```
     9
☐    3
─────
     6
```

⁴⁶
```
     1
☐    5
─────
     6
```

⁴⁷
```
     8
☐    4
─────
     4
```

⁴⁸
```
     9
☐    1
─────
     8
```

⁴⁹
```
     4
☐    2
─────
     6
```

⁵⁰
```
     3
☐    6
─────
     9
```

Fill in the numbers.

⁵¹ 6 + ☐ = 7

⁵² 1 + ☐ = 4

⁵³ 6 − ☐ = 2

⁵⁴ 7 − ☐ = 3

⁵⁵ 4 + ☐ = 8

⁵⁶ 2 + ☐ = 5

ISBN: 978-1-897164-11-2

Complete.

57. 10 🐦 are in the sky. 2 🐦 land on the grass. How many 🐦 are left in the sky?

_____ 🐦 left.

58. 6 🐸 are in a pond. 3 🐸 jump away. How many 🐸 are left in the pond?

_____ 🐸 left.

59. 5 🪰 are in the sky. 4 🪰 are on the water. How many 🪰 are there in all?

_____ 🪰 in all.

60. There are 2 🌹 and 6 🌹 . How many 🌹 🌹 are there in all?

_____ 🌹 🌹 in all.

61. 4 🐒 are in the tree. 3 🐒 are on the grass. How many 🐒 are there in all?

_____ 🐒 in all.

62. 8 🍌 are in the tree. The 🐒 eats 4 🍌. How many 🍌 are left in the tree?

_____ 🍌 left.

ISBN: 978-1-897164-11-2

9 Addition Facts to 15

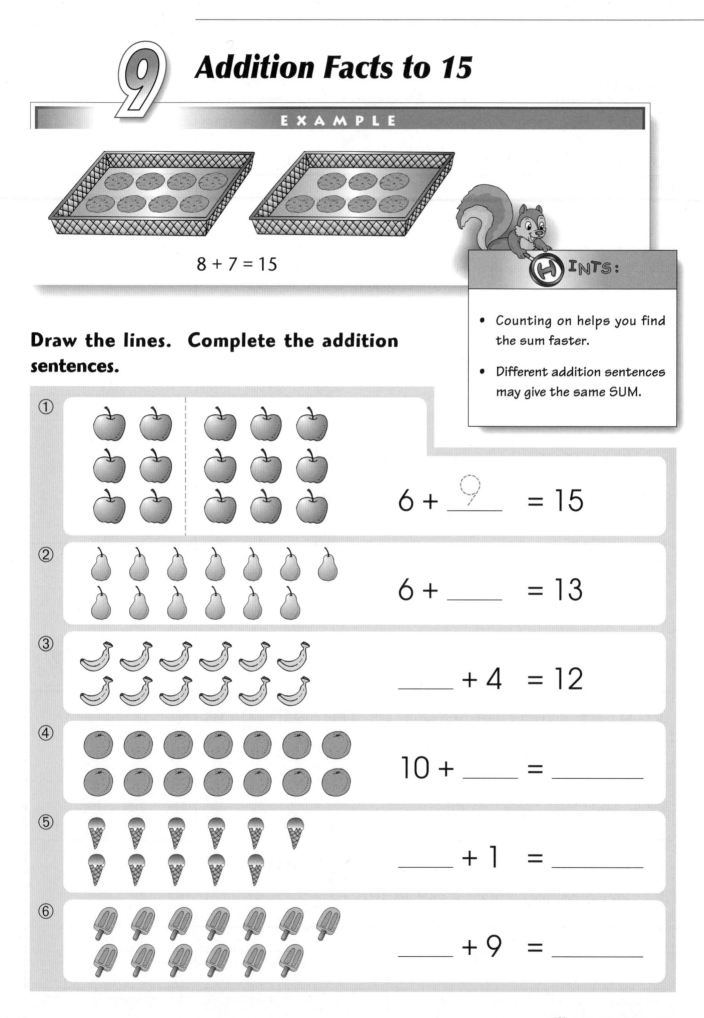

$8 + 7 = 15$

HINTS:

- Counting on helps you find the sum faster.
- Different addition sentences may give the same SUM.

Draw the lines. Complete the addition sentences.

① $6 + \underline{9} = 15$

② $6 + \underline{} = 13$

③ $\underline{} + 4 = 12$

④ $10 + \underline{} = \underline{}$

⑤ $\underline{} + 1 = \underline{}$

⑥ $\underline{} + 9 = \underline{}$

ISBN: 978-1-897164-11-2

Add.

⑦ $12 + 3 =$ ☐ ⑧ $11 + 2 =$ ☐

⑨ $10 + 4 =$ ☐ ⑩ $9 + 6 =$ ☐

⑪ $8 + 6 =$ ☐ ⑫ $7 + 5 =$ ☐

⑬ $9 + 3 =$ ☐ ⑭ $6 + 7 =$ ☐

⑮ $14 + 0 =$ ☐ ⑯ $2 + 9 =$ ☐

⑰ $3 + 8 =$ ☐ ⑱ $5 + 6 =$ ☐

⑲ $7 + 7 =$ ☐ ⑳ $13 + 2 =$ ☐

㉑
$$\begin{array}{r} 4 \\ + \ 9 \\ \hline \end{array}$$

㉒
$$\begin{array}{r} 11 \\ + \ 4 \\ \hline \end{array}$$

㉓
$$\begin{array}{r} 6 \\ + \ 6 \\ \hline \end{array}$$

㉔
$$\begin{array}{r} 7 \\ + \ 4 \\ \hline \end{array}$$

㉕
$$\begin{array}{r} 8 \\ + \ 4 \\ \hline \end{array}$$

㉖
$$\begin{array}{r} 9 \\ + \ 5 \\ \hline \end{array}$$

㉗
$$\begin{array}{r} 5 \\ + \ 8 \\ \hline \end{array}$$

㉘
$$\begin{array}{r} 11 \\ + \ 3 \\ \hline \end{array}$$

㉙
$$\begin{array}{r} 14 \\ + \ 1 \\ \hline \end{array}$$

㉚
$$\begin{array}{r} 7 \\ + \ 8 \\ \hline \end{array}$$

㉛
$$\begin{array}{r} 9 \\ + \ 6 \\ \hline \end{array}$$

㉜
$$\begin{array}{r} 12 \\ + \ 2 \\ \hline \end{array}$$

ISBN: 978-1-897164-11-2

Fill in the missing numbers.

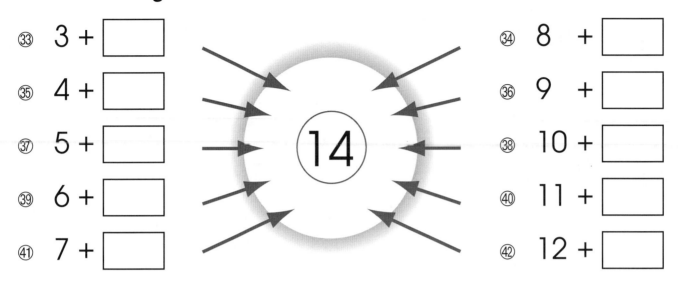

㉝ 3 + ☐

㉟ 4 + ☐

㊲ 5 + ☐

㊴ 6 + ☐

㊶ 7 + ☐

(14)

㉞ 8 + ☐

㊱ 9 + ☐

㊳ 10 + ☐

㊵ 11 + ☐

㊷ 12 + ☐

Complete. Colour the balloon with the largest sum in each group.

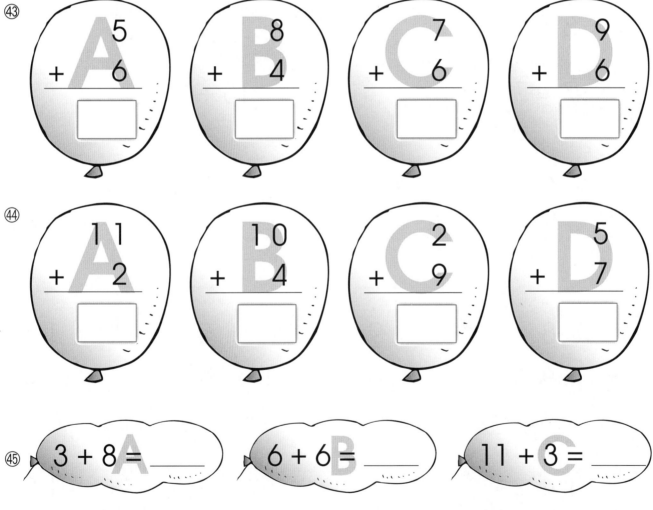

㊸

A
  5
+ 6
☐

B
  8
+ 4
☐

C
  7
+ 6
☐

D
  9
+ 6
☐

㊹

A
  11
+ 2
☐

B
  10
+ 4
☐

C
  2
+ 9
☐

D
  5
+ 7
☐

㊺ 3 + 8 A = _____

6 + 6 B = _____

11 + 3 C = _____

㊻ 12 + 3 A = _____

6 + 8 B = _____

9 + 3 C = _____

ISBN: 978-1-897164-11-2

Complete.

47 There are 8 red 🍎 and 6 green 🍏 . How many 🍎 🍏 are there in all? _____ 🍎 🍏 in all.		8 + 6
48 10 🍪 are on the plate. 3 🍪 are in the bag. How many 🍪 are there in all? _____ 🍪 in all.		
49 12 ⚽ are in the basket. 0 ⚽ are on the table. How many ⚽ are there in all? _____ ⚽ in all.		
50 4 🎈 are in Sam's left hand. 7 🎈 are in his right hand. How many 🎈 does Sam have in all? _____ 🎈 in all.		

Just for Fun

Complete.

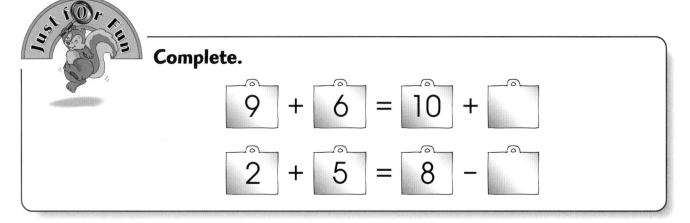

$$9 + 6 = 10 + \boxed{}$$

$$2 + 5 = 8 - \boxed{}$$

ISBN: 978-1-897164-11-2

10 *Subtraction Facts to 15*

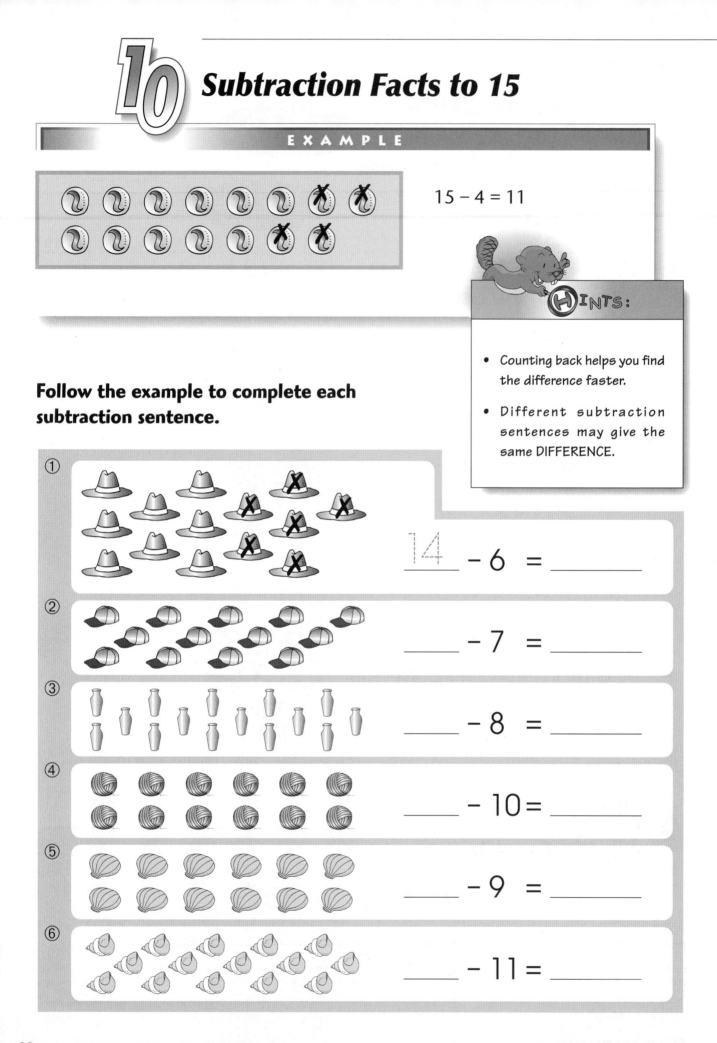

15 − 4 = 11

HINTS:

- Counting back helps you find the difference faster.
- Different subtraction sentences may give the same DIFFERENCE.

Follow the example to complete each subtraction sentence.

① 14 − 6 = _____

② ____ − 7 = _____

③ ____ − 8 = _____

④ ____ − 10 = _____

⑤ ____ − 9 = _____

⑥ ____ − 11 = _____

ISBN: 978-1-897164-11-2

Subtract.

⑦	13 − 4 = ☐	⑧	12 − 6 = ☐
⑨	15 − 7 = ☐	⑩	14 − 9 = ☐
⑪	11 − 6 = ☐	⑫	13 − 8 = ☐
⑬	12 − 8 = ☐	⑭	15 − 9 = ☐
⑮	14 − 4 = ☐	⑯	13 − 0 = ☐
⑰	13 − 2 = ☐	⑱	11 − 3 = ☐
⑲	15 − 13 = ☐	⑳	12 − 3 = ☐

㉑
$$\begin{array}{r} 11 \\ -\ 7 \\ \hline \end{array}$$

㉒
$$\begin{array}{r} 13 \\ -\ 1 \\ \hline \end{array}$$

㉓
$$\begin{array}{r} 15 \\ -\ 5 \\ \hline \end{array}$$

㉔
$$\begin{array}{r} 12 \\ -\ 12 \\ \hline \end{array}$$

㉕
$$\begin{array}{r} 14 \\ -\ 10 \\ \hline \end{array}$$

㉖
$$\begin{array}{r} 15 \\ -\ 9 \\ \hline \end{array}$$

㉗
$$\begin{array}{r} 12 \\ -\ 4 \\ \hline \end{array}$$

㉘
$$\begin{array}{r} 11 \\ -\ 4 \\ \hline \end{array}$$

㉙
$$\begin{array}{r} 13 \\ -\ 9 \\ \hline \end{array}$$

㉚
$$\begin{array}{r} 14 \\ -\ 12 \\ \hline \end{array}$$

㉛
$$\begin{array}{r} 11 \\ -\ 5 \\ \hline \end{array}$$

㉜
$$\begin{array}{r} 12 \\ -\ 7 \\ \hline \end{array}$$

ISBN: 978-1-897164-11-2

Subtract. Help Baby Bear find Mother Bear.

33. 14 − 7 = ☐

34. 13 − 5 = ☐

35.
$$\begin{array}{r} 12 \\ -\ \ 5 \\ \hline \square \end{array}$$

36. 15 − 6 = ☐

37. 11 − 2 = ☐

38.
$$\begin{array}{r} 13 \\ -\ 11 \\ \hline \square \end{array}$$

39. 14 − 8 = ☐

40. 12 − 2 = ☐

41. 13 − 3 = ☐

42.
$$\begin{array}{r} 11 \\ -\ \ 8 \\ \hline \square \end{array}$$

43. 14 − 5 = ☐

ISBN: 978-1-897164-11-2

Complete.

44 There are 14 🍎. 8 🍎 are eaten. How many 🍎 are left? _____ 🍎 left.	$\begin{array}{r} 14 \\ -8 \\ \hline \end{array}$
45 Sue has 12 🌰. Sam has 7 🌰. How many more 🌰 does Sue have than Sam? _____ more 🌰.	
46 There are 13 🍪 on the plate and 5 🍪 in the bag. How many more 🍪 are there on the plate? _____ more 🍪.	
47 There are 15 🎈. 6 🎈 burst. How many 🎈 are left? _____ 🎈 left.	

Just for Fun

Count on to find the path for the monkey. Colour the path.

12	18	16	17	15
14	16	15	18	17
15	13	14	19	20
11	12	17	18	16
17	13	12	11	12

11 Addition and Subtraction Facts to 15

There are 12 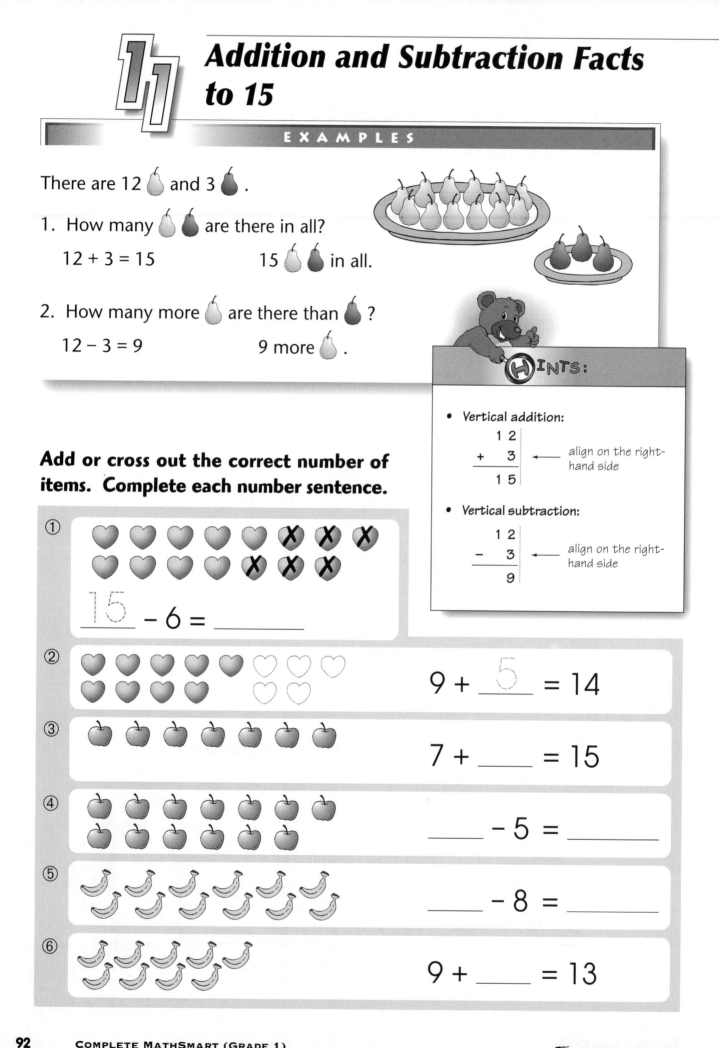 and 3 .

1. How many are there in all?

   12 + 3 = 15   15 in all.

2. How many more are there than ?

   12 − 3 = 9   9 more .

HINTS:

- Vertical addition:

  ```
    1 2
  +   3   ← align on the right-hand side
  -----
    1 5
  ```

- Vertical subtraction:

  ```
    1 2
  −   3   ← align on the right-hand side
  -----
      9
  ```

Add or cross out the correct number of items. Complete each number sentence.

① $\underline{15} - 6 = \underline{}$

② $9 + \underline{5} = 14$

③ $7 + \underline{} = 15$

④ $\underline{} - 5 = \underline{}$

⑤ $\underline{} - 8 = \underline{}$

⑥ $9 + \underline{} = 13$

Add or subtract.

⑦ $13 - 7 =$ ▢

⑧ $8 + 5 =$ ▢

⑨ $6 + 8 =$ ▢

⑩ $11 - 7 =$ ▢

⑪ $5 + 10 =$ ▢

⑫ $12 - 6 =$ ▢

⑬ $14 - 6 =$ ▢

⑭ $8 + 3 =$ ▢

⑮ $15 - 9 =$ ▢

⑯ $7 + 7 =$ ▢

⑰ $11 - 10 =$ ▢

⑱ $15 + 0 =$ ▢

⑲ $12 + 3 =$ ▢

⑳ $15 - 6 =$ ▢

㉑
$$\begin{array}{r} 4 \\ +\ 9 \\ \hline \end{array}$$

㉒
$$\begin{array}{r} 14 \\ -\ 9 \\ \hline \end{array}$$

㉓
$$\begin{array}{r} 11 \\ +\ 2 \\ \hline \end{array}$$

㉔
$$\begin{array}{r} 12 \\ -\ 10 \\ \hline \end{array}$$

㉕
$$\begin{array}{r} 9 \\ -\ 6 \\ \hline \end{array}$$

㉖
$$\begin{array}{r} 12 \\ -\ 5 \\ \hline \end{array}$$

㉗
$$\begin{array}{r} 13 \\ -\ 11 \\ \hline \end{array}$$

㉘
$$\begin{array}{r} 13 \\ +\ 2 \\ \hline \end{array}$$

㉙
$$\begin{array}{r} 15 \\ -\ 12 \\ \hline \end{array}$$

㉚
$$\begin{array}{r} 6 \\ +\ 8 \\ \hline \end{array}$$

㉛
$$\begin{array}{r} 7 \\ +\ 5 \\ \hline \end{array}$$

㉜
$$\begin{array}{r} 14 \\ -\ 8 \\ \hline \end{array}$$

ISBN: 978-1-897164-11-2

Complete the tables.

③③

+	4	5	6
7			
8			
9			15

③④

13	14	15	–
			7
			8
		6	9

Match.

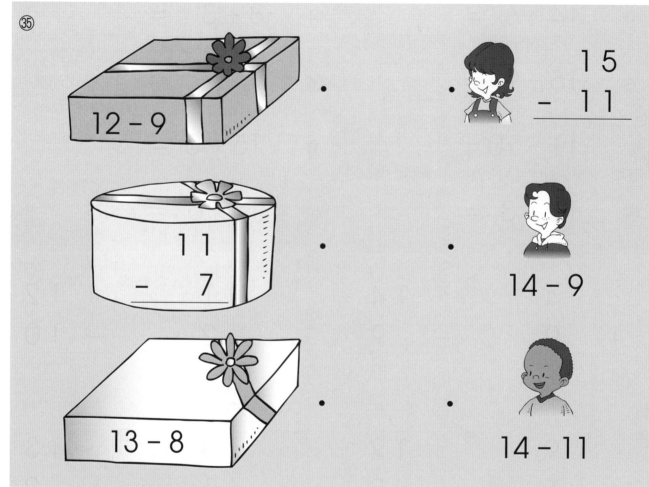

③⑤

In each group, colour the two numbers that give the sum in the centre.

③⑥   ③⑦

ISBN: 978-1-897164-11-2

Complete.

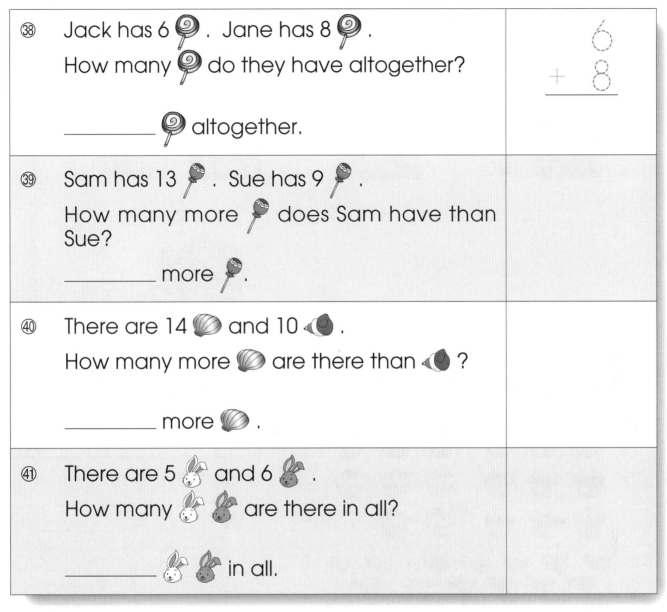

38 Jack has 6 🍭 . Jane has 8 🍭 .
    How many 🍭 do they have altogether?

    _____ 🍭 altogether.

    6
    $+\ 8$

39 Sam has 13 🍭 . Sue has 9 🍭 .
    How many more 🍭 does Sam have than Sue?

    _____ more 🍭 .

40 There are 14 🐚 and 10 🐚 .
    How many more 🐚 are there than 🐚 ?

    _____ more 🐚 .

41 There are 5 🐰 and 6 🐰 .
    How many 🐰 🐰 are there in all?

    _____ 🐰 🐰 in all.

Colour the path for Little Ant to get the food.
Start from 0. Count by 5's to 50.

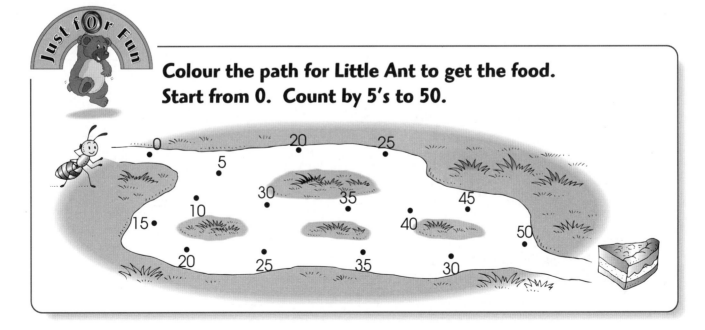

12 Addition Facts to 20

EXAMPLE

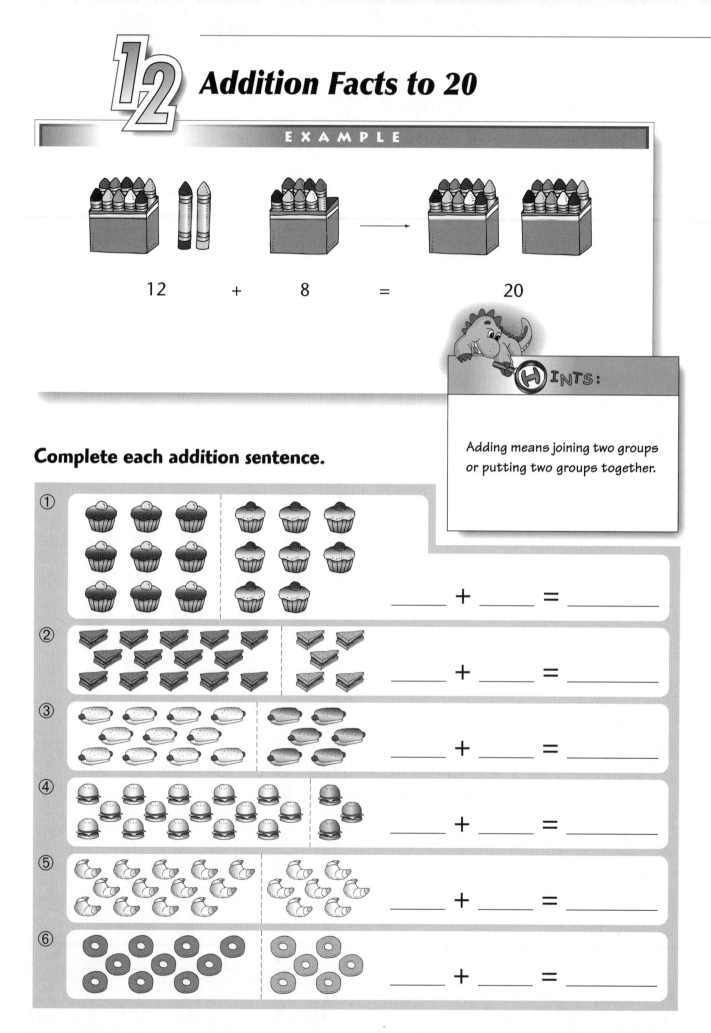

12   +   8   =   20

HINTS:

Adding means joining two groups or putting two groups together.

Complete each addition sentence.

① _____ + _____ = _____

② _____ + _____ = _____

③ _____ + _____ = _____

④ _____ + _____ = _____

⑤ _____ + _____ = _____

⑥ _____ + _____ = _____

ISBN: 978-1-897164-11-2

Add.

⑦ 16 + 4 = ☐	⑧ 13 + 6 = ☐
⑨ 11 + 8 = ☐	⑩ 15 + 4 = ☐
⑪ 12 + 7 = ☐	⑫ 17 + 3 = ☐
⑬ 10 + 9 = ☐	⑭ 14 + 4 = ☐
⑮ 8 + 9 = ☐	⑯ 19 + 1 = ☐
⑰ 15 + 2 = ☐	⑱ 12 + 5 = ☐
⑲ 13 + 4 = ☐	⑳ 11 + 9 = ☐

㉑
```
  17
+  2
-----
```
☐

㉒
```
  10
+  8
-----
```
☐

㉓
```
  15
+  5
-----
```
☐

㉔
```
  12
+  6
-----
```
☐

㉕
```
  11
+  5
-----
```
☐

㉖
```
  13
+  6
-----
```
☐

㉗
```
  14
+  3
-----
```
☐

㉘
```
  16
+  3
-----
```
☐

㉙
```
  18
+  2
-----
```
☐

㉚
```
   9
+  7
-----
```
☐

㉛
```
  19
+  1
-----
```
☐

㉜
```
  10
+ 10
-----
```
☐

ISBN: 978-1-897164-11-2

Match and complete. Write the letters in ㊸ to solve the riddle.

㉝ 15 + 3 = _____ •   • (n) 13 + 3 = _____

㉞ 10 + 6 = _____ •   • (k) 12 + 2 = _____

㉟ 9 + 5 = _____ •   • (r) 16 + 2 = _____

㊱ 11 + 6 = _____ •   • (h) 16 + 4 = _____

㊲ 12 + 8 = _____ •   • (c) 16 + 1 = _____

㊳ 13 + 2 = _____ •   • (e) 15 + 4 = _____

㊴ 16 + 3 = _____ •   • (d) 14 + 1 = _____

㊵ 11 + 1 = _____ •   • (a) 6 + 5 = _____

㊶ 9 + 4 = _____ •   • (f) 10 + 2 = _____

㊷ 7 + 4 = _____ •   • (i) 6 + 7 = _____

Riddle: What do you need when you sweat?

㊸

20	11	16	15	14	19	18	17	20	13	19	12
A	h											.

ISBN: 978-1-897164-11-2

Complete.

㊸ There are 10 🎂 and 10 🍰 in the bakery.
How many 🎂🍰 are there in all?

_____ = _____   _____ 🎂🍰 in all.

㊺ There are 12 🥧 and 6 🥟 .
How many 🥧🥟 are there in all?

_____ = _____   _____ 🥧🥟 in all.

㊻ There are 8 🧁 and 8 🧁 .
How many 🧁🧁 are there in all?

_____ = _____   _____ 🧁🧁 in all.

㊼ There are 9 🥖 . The baker makes 10 more 🥖 .
How many 🥖 are there in all?

_____ = _____   _____ 🥖 in all.

㊽ There are 13 🍩 in 🍱 and 4 🍩 in 📦 .
How many 🍩 are there in all?

_____ = _____   _____ 🍩 in all.

Just for Fun

Colour the path for Sam to get his bike. Start from 10. Count by 10's to 100.

10	30	60	70	50
10	40	50	80	90
20	30	60	60	100
10	20	30	70	80

ISBN: 978-1-897164-11-2

13 Subtraction Facts to 20

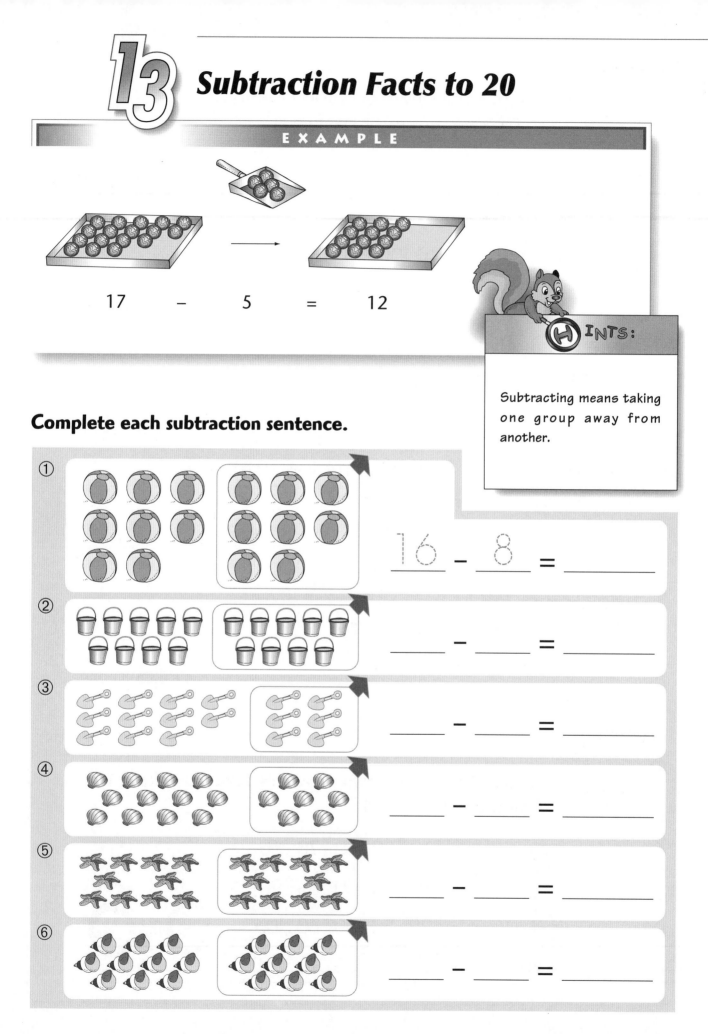

17 – 5 = 12

HINTS:

Subtracting means taking one group away from another.

Complete each subtraction sentence.

① 16 – 8 = _____

② _____ – _____ = _____

③ _____ – _____ = _____

④ _____ – _____ = _____

⑤ _____ – _____ = _____

⑥ _____ – _____ = _____

ISBN: 978-1-897164-11-2

Add or subtract.

⑦ 18 – 7 = ▢   ⑧ 16 – 9 = ▢

⑨ 20 – 11 = ▢   ⑩ 19 – 4 = ▢

⑪ 17 – 8 = ▢   ⑫ 18 – 12 = ▢

⑬ 16 – 4 = ▢   ⑭ 20 – 6 = ▢

⑮ 19 – 17 = ▢   ⑯ 17 – 4 = ▢

⑰ 20 – 2 = ▢   ⑱ 16 – 13 = ▢

⑲ 18 – 4 = ▢   ⑳ 17 – 11 = ▢

㉑
$$\begin{array}{r} 19 \\ -\ 3 \\ \hline \end{array}$$

㉒
$$\begin{array}{r} 16 \\ -\ 10 \\ \hline \end{array}$$

㉓
$$\begin{array}{r} 18 \\ -\ 8 \\ \hline \end{array}$$

㉔
$$\begin{array}{r} 17 \\ -\ 5 \\ \hline \end{array}$$

㉕
$$\begin{array}{r} 20 \\ -\ 5 \\ \hline \end{array}$$

㉖
$$\begin{array}{r} 17 \\ -\ 8 \\ \hline \end{array}$$

㉗
$$\begin{array}{r} 16 \\ -\ 9 \\ \hline \end{array}$$

㉘
$$\begin{array}{r} 19 \\ -\ 13 \\ \hline \end{array}$$

㉙
$$\begin{array}{r} 18 \\ -\ 15 \\ \hline \end{array}$$

㉚
$$\begin{array}{r} 16 \\ -\ 12 \\ \hline \end{array}$$

㉛
$$\begin{array}{r} 19 \\ -\ 5 \\ \hline \end{array}$$

㉜
$$\begin{array}{r} 20 \\ -\ 7 \\ \hline \end{array}$$

ISBN: 978-1-897164-11-2

Subtract. Help Little Bunny go through the forest.

㉝ 16 − 10 = ☐

㉞ 20 − 13 = ☐

㉟
$$\begin{array}{r} 1\,8 \\ -\ \ 7 \\ \hline \end{array}$$
☐

㊱ 17 − 12 = ☐

㊲ 16 − 11 = ☐

㊳
$$\begin{array}{r} 1\,6 \\ -\ 1\,5 \\ \hline \end{array}$$
☐

㊴ 18 − 16 = ☐

㊵ 19 − 14 = ☐

㊶
$$\begin{array}{r} 1\,7 \\ -\ 1\,5 \\ \hline \end{array}$$
☐

㊷ 18 − 11 = ☐

㊸
$$\begin{array}{r} 1\,9 \\ -\ 1\,0 \\ \hline \end{array}$$
☐

㊹ 18 − 6 = ☐

ISBN: 978-1-897164-11-2

Complete.

45   Sue bought 18 ✏. Sam bought 12 ✏.

How many more ✏ did Sue buy than Sam?

_____ = _____   _____ more ✏ .

46   Jack has 17 📓. Jane has 9 📓.

How many more 📓 does Jack have than Jane?

_____ = _____   _____ more 📓 .

47   Bob has 20 🧱. Ben has 18 🧱.

How many more 🧱 does Bob have than Ben?

_____ = _____   _____ more 🧱 .

48   There are 16 🎱 on the table. 5 🎱 roll off.

How many 🎱 are left on the table?

_____ = _____   _____ 🎱 left.

49   There are 19 children in the playground. 9 of them are boys.

How many girls are there in the playground?

_____ = _____   _____ girls.

Just for Fun

Colour the cards with the same answers.

18 − 4	12 − 8	16 − 11

19 − 5	17 − 4	20 − 6	14 − 10

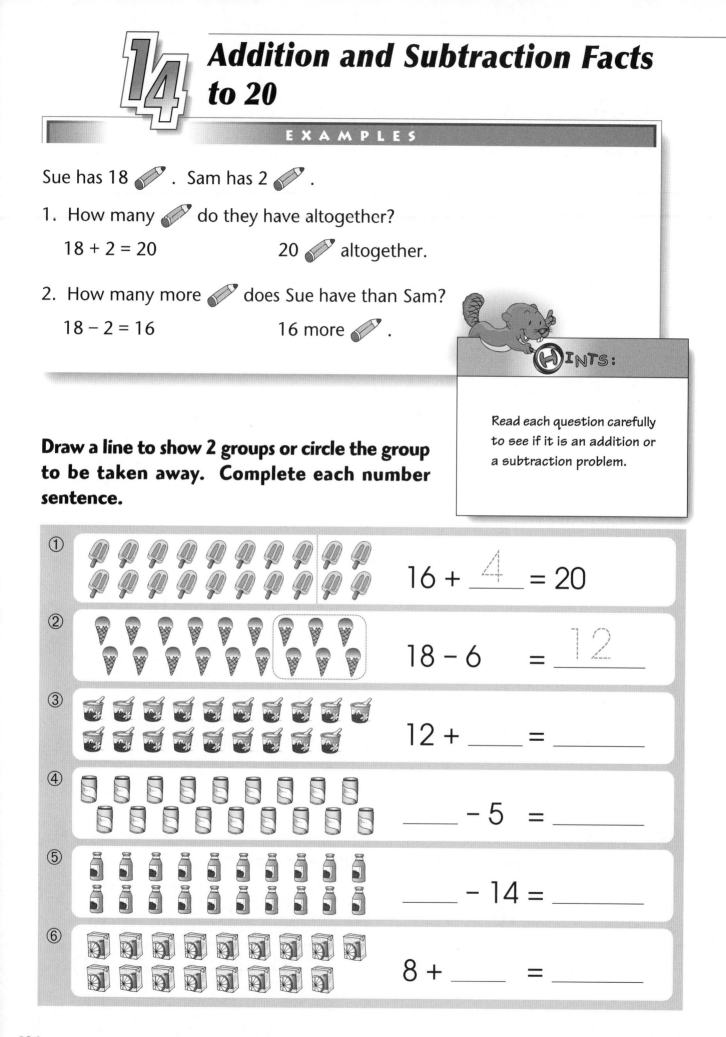

Addition and Subtraction Facts to 20

Sue has 18 ✏ . Sam has 2 ✏ .

1. How many ✏ do they have altogether?

    18 + 2 = 20   20 ✏ altogether.

2. How many more ✏ does Sue have than Sam?

    18 − 2 = 16   16 more ✏ .

HINTS:

Read each question carefully to see if it is an addition or a subtraction problem.

Draw a line to show 2 groups or circle the group to be taken away. Complete each number sentence.

① 16 + _4_ = 20

② 18 − 6 = _12_

③ 12 + ___ = _____

④ ___ − 5 = _____

⑤ ___ − 14 = _____

⑥ 8 + ___ = _____

ISBN: 978-1-897164-11-2

Add or subtract.

⑦ 18 – 4 = ☐   ⑧ 16 + 3 = ☐

⑨ 15 + 4 = ☐   ⑩ 19 – 12 = ☐

⑪ 12 – 9 = ☐   ⑫ 20 – 8 = ☐

⑬ 17 – 14 = ☐   ⑭ 17 + 2 = ☐

⑮ 16 – 12 = ☐   ⑯ 15 + 5 = ☐

⑰ 19 + 1 = ☐   ⑱ 18 – 11 = ☐

⑲ 20 + 0 = ☐   ⑳ 17 – 9 = ☐

㉑
```
  1 5
+   2
-----
```
☐

㉒
```
  1 6
-   9
-----
```
☐

㉓
```
  1 7
+   3
-----
```
☐

㉔
```
  2 0
-   9
-----
```
☐

㉕
```
  1 8
- 1 5
-----
```
☐

㉖
```
  1 6
+   4
-----
```
☐

㉗
```
  1 7
- 1 3
-----
```
☐

㉘
```
  1 9
-   9
-----
```
☐

㉙
```
  2 0
-   4
-----
```
☐

㉚
```
  1 7
-   5
-----
```
☐

㉛
```
  1 8
+   2
-----
```
☐

㉜
```
  1 5
+   3
-----
```
☐

ISBN: 978-1-897164-11-2

In each group, colour the plates that match the number.

㉝ 19 | 12 + 7 | 20 – 1 | 14 + 4 | 13 + 6

㉞ 16 | 20 – 4 | 12 + 3 | 19 – 3 | 9 + 7

㉟ 13 | 9 + 5 | 19 – 6 | 17 – 4 | 7 + 6

㊱ 15 | 18 – 3 | 9 + 7 | 17 – 2 | 11 + 4

㊲ 18 | 18 – 0 | 20 – 2 | 10 + 8 | 12 + 5

㊳ 11 | 16 – 4 | 7 + 4 | 17 – 6 | 9 + 2

㊴ 12 | 8 + 4 | 19 – 7 | 6 + 5 | 16 – 4

ISBN: 978-1-897164-11-2

Complete.

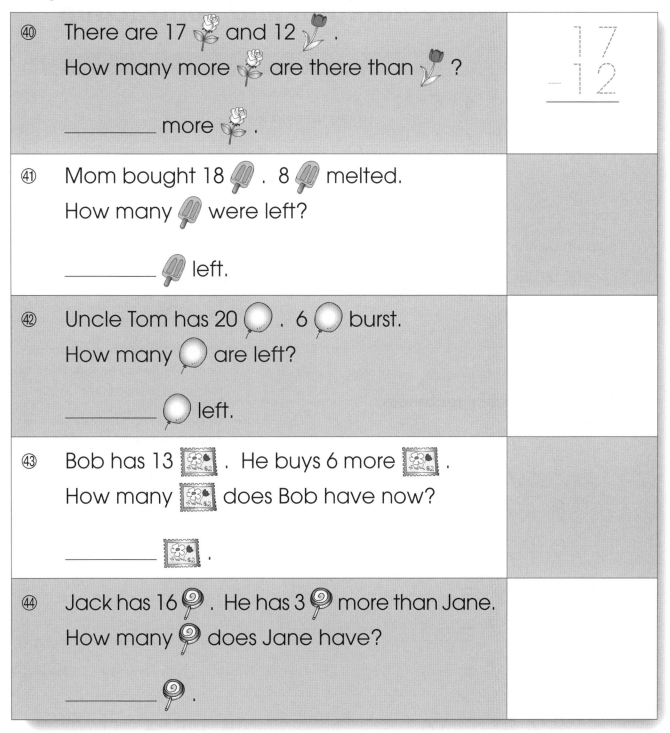

④⓪ There are 17 🌹 and 12 🌷.
How many more 🌹 are there than 🌷?

17
−12

_____ more 🌹.

④① Mom bought 18 🍦. 8 🍦 melted.
How many 🍦 were left?

_____ 🍦 left.

④② Uncle Tom has 20 🎈. 6 🎈 burst.
How many 🎈 are left?

_____ 🎈 left.

④③ Bob has 13 📮. He buys 6 more 📮.
How many 📮 does Bob have now?

_____ 📮.

④④ Jack has 16 🍭. He has 3 🍭 more than Jane.
How many 🍭 does Jane have?

_____ 🍭.

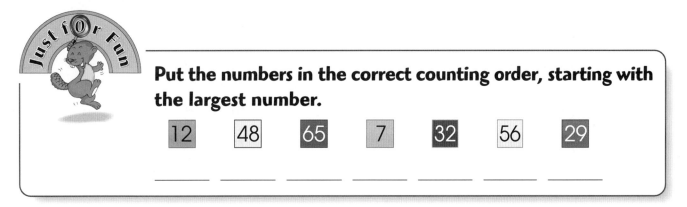

Put the numbers in the correct counting order, starting with the largest number.

| 12 | 48 | 65 | 7 | 32 | 56 | 29 |

_____ _____ _____ _____ _____ _____ _____

ISBN: 978-1-897164-11-2

15 More Addition and Subtraction

1.

goes up by one

goes up by one

$\quad 6 + 6 = 12$

$\quad 7 + 6 = 13$

$\quad 8 + 6 = 14$

goes up by one

goes up by one

2.

goes up by one

goes up by one

$\quad 12 - 7 = 5$

$\quad 13 - 7 = 6$

$\quad 14 - 7 = 7$

goes up by one

goes up by one

HINTS:

- Knowing the addition or subtraction patterns may help you find the sum or difference faster.

- Using tens may also help you find the sum and difference faster.

  e.g. $7 + 5 = 7 + 3 + 2$

  $\qquad = 10 + 2$

  $\qquad = 12$

  $12 - 4 = 10 + 2 - 4$

  $\qquad = 10 - 4 + 2$

  $\qquad = 6 + 2$

  $\qquad = 8$

Complete the number sentences.

①

$\quad 7 + 7 \ = 14$

a. $\ 8 + 7 \ = $ _____

b. $\ 9 + 7 \ = $ _____

c. $\ 10 + 7 = $ _____

d. $\ 11 + 7 = $ _____

e. $\ 12 + 7 = $ _____

②

$\quad 8 + 8 \ = 16$

a. $\ 8 + 9 \ = $ _____

b. $\ 8 + 10 = $ _____

c. $\ 8 + 11 = $ _____

d. $\ 8 + 12 = $ _____

③

$\quad 5 + 5 = 10$

a. $\ 5 + 6 = $ _____

b. $\ 5 + 7 = $ _____

c. $\ 5 + 8 = $ _____

d. $\ 5 + 9 = $ _____

ISBN: 978-1-897164-11-2

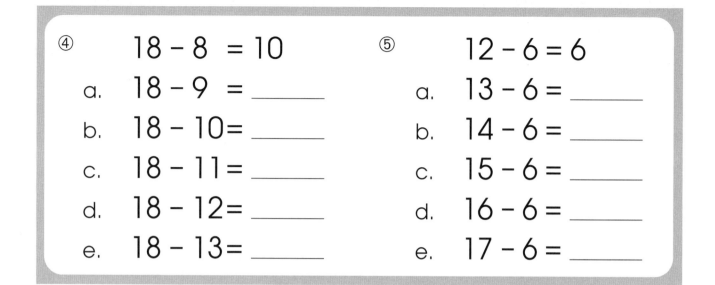

④ $18 - 8 = 10$

   a. $18 - 9 =$ _____

   b. $18 - 10 =$ _____

   c. $18 - 11 =$ _____

   d. $18 - 12 =$ _____

   e. $18 - 13 =$ _____

⑤ $12 - 6 = 6$

   a. $13 - 6 =$ _____

   b. $14 - 6 =$ _____

   c. $15 - 6 =$ _____

   d. $16 - 6 =$ _____

   e. $17 - 6 =$ _____

Draw and complete.

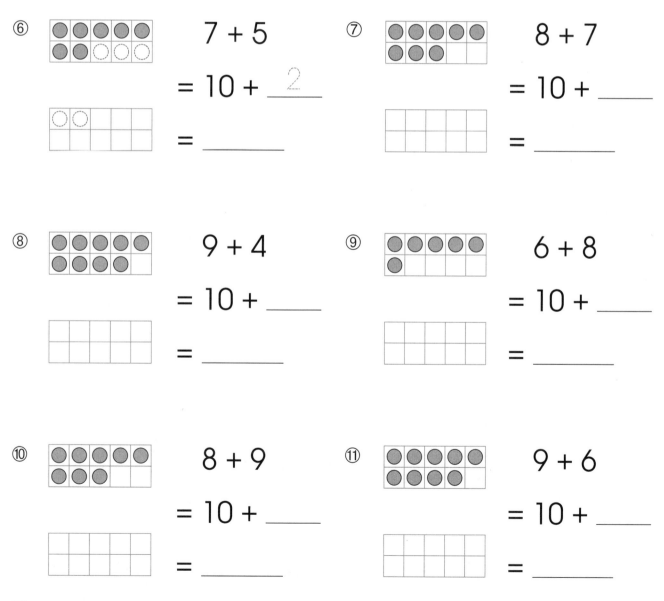

⑥ $7 + 5$

$= 10 + \underline{2}$

$= \underline{\hphantom{000}}$

⑦ $8 + 7$

$= 10 + \underline{\hphantom{00}}$

$= \underline{\hphantom{000}}$

⑧ $9 + 4$

$= 10 + \underline{\hphantom{00}}$

$= \underline{\hphantom{000}}$

⑨ $6 + 8$

$= 10 + \underline{\hphantom{00}}$

$= \underline{\hphantom{000}}$

⑩ $8 + 9$

$= 10 + \underline{\hphantom{00}}$

$= \underline{\hphantom{000}}$

⑪ $9 + 6$

$= 10 + \underline{\hphantom{00}}$

$= \underline{\hphantom{000}}$

ISBN: 978-1-897164-11-2

Cross out the correct number of items and complete the subtraction sentences.

⑫

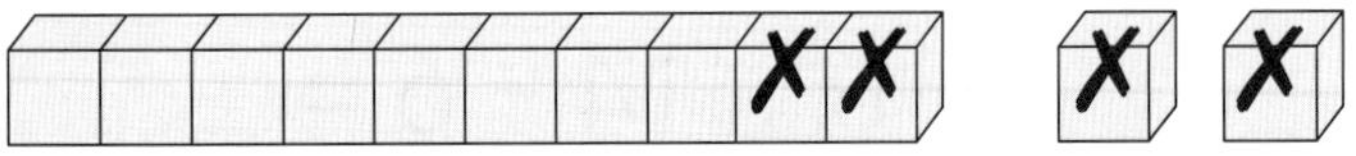

$12 - 4$
$= 10 - \underline{2}$
$= \underline{}$

⑬

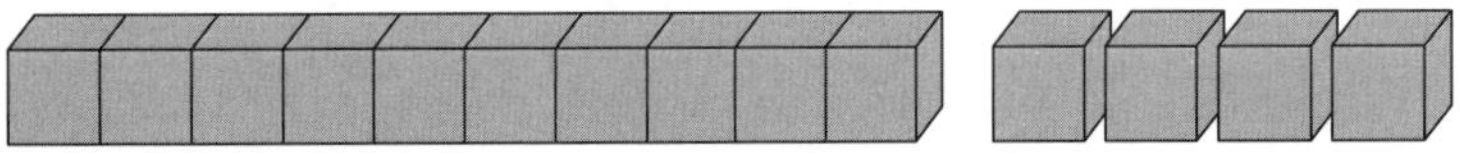

$14 - 6$
$= 10 - \underline{}$
$= \underline{}$

⑭

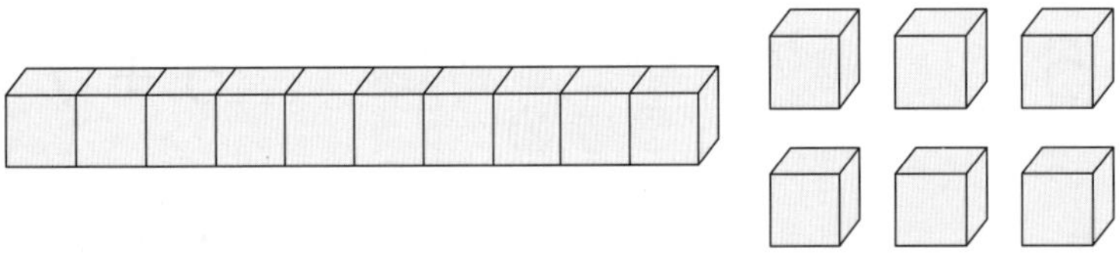

$16 - 9$
$= 10 - \underline{}$
$= \underline{}$

⑮

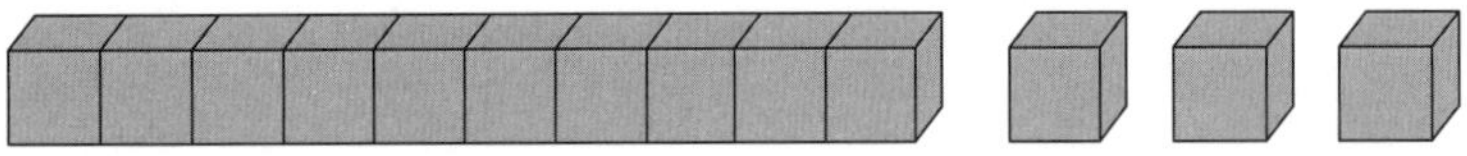

$13 - 7$
$= 10 - \underline{}$
$= \underline{}$

⑯

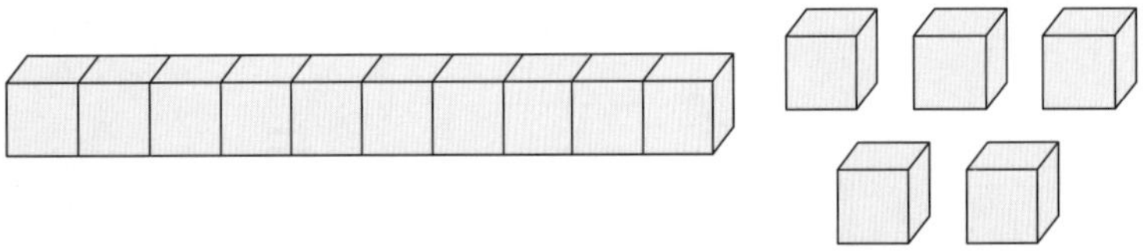

$15 - 8$
$= 10 - \underline{}$
$= \underline{}$

⑰

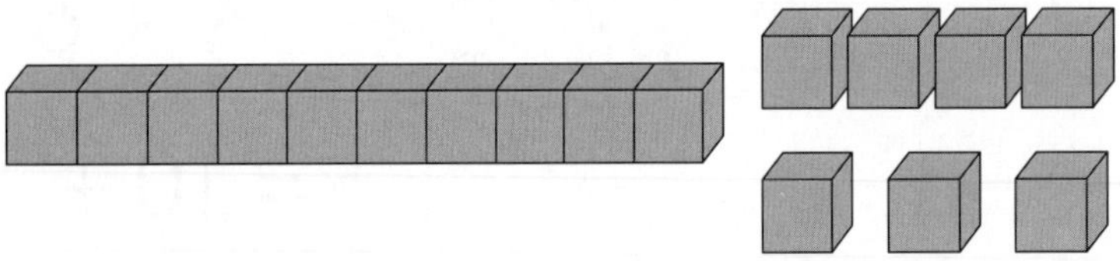

$17 - 9$
$= 10 - \underline{}$
$= \underline{}$

ISBN: 978-1-897164-11-2

Add.

⑱
```
   2
   4
+  8
─────
```

⑲
```
   3
   2
+  7
─────
```

⑳
```
   7
   2
+  9
─────
```

㉑
```
   8
   0
+  7
─────
```

㉒
```
   9
   1
+  6
─────
```

㉓
```
   5
   5
+  7
─────
```

㉔
```
   2
   8
+  9
─────
```

㉕
```
   3
   7
+  5
─────
```

Just for Fun

Complete. Colour the party hats red if the answers are odd numbers. Colour the hats yellow if the answers are even numbers.

```
  12
+  7
─────
```

```
  18
-  6
─────
```

```
  13
+  5
─────
```

```
  20
-  4
─────
```

```
  19
-  4
─────
```

ISBN: 978-1-897164-11-2

Addition and Subtraction with Money

EXAMPLES

How many cents are there in the piggy bank?

$5 + 1 + 1$
$= 7$

There are 7¢ in the piggy bank.

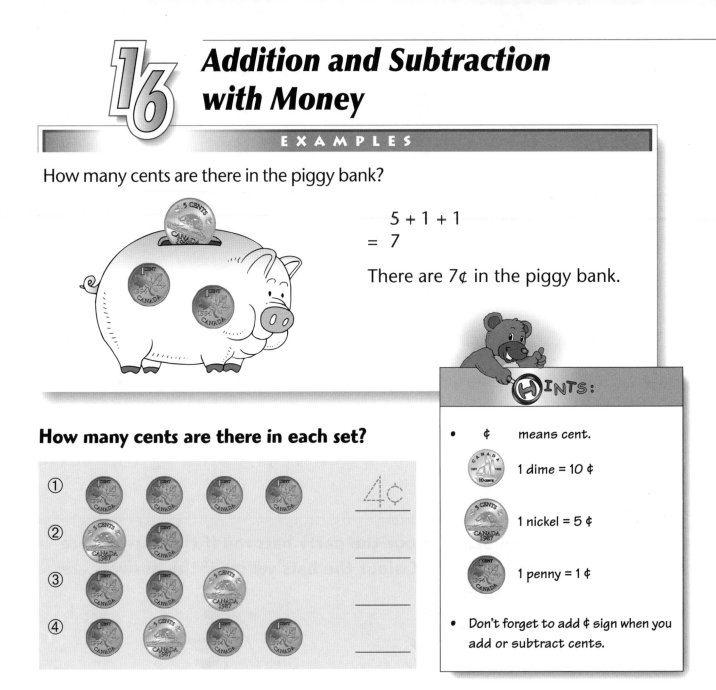

HINTS:

- ¢ means cent.
- 1 dime = 10 ¢
- 1 nickel = 5 ¢
- 1 penny = 1 ¢
- Don't forget to add ¢ sign when you add or subtract cents.

How many cents are there in each set?

① 4¢

② _____

③ _____

④ _____

The children go to a garage sale. Circle the coins needed to buy each item.

⑤ 4 ¢

⑥ 8 ¢

⑦ 10 ¢

⑧ 5 ¢

ISBN: 978-1-897164-11-2

How much change do they get?

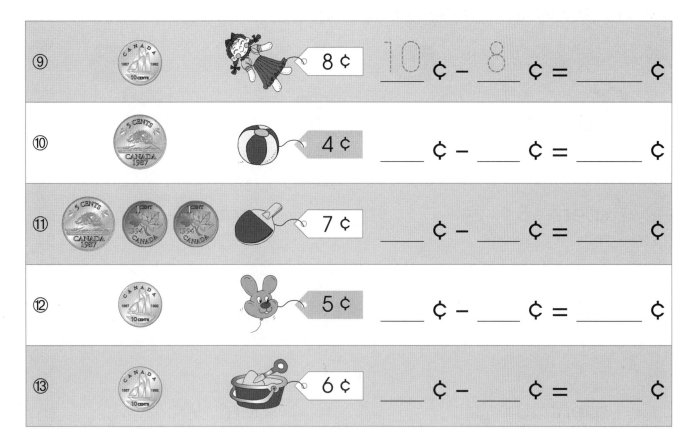

⑨ 8 ¢   10 ¢ – 8 ¢ = _____ ¢

⑩ 4 ¢   ___ ¢ – ___ ¢ = _____ ¢

⑪ 7 ¢   ___ ¢ – ___ ¢ = _____ ¢

⑫ 5 ¢   ___ ¢ – ___ ¢ = _____ ¢

⑬ 6 ¢   ___ ¢ – ___ ¢ = _____ ¢

How much more do they need?

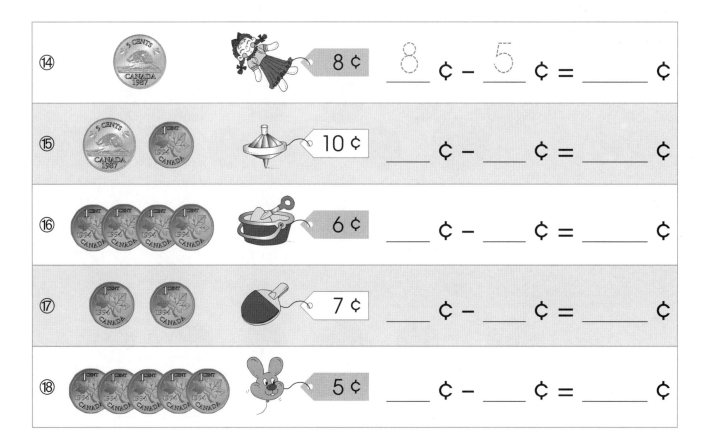

⑭ 8 ¢   8 ¢ – 5 ¢ = _____ ¢

⑮ 10 ¢   ___ ¢ – ___ ¢ = _____ ¢

⑯ 6 ¢   ___ ¢ – ___ ¢ = _____ ¢

⑰ 7 ¢   ___ ¢ – ___ ¢ = _____ ¢

⑱ 5 ¢   ___ ¢ – ___ ¢ = _____ ¢

ISBN: 978-1-897164-11-2

The children spent the exact amounts to buy the garage sale items. Write the letters in the boxes to tell what they bought.

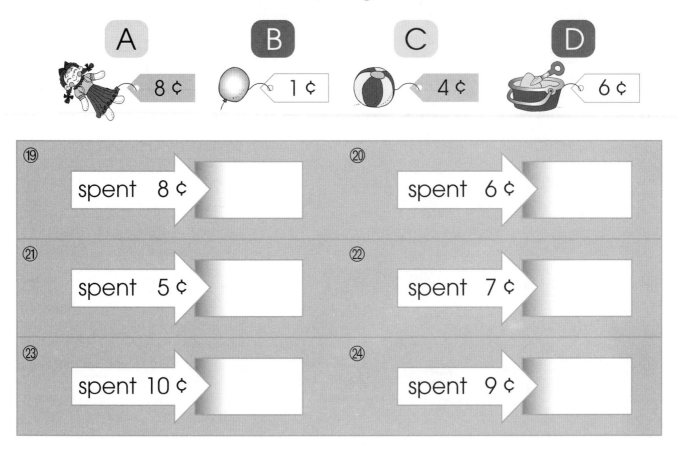

A — doll 8 ¢
B — balloon 1 ¢
C — ball 4 ¢
D — pail 6 ¢

⑲ spent 8 ¢

⑳ spent 6 ¢

㉑ spent 5 ¢

㉒ spent 7 ¢

㉓ spent 10 ¢

㉔ spent 9 ¢

Show 3 different ways to make 10¢ with nickels and pennies. Circle the correct number of coins.

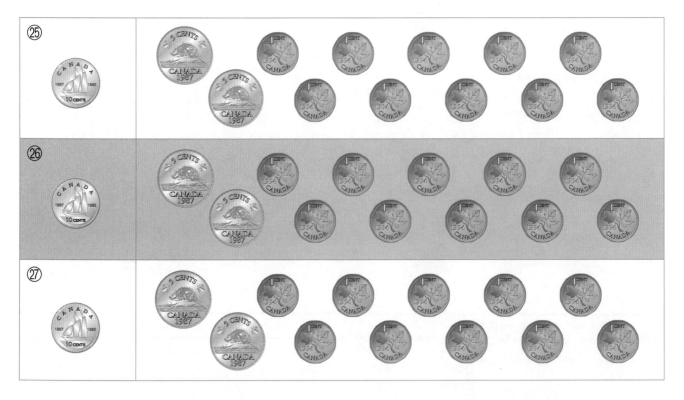

㉕

㉖

㉗

ISBN: 978-1-897164-11-2

Complete.

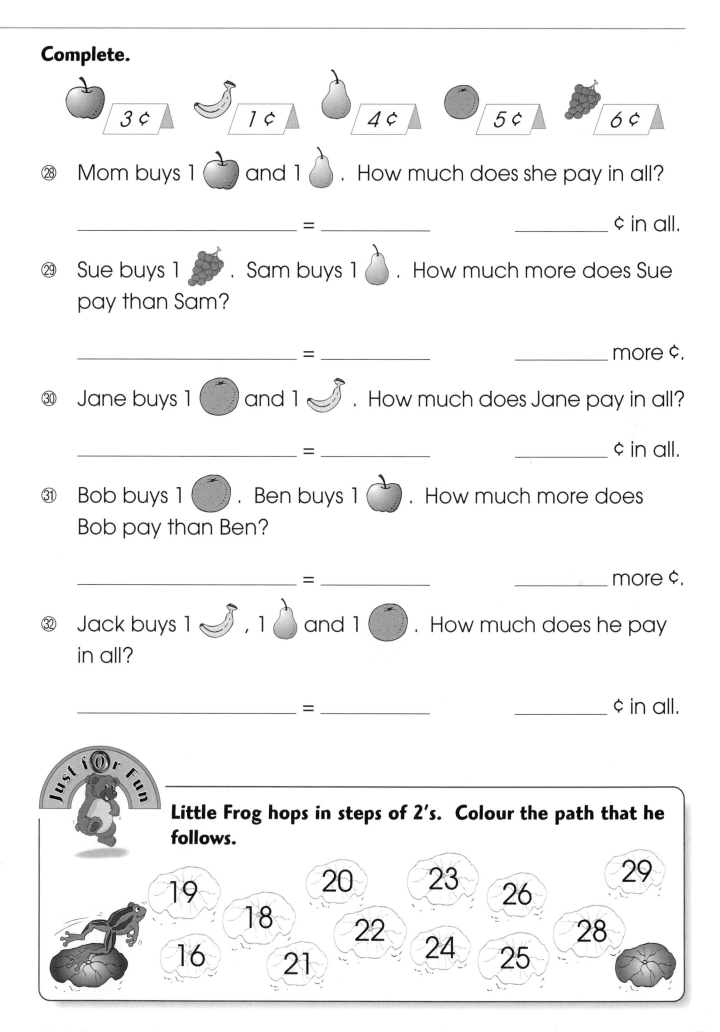

| | 3 ¢ | | 1 ¢ | | 4 ¢ | | 5 ¢ | | 6 ¢ |

㉘ Mom buys 1 🍎 and 1 🍐. How much does she pay in all?

_____ = _____ _____ ¢ in all.

㉙ Sue buys 1 🍇. Sam buys 1 🍐. How much more does Sue pay than Sam?

_____ = _____ _____ more ¢.

㉚ Jane buys 1 🍊 and 1 🍌. How much does Jane pay in all?

_____ = _____ _____ ¢ in all.

㉛ Bob buys 1 🍊. Ben buys 1 🍎. How much more does Bob pay than Ben?

_____ = _____ _____ more ¢.

㉜ Jack buys 1 🍌, 1 🍐 and 1 🍊. How much does he pay in all?

_____ = _____ _____ ¢ in all.

Just for Fun

Little Frog hops in steps of 2's. Colour the path that he follows.

19 20 23 29
18 26
16 21 22 24 25 28

Final Review

Add or subtract.

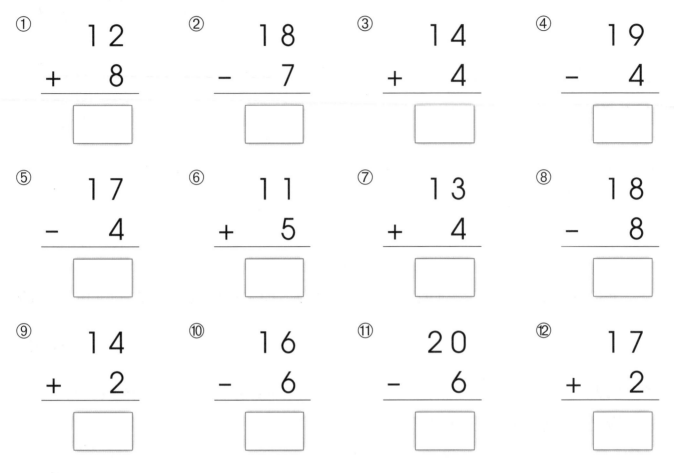

①
12
+ 8

②
18
− 7

③
14
+ 4

④
19
− 4

⑤
17
− 4

⑥
11
+ 5

⑦
13
+ 4

⑧
18
− 8

⑨
14
+ 2

⑩
16
− 6

⑪
20
− 6

⑫
17
+ 2

⑬ − 9

20	
17	
15	
18	

⑭ + 3

16	
15	
13	
17	

⑮ − 6

19	
16	
12	
18	

⑯ 8 + 2 + 9 = _____

⑰ 3 + 4 + 6 = _____

ISBN: 978-1-897164-11-2

Complete and match. Write the letters in ㉖ to solve the riddle.

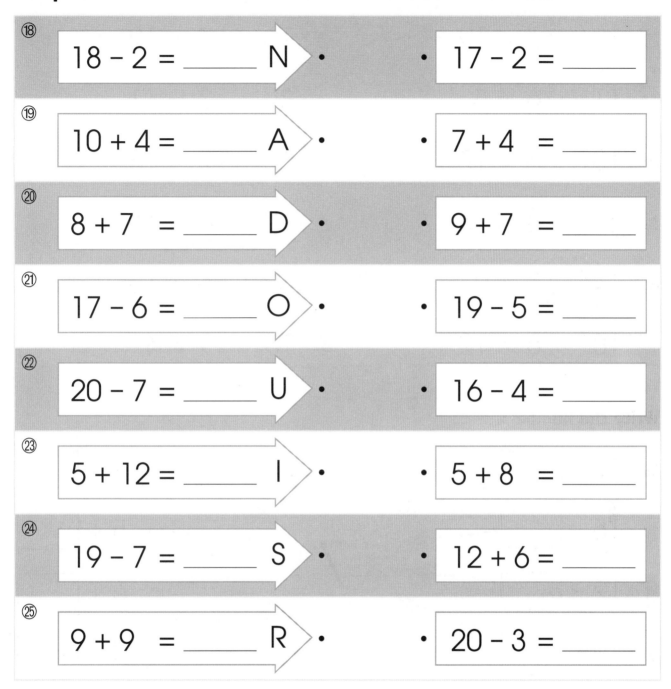

⑱ 18 − 2 = _____ N •   • 17 − 2 = _____

⑲ 10 + 4 = _____ A •   • 7 + 4 = _____

⑳ 8 + 7 = _____ D •   • 9 + 7 = _____

㉑ 17 − 6 = _____ O •   • 19 − 5 = _____

㉒ 20 − 7 = _____ U •   • 16 − 4 = _____

㉓ 5 + 12 = _____ I •   • 5 + 8 = _____

㉔ 19 − 7 = _____ S •   • 12 + 6 = _____

㉕ 9 + 9 = _____ R •   • 20 − 3 = _____

Riddle: A large reptile which is extinct.

㉖

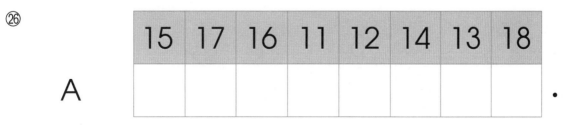

	15	17	16	11	12	14	13	18
A								

Put + or – in ◯ .

㉗ 12 ◯ 7 = 19   ㉘ 16 ◯ 4 = 12

㉙ 11 ◯ 6 = 5   ㉚ 8 ◯ 3 = 11

㉛ 13 ◯ 5 = 18   ㉜ 15 ◯ 2 = 13

㉝ 6 ◯ 8 = 14   ㉞ 10 ◯ 6 = 16

㉟ 14 ◯ 5 = 9   ㊱ 7 ◯ 6 = 13

㊲ 18 ◯ 6 = 12   ㊳ 13 ◯ 9 = 4

Write the numbers.

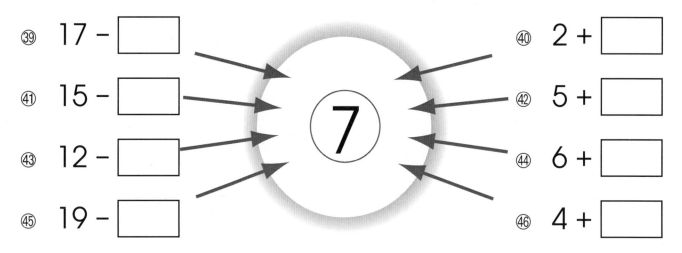

㊴ 17 – ☐   ㊵ 2 + ☐

㊶ 15 – ☐   ㊷ 5 + ☐

㊸ 12 – ☐   ㊹ 6 + ☐

㊺ 19 – ☐   ㊻ 4 + ☐

Put the sums of the pairs of cards in order, starting with the smallest number first. Write 1st, 2nd, 3rd or 4th in ☐ .

㊼

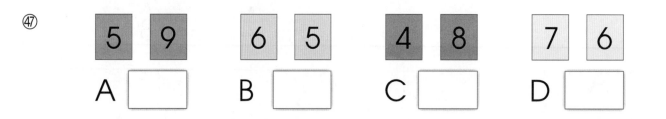

5 9	6 5	4 8	7 6
A ☐	B ☐	C ☐	D ☐

ISBN: 978-1-897164-11-2

Complete the number sentences.

④⑧
6 + 6 = 12
a.   6 + 7 = _____
b.   6 + 8 = _____
c.   6 + 9 = _____

④⑨
14 – 7 = 7
a.   15 – 7 = _____
b.   16 – 7 = _____
c.   17 – 7 = _____

Draw and complete.

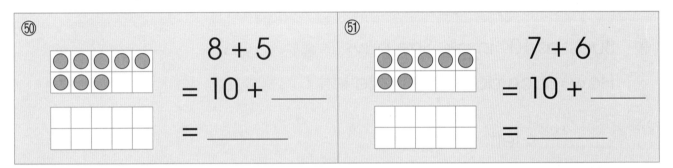

⑤⓪
8 + 5
= 10 + ____
= _____

⑤①
7 + 6
= 10 + ____
= _____

Cross out the correct number of items and complete the subtraction sentences.

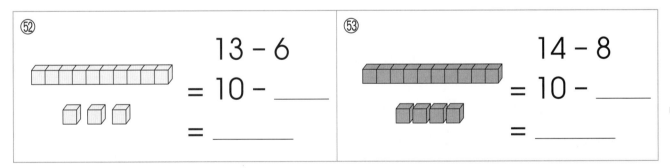

⑤②
13 – 6
= 10 – ____
= _____

⑤③
14 – 8
= 10 – ____
= _____

Circle the coins needed to buy each item.

⑤④   9 ¢

⑤⑤   7 ¢

ISBN: 978-1-897164-11-2

Complete.

56. There are 18 🐚 on the table. 6 🐚 roll off.
How many 🐚 are left on the table?

_____ 🐚 left.

57. There are 6 🥐 in the box. Mom makes 12 more 🥐.
How many 🥐 are there in all?

_____ 🥐 in all.

58. Sue has 10¢ in all. She buys 1 �⚽ 5¢.
How much does Sue have left?

_____ ¢ left.

59. Sam has 6 🎈 and 5 🎈.
How many 🎈🎈 does Sam have altogether?

_____ 🎈🎈 altogether.

60. Bob has 15 🍭. Ben has 9 🍭.
How many more 🍭 does Bob have than Ben?

_____ more 🍭.

61. Jack buys 1 🚗 7¢. Jane buys 1 ✈ 9¢.
How much more does Jane spend than Jack?

_____ ¢ more.

ISBN: 978-1-897164-11-2

Overview

In Section II, addition and subtraction skills were developed.

In this section, additional opportunities are provided for children to practise these skills in meaningful contexts.

The concepts of shape and symmetry are also developed. Children learn to recognize 2-dimensional shapes such as rectangles, squares, triangles, hexagons and circles, and 3-dimensional shapes such as spheres, prisms, cones, cylinders and pyramids.

In addition, topics such as measurement, money, graphs and probability are introduced. At this stage, children should be able to use "mathematical language" to express their thinking.

Review

Quick Tip

Numbers in words:

1	2	3	4	5	6	7	8	9	10
one	two	three	four	five	six	seven	eight	nine	ten

Some words telling the order of things:

1st	2nd	3rd	4th	5th	6th	7th	8th	9th	10th
first	second	third	fourth	fifth	sixth	seventh	eighth	ninth	tenth

Count and write the numbers in the boxes. Then write the numbers in words.

① ② ③ ④

Look at the aliens and fill in the blanks.

Sam   Wilson   Alex   Tim   Lucy   Eric   Paul   George

⑤ _____ is the 3rd and _____ is the 7th on the line.

⑥ Lucy is the _____ and George is the _____ on the line.

⑦ There are _____ aliens on the line.

ISBN: 978-1-897164-11-2

What comes next? Colour the correct picture for each group.

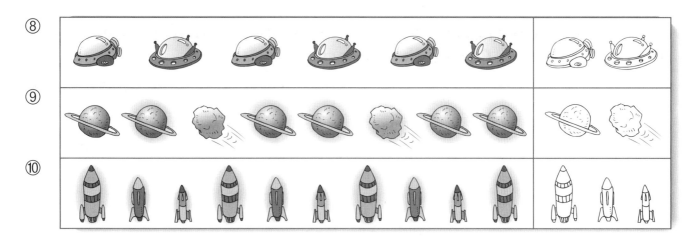

Fill in the missing numbers in each group.

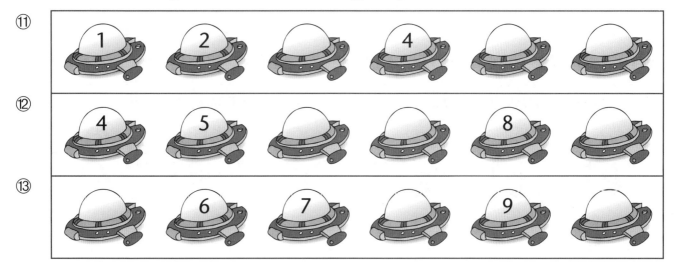

Circle the correct words.

⑭ Sam the alien is inside / outside the 🛸 .

⑮ Sam the alien is behind / in front of the 🪐 .

⑯ Sam the alien is above / below the 🪐 .

⑰ Sam the alien is wearing a 🪖 on / in its head.

ISBN: 978-1-897164-11-2

Sam the alien is visiting a farm. Help him find the objects that match the words. Colour the correct ones.

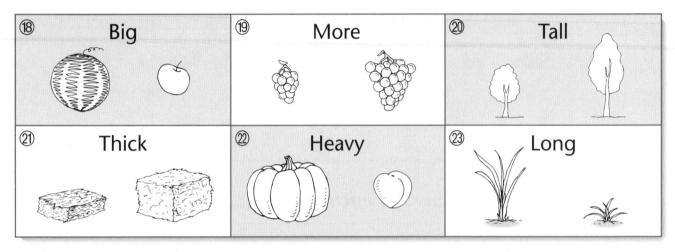

⑱ Big

⑲ More

⑳ Tall

㉑ Thick

㉒ Heavy

㉓ Long

Help Sam the alien put the pictures in order. Write the letters.

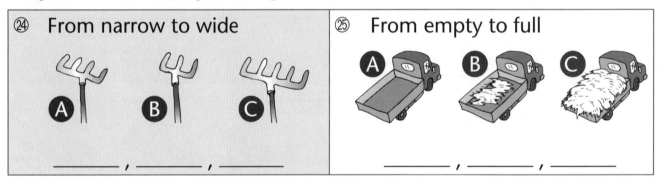

㉔ From narrow to wide

A   B   C

_____ , _____ , _____

㉕ From empty to full

A   B   C

_____ , _____ , _____

Sort the objects in each group. Cross out X the one that does not belong.

㉖

㉗

㉘

㉙

Join the matching solids with lines for Sam.

③⓪

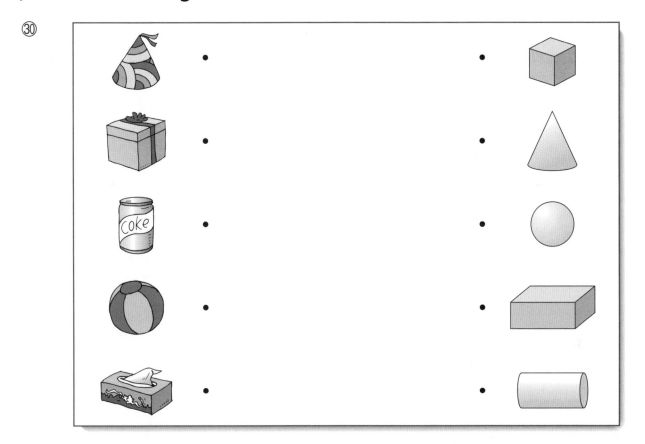

Help Sam the alien trace and colour the shapes. Then colour the shapes in the picture with the same colours used for colouring the shapes in ③①.

③①

Rectangle - blue	Triangle - green	Circle - yellow	Square - red

③②

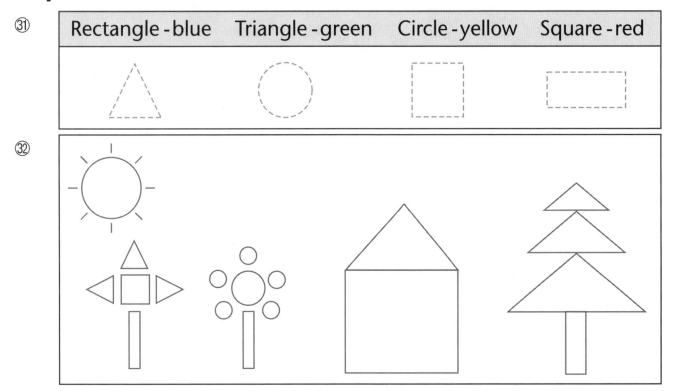

ISBN: 978-1-897164-11-2

Numbers 1 - 20

Count and write the number of toys in each group in the box. Then put a check mark ✔ in the circle to show which group has more.

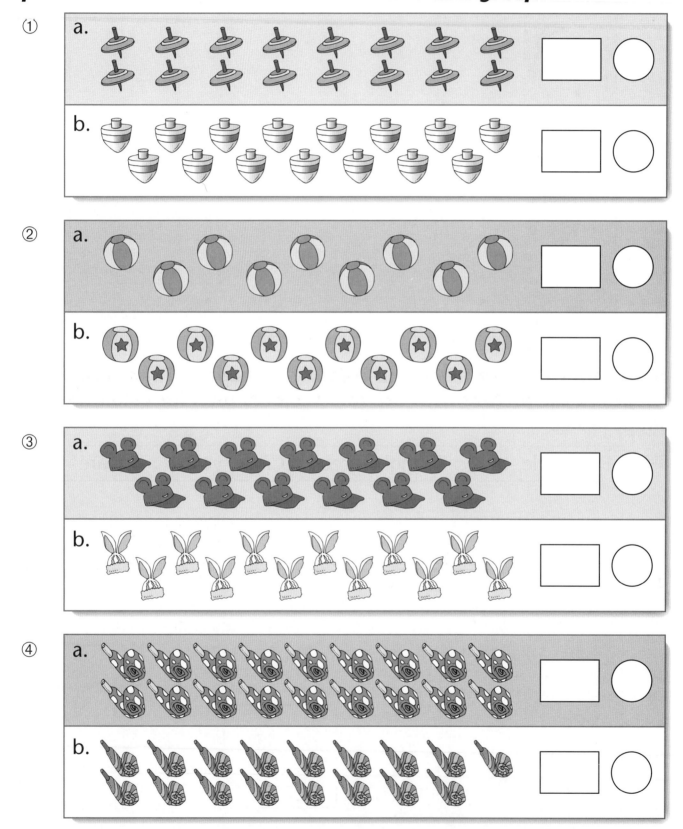

ISBN: 978-1-897164-11-2

Count the toys. Then write the numbers in the boxes.

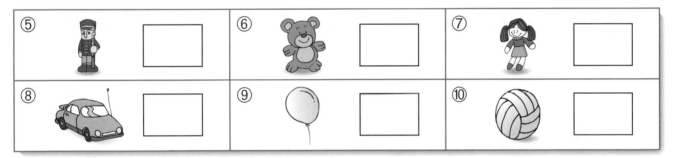

⑤ [ ]   ⑥ [ ]   ⑦ [ ]

⑧ [ ]   ⑨ [ ]   ⑩ [ ]

Circle the correct words.

⑪ Eleven / Thirteen is one more than twelve.

⑫ Seventeen is one less than sixteen / eighteen .

⑬ Eighteen / Fourteen is two more than sixteen.

⑭ Thirteen is one / two / three less than fifteen.

⑮ Twenty is one / two / three more than nineteen.

Quick Tip

eleven	11
twelve	12
thirteen	13
fourteen	14
fifteen	15
sixteen	16
seventeen	17
eighteen	18
nineteen	19
twenty	20

ISBN: 978-1-897164-11-2

Add picture(s) to each group to match the number in the circle.

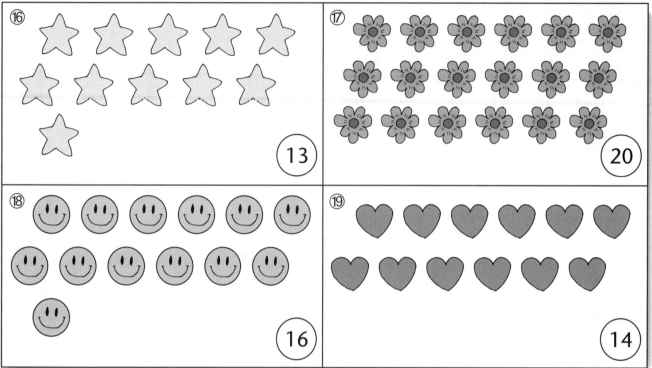

Cross out X picture(s) in each group to match the number in the circle.

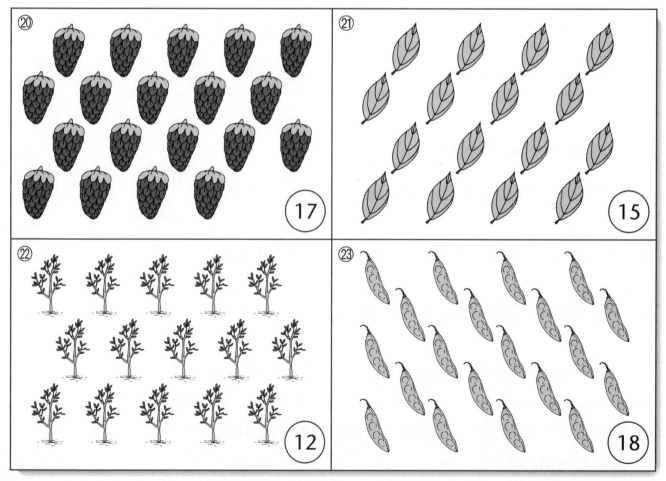

   ISBN: 978-1-897164-11-2

Look at the pictures. Write the numbers.

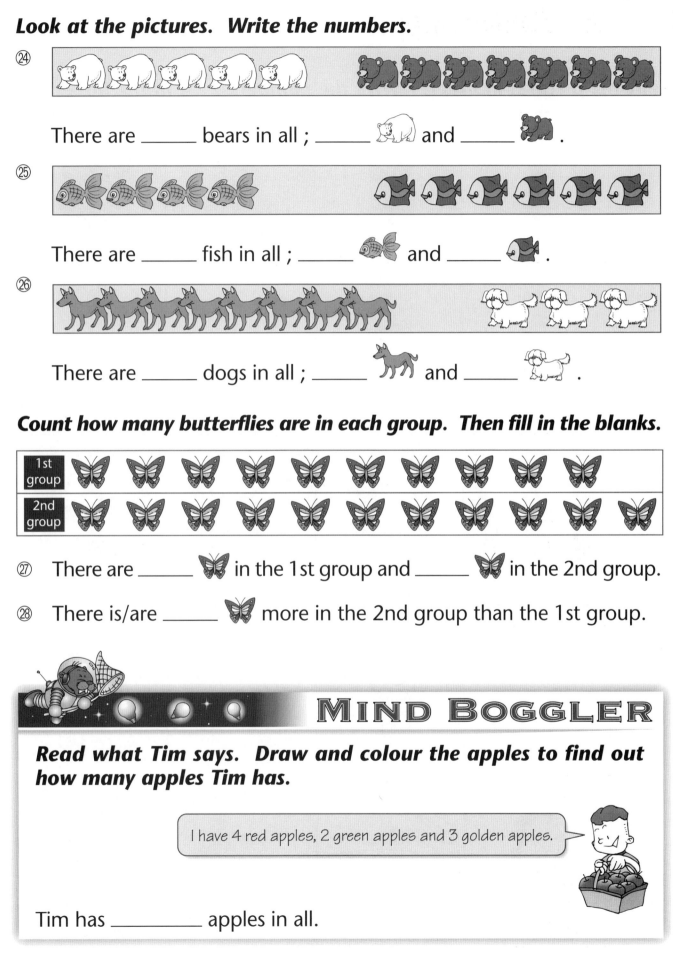

24 There are _____ bears in all ; _____ 🐻 and _____ 🐻 .

25 There are _____ fish in all ; _____ 🐟 and _____ 🐟 .

26 There are _____ dogs in all ; _____ 🐕 and _____ 🐕 .

Count how many butterflies are in each group. Then fill in the blanks.

27 There are _____ 🦋 in the 1st group and _____ 🦋 in the 2nd group.

28 There is/are _____ 🦋 more in the 2nd group than the 1st group.

MIND BOGGLER

Read what Tim says. Draw and colour the apples to find out how many apples Tim has.

I have 4 red apples, 2 green apples and 3 golden apples.

Tim has _____ apples in all.

ISBN: 978-1-897164-11-2

Sequencing

Put the pictures in order. Write the numbers 1 - 4 in the boxes.

ISBN: 978-1-897164-11-2

Look at the patterns. Draw the missing shapes in the blanks.

⑥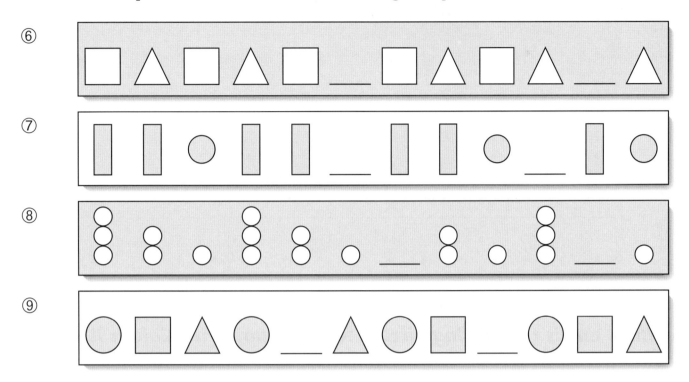

⑦

⑧

⑨

Draw the patterns.

⑩ Use 3 circles to make 2 more patterns which are different from the one below.

⑪ Use 4 squares to make 2 more patterns which are different from the one below.

⑫ Use 1 square and 2 triangles to make 2 more patterns which are different from the one below.

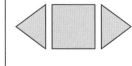

ISBN: 978-1-897164-11-2

Complete the patterns.

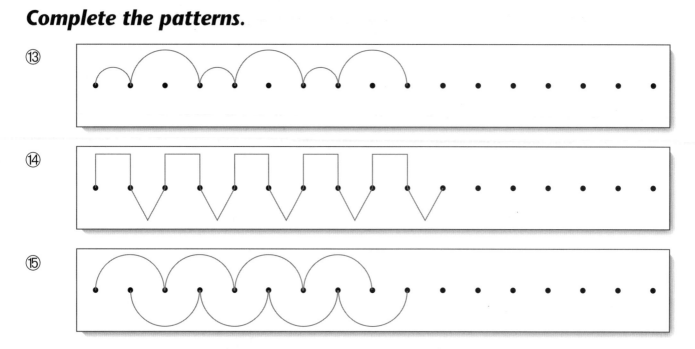

⑬

⑭

⑮

Which one is the missing picture for each pattern? Colour it.

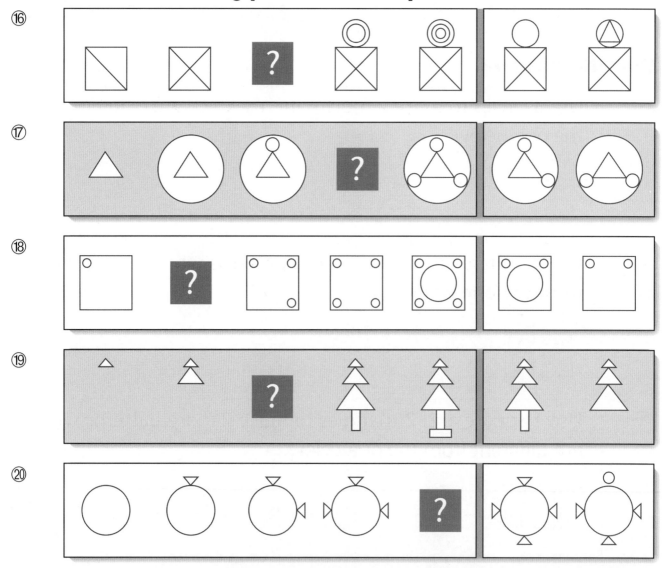

⑯

⑰

⑱

⑲

⑳

ISBN: 978-1-897164-11-2

Use the cubes to help you find the answers.

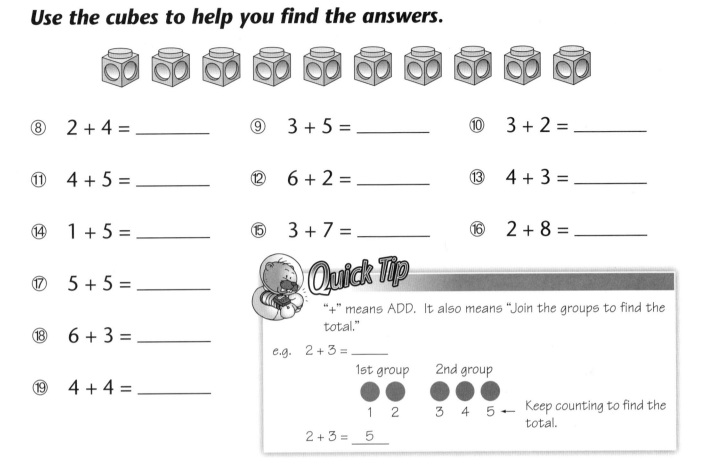

⑧   2 + 4 = _____

⑨   3 + 5 = _____

⑩   3 + 2 = _____

⑪   4 + 5 = _____

⑫   6 + 2 = _____

⑬   4 + 3 = _____

⑭   1 + 5 = _____

⑮   3 + 7 = _____

⑯   2 + 8 = _____

⑰   5 + 5 = _____

⑱   6 + 3 = _____

⑲   4 + 4 = _____

Quick Tip

"+" means ADD. It also means "Join the groups to find the total."

e.g.   2 + 3 = _____

1st group   2nd group

●●   ●●●

1   2   3   4   5 ← Keep counting to find the total.

2 + 3 = 5

Complete the addition table.

⑳

+	1	2	3	4	5
1		3			
2					
3					8
4					
5			8		

Column number: 2
Row number: 1
2 + 1 = 3

Column number: 5
Row number: 3
5 + 3 = 8

Column number: 3
Row number: 5
3 + 5 = 8

ISBN: 978-1-897164-11-2

See how Nancy puts her stickers into groups. Count and write the number of stickers in each group. Then do the addition.

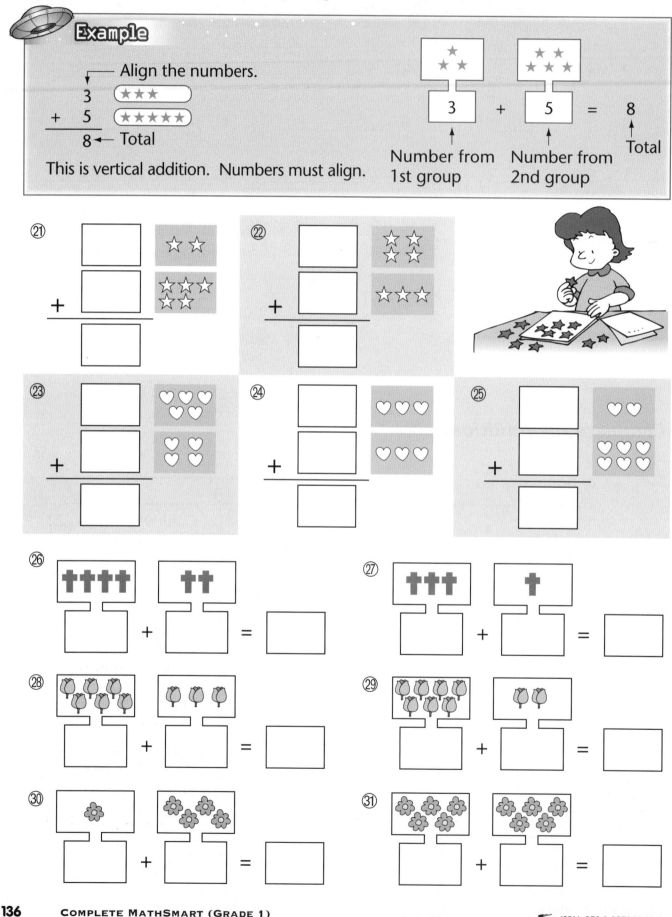

Example

Align the numbers.

3   ★★★
+ 5   ★★★★★
―――――
8 ← Total

This is vertical addition. Numbers must align.

3 + 5 = 8

Number from 1st group   Number from 2nd group   Total

ISBN: 978-1-897164-11-2

Andy and his friends are going fishing. Look at the fish they catch. Read the sentences and add the fish. Then write the children's names.

③② Andy catches _____ fish and then _____ more.

He catches _____ fish in all.

```
   □
 + □
 ──
   □
```

③③ Richard catches _____ fish and then _____ more.

He catches _____ fish in all.

```
   □
 + □
 ──
   □
```

③④ Ann catches _____ fish and then _____ more.

She catches _____ fish in all.

```
   □
 + □
 ──
   □
```

③⑤ _____ catches the most fish.

③⑥ _____ catches the fewest fish.

MIND BOGGLER

Who catches more fish?

George: I catch 2 sunfish and 7 bass.

Louis: I catch 4 sunfish and 4 bass.

_____ es more fish.

4 Subtraction

See how much food Jill is going to take. Cross out ✗ the food and write how much food is left.

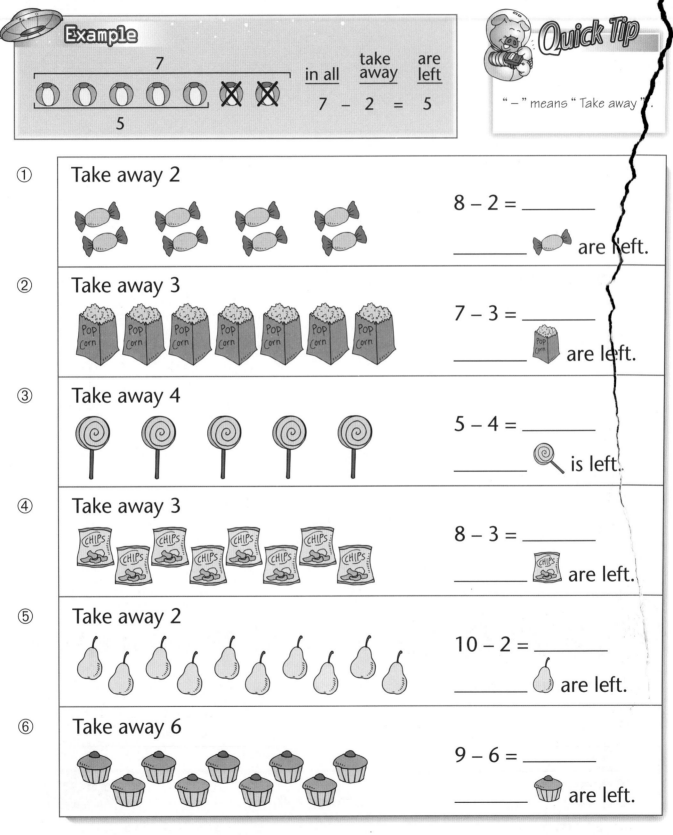

Example

	in all	take away	are left
	7	– 2	= 5

7

5

Quick Tip

" – " means " Take away ".

① Take away 2

8 – 2 = _____

_____ are left.

② Take away 3

7 – 3 = _____

_____ are left.

③ Take away 4

5 – 4 = _____

_____ is left.

④ Take away 3

8 – 3 = _____

_____ are left.

⑤ Take away 2

10 – 2 = _____

_____ are left.

⑥ Take away 6

9 – 6 = _____

_____ are left.

ISBN: 978-1-897164-11-2

Write how many shapes are crossed out and find the answers.

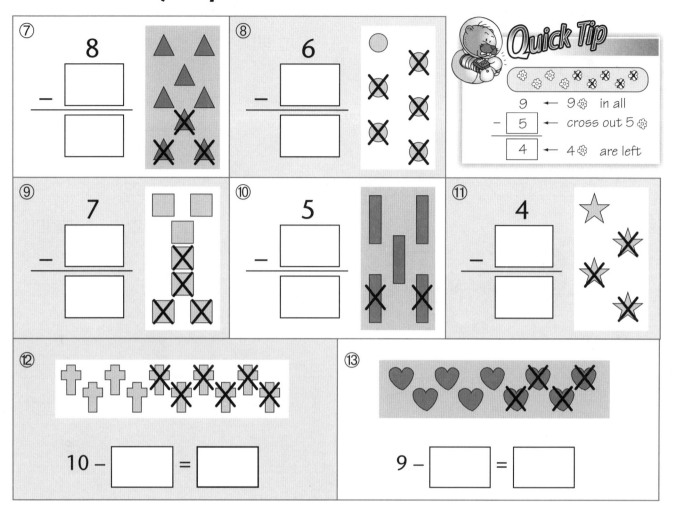

Use the building blocks to help you find the answers.

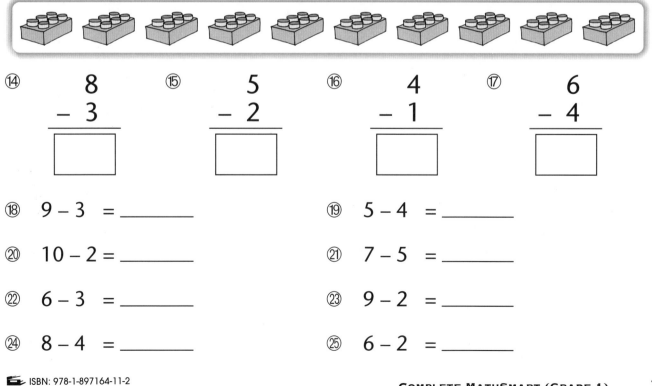

⑭
$$\begin{array}{r} 8 \\ -\ 3 \\ \hline \end{array}$$

⑮
$$\begin{array}{r} 5 \\ -\ 2 \\ \hline \end{array}$$

⑯
$$\begin{array}{r} 4 \\ -\ 1 \\ \hline \end{array}$$

⑰
$$\begin{array}{r} 6 \\ -\ 4 \\ \hline \end{array}$$

⑱ 9 – 3 = _____

⑲ 5 – 4 = _____

⑳ 10 – 2 = _____

㉑ 7 – 5 = _____

㉒ 6 – 3 = _____

㉓ 9 – 2 = _____

㉔ 8 – 4 = _____

㉕ 6 – 2 = _____

ISBN: 978-1-897164-11-2

Look at the birds. See how many birds fly away. Write the numbers.

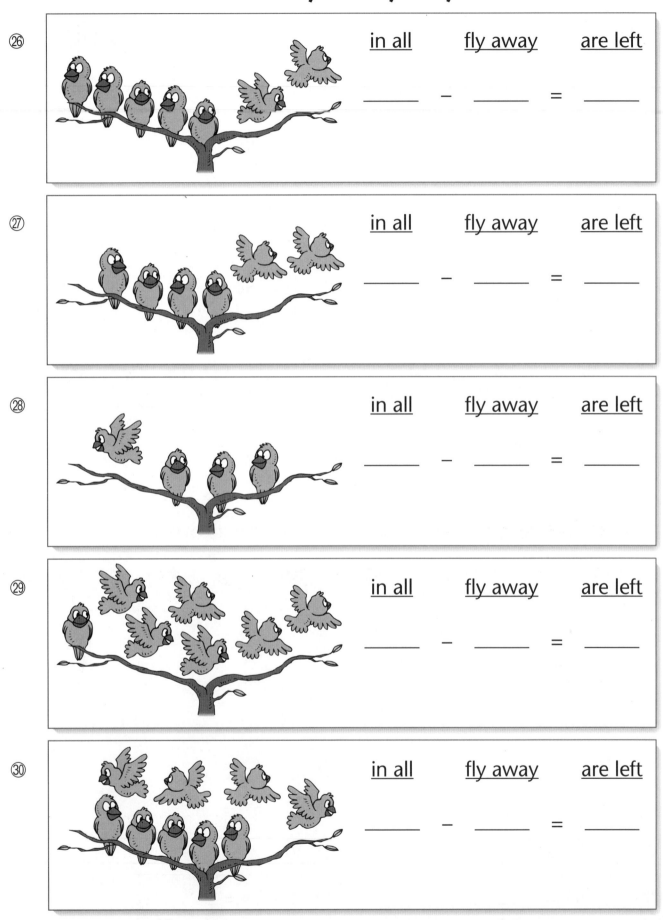

㉖   <u>in all</u>   <u>fly away</u>   <u>are left</u>

_____ – _____ = _____

㉗   <u>in all</u>   <u>fly away</u>   <u>are left</u>

_____ – _____ = _____

㉘   <u>in all</u>   <u>fly away</u>   <u>are left</u>

_____ – _____ = _____

㉙   <u>in all</u>   <u>fly away</u>   <u>are left</u>

_____ – _____ = _____

㉚   <u>in all</u>   <u>fly away</u>   <u>are left</u>

_____ – _____ = _____

ISBN: 978-1-897164-11-2

Read what Tommy Turtle says. Write the numbers.

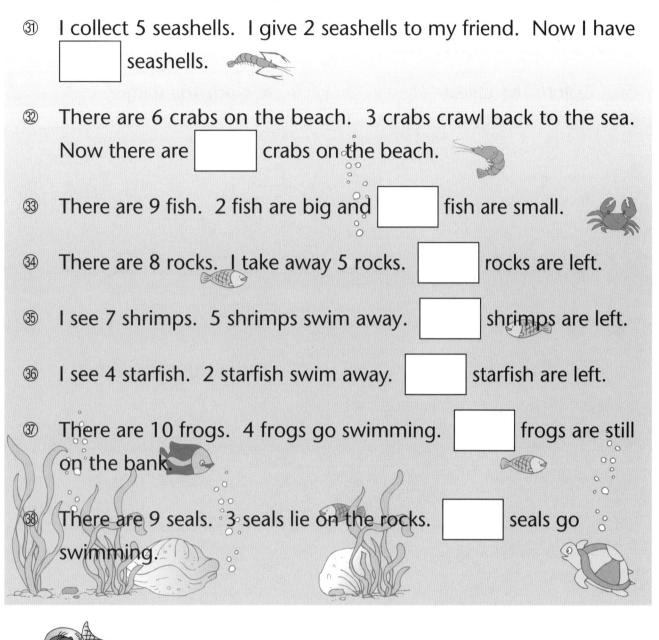

③ I collect 5 seashells. I give 2 seashells to my friend. Now I have ☐ seashells.

③ There are 6 crabs on the beach. 3 crabs crawl back to the sea. Now there are ☐ crabs on the beach.

③ There are 9 fish. 2 fish are big and ☐ fish are small.

③ There are 8 rocks. I take away 5 rocks. ☐ rocks are left.

③ I see 7 shrimps. 5 shrimps swim away. ☐ shrimps are left.

③ I see 4 starfish. 2 starfish swim away. ☐ starfish are left.

③ There are 10 frogs. 4 frogs go swimming. ☐ frogs are still on the bank.

③ There are 9 seals. 3 seals lie on the rocks. ☐ seals go swimming.

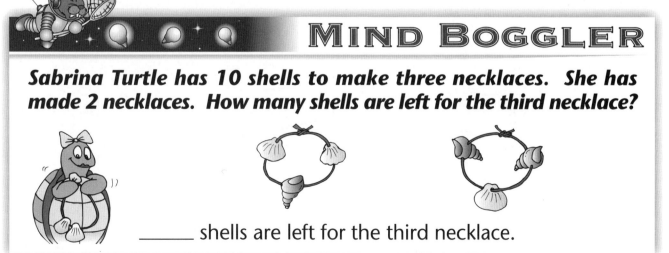

MIND BOGGLER

Sabrina Turtle has 10 shells to make three necklaces. She has made 2 necklaces. How many shells are left for the third necklace?

_____ shells are left for the third necklace.

ISBN: 978-1-897164-11-2

5 Measurement I

Colour the correct pictures.

① Colour the tallest.

② Colour the widest.

③ Colour the heaviest.

④ Colour the longest.

⑤ Colour the thinnest.

⑥ Colour the biggest.

ISBN: 978-1-897164-11-2

Ricky has cards of different shapes. See how he uses pennies to cover one of the cards. Then follow his way to measure the cards below.

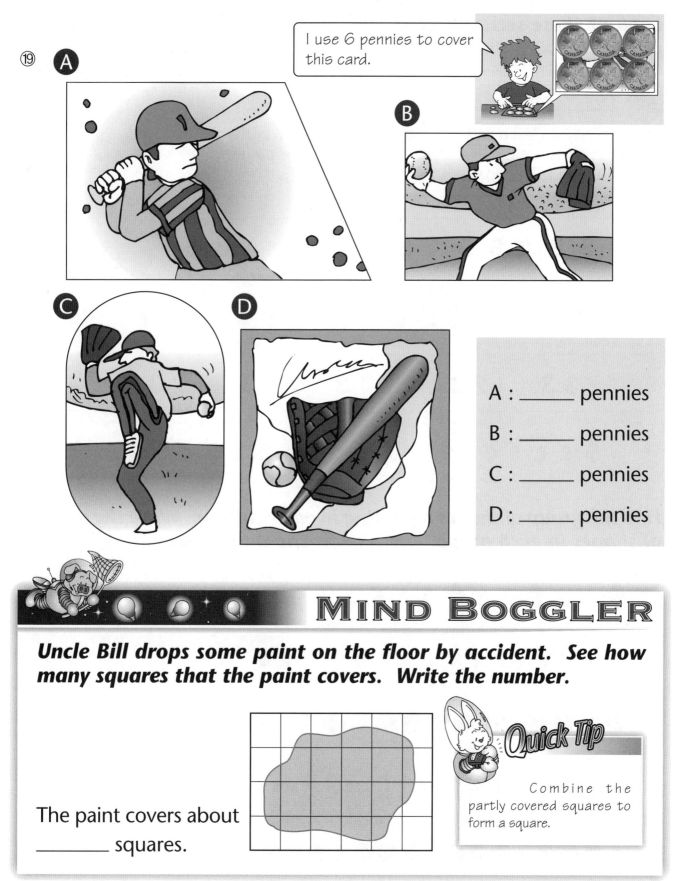

⑲ Ⓐ

I use 6 pennies to cover this card.

Ⓑ

Ⓒ Ⓓ

A : _____ pennies

B : _____ pennies

C : _____ pennies

D : _____ pennies

MIND BOGGLER

Uncle Bill drops some paint on the floor by accident. See how many squares that the paint covers. Write the number.

The paint covers about _____ squares.

Quick Tip

Combine the partly covered squares to form a square.

ISBN: 978-1-897164-11-2

6 Patterns

Look at these sets. Check ✔ the one that is a pattern. Otherwise, put a cross ✗ in the circle.

Quick Tip

A pattern is a way in which something happens again and again.

Examples

① Is ABABABABAB a pattern?
AB repeats itself.
ABABABABAB is a pattern.

② Is 13452314 a pattern?
No, it is not a pattern.

① A B B A B B A B B A B B A B B A B B ◯

② ▲ ■ ● ● ▲ ■ ● ● ▲ ■ ● ● ▲ ■ ● ● ◯

③ 1 2 3 3 1 1 2 3 1 3 2 1 3 1 2 2 3 1 1 2 3 1 ◯

④ $ $ ¢ ¢ $ ¢ $ ¢ ¢ $ $ ¢ ¢ $ $ ¢ $ ¢ $ $ ◯

Find the group of shapes repeating in each pattern. Write the number of shapes in each group. Then draw the shapes out.

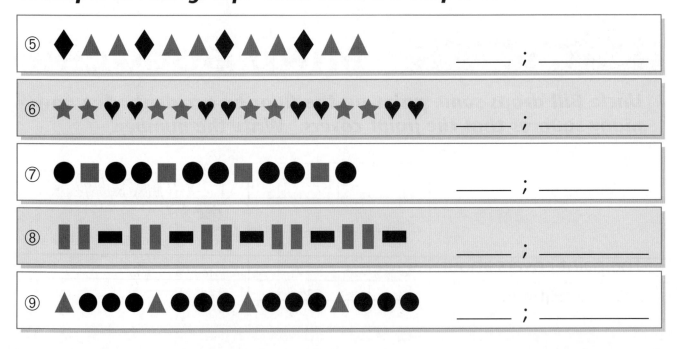

⑤ ◆ ▲ ▲ ◆ ▲ ▲ ◆ ▲ ▲ ◆ ▲ ▲ _____ ; _____

⑥ ★ ★ ♥ ♥ ★ ★ ♥ ♥ ★ ★ ♥ ♥ ★ ★ ♥ ♥ _____ ; _____

⑦ ● ■ ● ● ■ ● ● ■ ● ● ■ ● _____ ; _____

⑧ ▌▌ ■ ▌ ▌ ■ ▌▌ ■ ▌ ▌ ■ ▌▌ ■ ▌ _____ ; _____

⑨ ▲ ● ● ● ▲ ● ● ● ▲ ● ● ● ▲ ● ● ● _____ ; _____

ISBN: 978-1-897164-11-2

Extend the patterns.

⑩ ◯ ✕ ◯ ✕ ◯ ✕ ◯ ✕ _____ _____ _____

⑪ **4 6 3 4 4 6 3 4** _____ _____ _____

⑫ T P G G T P G G _____ _____ _____

⑬ ◯ ◯ ∘ ◯ ◯ ∘ ◯ ◯ ∘ _____ _____ _____

⑭ △ ▲ ▽ △ ▲ ▽ △ ▲ ▽ _____ _____ _____

Ben and Jill are painting a pattern. Help them choose the shapes from the pattern code and colour the shapes.

1 = yellow △   2 = red ◯   3 = blue ☐

4 = green ☐   5 = purple ⬡

⑮ _____ _____ _____ _____ _____ _____ _____ _____
    1   2   2   3   1   2   2   3

⑯ _____ _____ _____ _____ _____ _____ _____ _____
    4   2   5   4   2   5   4   2

⑰ _____ _____ _____ _____ _____ _____ _____ _____
    4   3   1   4   3   3   1

⑱ _____ _____ _____ _____ _____ _____ _____ _____
    5   4   3   5   2   4   3

ISBN: 978-1-897164-11-2

Write the number of shaded triangles in each picture and follow the pattern to draw and shade the next picture. Then circle the correct answers.

⑲ a.

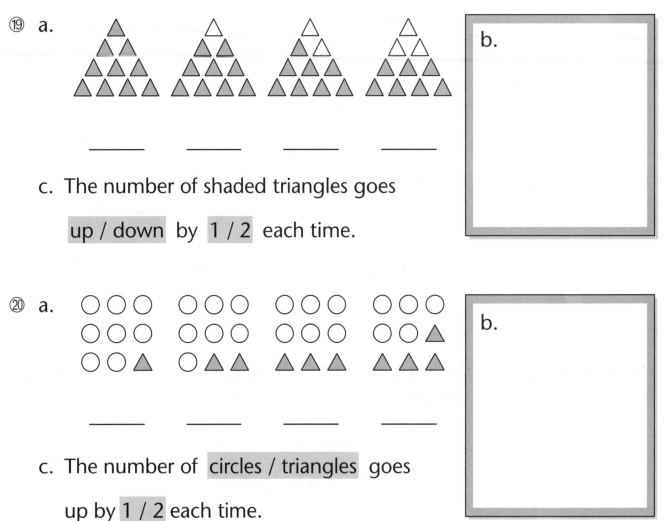

_____   _____   _____   _____

b.

c. The number of shaded triangles goes

up / down by 1 / 2 each time.

⑳ a.

_____   _____   _____   _____

b.

c. The number of circles / triangles goes

up by 1 / 2 each time.

Look at the two magic washing machines. After washing the clothes, how do the numbers on the clothes change? Write the new numbers.

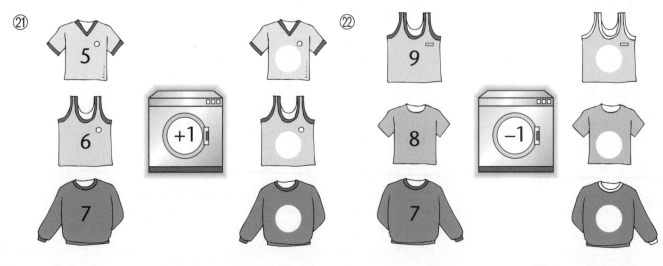

㉑ 5   6   +1   7

㉒ 9   8   −1   7

ISBN: 978-1-897164-11-2

Cross out ✗ one of the pictures in each set so that it follows a pattern.

㉓

㉔

㉕

Colour the hearts and answer the questions.

㉖ a. For the 1st row, colour the 1st, 4th and 7th hearts green and the rest blue.

 b. For the 2nd row, colour the 2nd, 5th and 8th hearts green and the rest blue.

 c. For the 3rd row, colour the 3rd and 6th hearts green and the rest blue.

1st row								
2nd row								
3rd row								

 d. Do the rows have a pattern? _____

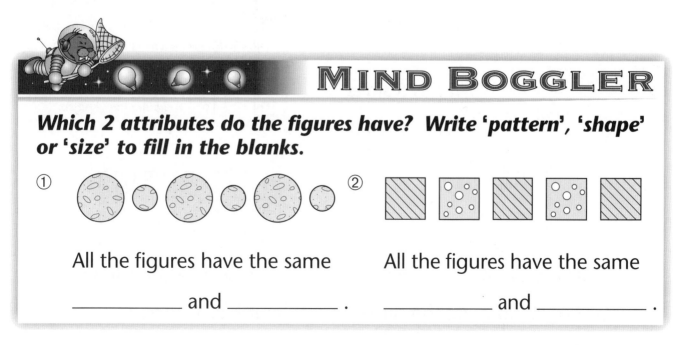

MIND BOGGLER

Which 2 attributes do the figures have? Write 'pattern', 'shape' or 'size' to fill in the blanks.

① ②

All the figures have the same   All the figures have the same

_____ and _____ .   _____ and _____ .

ISBN: 978-1-897164-11-2

7 2-D Figures

Colour the shapes that look like the one on the left.

Look at the shapes. Check ✔ the correct description for each shape.

⑤

Ⓐ It has 3 sides.

Ⓑ It has 4 sides.

Quick Tip

To prevent from counting repeatedly, you can write the numbers beside the sides, e.g.

2
1 □ 3   A square has 4 sides.
4

⑥

Ⓐ It has 5 sides.

Ⓑ It has 6 sides.

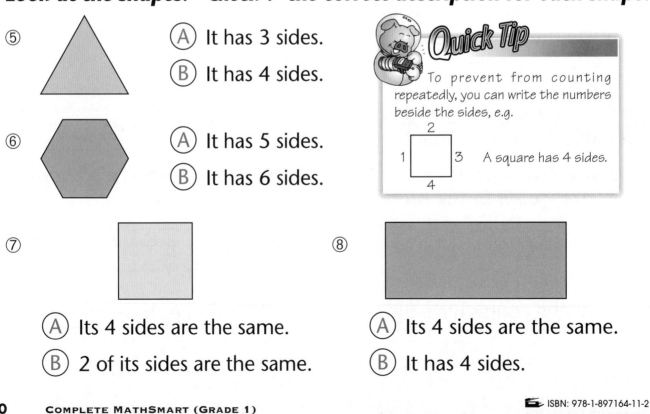

⑦

Ⓐ Its 4 sides are the same.

Ⓑ 2 of its sides are the same.

⑧

Ⓐ Its 4 sides are the same.

Ⓑ It has 4 sides.

   ISBN: 978-1-897164-11-2

Write the names of the shapes. Then write the numbers.

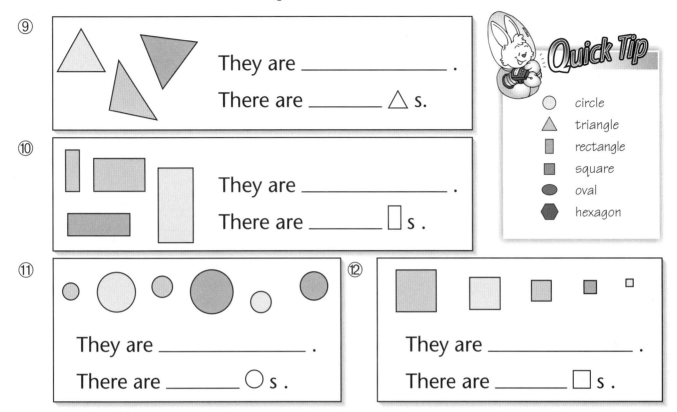

⑨ They are _____ .

There are _____ △ s.

⑩ They are _____ .

There are _____ ▢ s .

⑪ They are _____ .

There are _____ ○ s .

⑫ They are _____ .

There are _____ ▢ s .

Quick Tip

○ circle
△ triangle
▢ rectangle
▢ square
⬭ oval
⬡ hexagon

Are these pictures symmetric? Circle 'Yes' or 'No'.

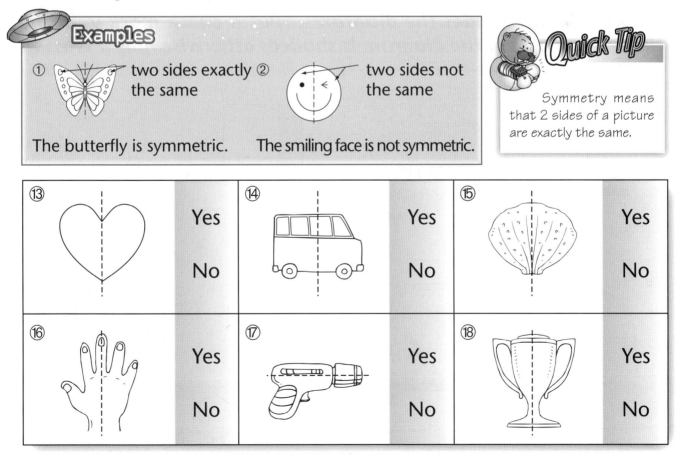

Examples

① two sides exactly the same

② two sides not the same

The butterfly is symmetric.   The smiling face is not symmetric.

Quick Tip

Symmetry means that 2 sides of a picture are exactly the same.

⑬ Yes   No

⑭ Yes   No

⑮ Yes   No

⑯ Yes   No

⑰ Yes   No

⑱ Yes   No

ISBN: 978-1-897164-11-2

Finish each picture to make it symmetric.

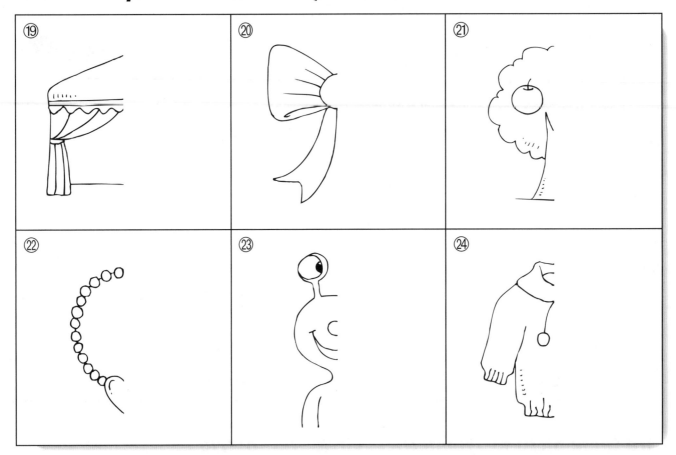

See how Jimmy shades the diagrams. Put a check mark ✔ in the circle if one half of the diagram is shaded; otherwise, put a cross **X**.

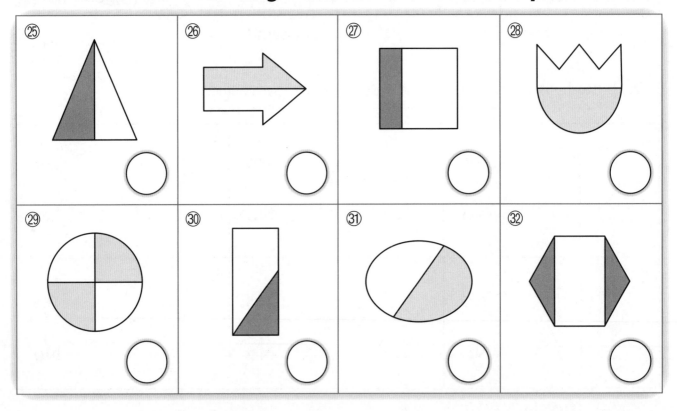

ISBN: 978-1-897164-11-2

Help Andy draw one shape on each piece of drawing paper on the board. Then answer the questions.

∽ An oval on the left and a rectangle on the right of the triangle
∽ A circle on the left of the oval
∽ A rectangle on the left and two circles on the right of the square
∽ A square under the rectangle
∽ A triangle on each side of the hexagon

㉝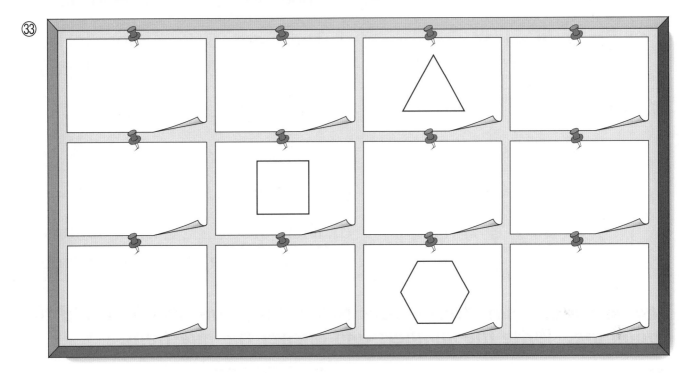

㉞ How many circles are there in all? _____

㉟ How many rectangles are there in all? _____

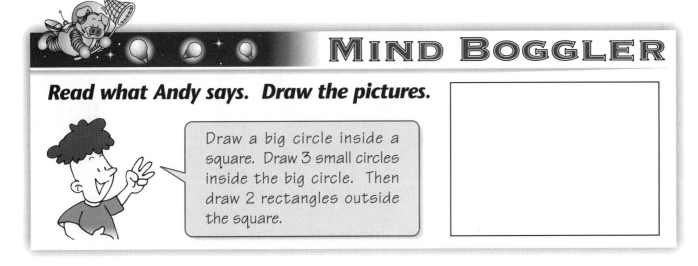

MIND BOGGLER

Read what Andy says. Draw the pictures.

Draw a big circle inside a square. Draw 3 small circles inside the big circle. Then draw 2 rectangles outside the square.

ISBN: 978-1-897164-11-2

Count the number of things for each group. Fill in the blanks.

①

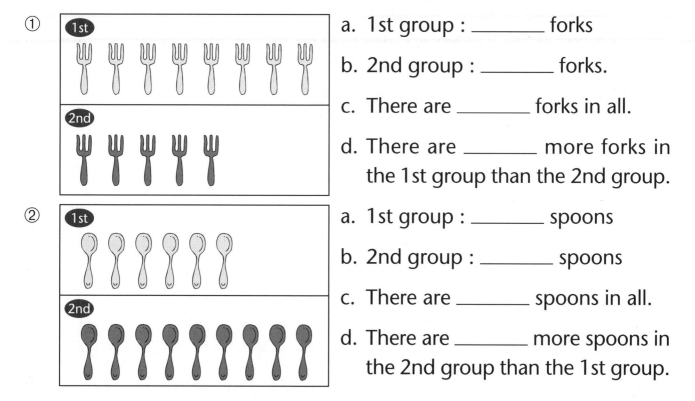

a. 1st group : _____ forks

b. 2nd group : _____ forks.

c. There are _____ forks in all.

d. There are _____ more forks in the 1st group than the 2nd group.

②

a. 1st group : _____ spoons

b. 2nd group : _____ spoons

c. There are _____ spoons in all.

d. There are _____ more spoons in the 2nd group than the 1st group.

See how many pins Shirley uses to tell how long the fork and the spoon are. Write the numbers and answer the questions.

③ _____ 📌 long

④ _____ 📌 long

⑤ Which one is longer, the fork or the spoon? _____

⑥ By how many 📌 is the fork longer than the spoon? _____ 📌

ISBN: 978-1-897164-11-2

Put the pictures in order. Write the numbers 1 - 4 in the boxes.

Do the addition or subtraction.

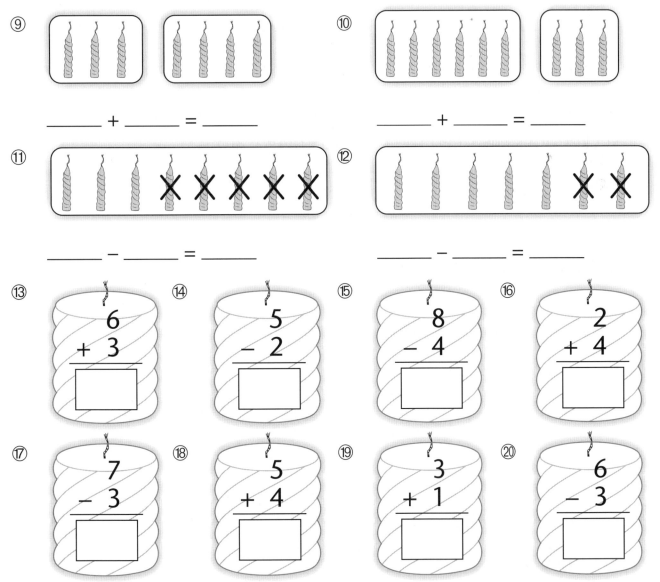

⑨ _____ + _____ = _____

⑩ _____ + _____ = _____

⑪ _____ − _____ = _____

⑫ _____ − _____ = _____

⑬ 6 + 3

⑭ 5 − 2

⑮ 8 − 4

⑯ 2 + 4

⑰ 7 − 3

⑱ 5 + 4

⑲ 3 + 1

⑳ 6 − 3

ISBN: 978-1-897164-11-2

Jill uses squares to measure the cards. Help her count how many squares each card covers and check ✔ the correct answers.

㉑ Card A : _____ squares ㉒ Card B : _____ squares

㉓ Which card covers more squares? Ⓐ Card A Ⓑ Card B

㉔ Jill uses one of the following stickers to do measurement. Which sticker does she need the most to cover Card A?

Ⓐ Ⓑ Ⓒ

Extend the patterns and name the shapes.

㉕ a. △ ▲ △ ▲ △ ▲ ___ ___ ___ ___ ___

  b. They are _____ .

㉖ a. ___ ___ ___ ___

  b. They are _____ .

㉗ a. ___ ___ ___ ___

  b. They are _____ .

ISBN: 978-1-897164-11-2

Write the numbers on the lines. Then solve the problems.

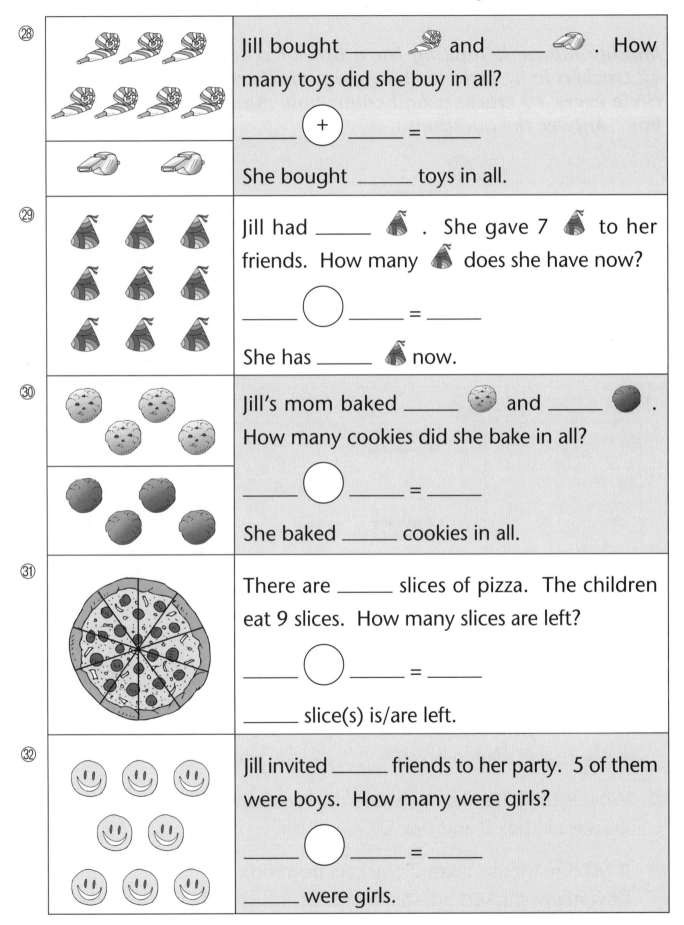

㉘ Jill bought _____ 🌀 and _____ 🔔 . How many toys did she buy in all?

_____ ⊕ _____ = _____

She bought _____ toys in all.

㉙ Jill had _____ 🎉 . She gave 7 🎉 to her friends. How many 🎉 does she have now?

_____ ◯ _____ = _____

She has _____ 🎉 now.

㉚ Jill's mom baked _____ 🍪 and _____ ● . How many cookies did she bake in all?

_____ ◯ _____ = _____

She baked _____ cookies in all.

㉛ There are _____ slices of pizza. The children eat 9 slices. How many slices are left?

_____ ◯ _____ = _____

_____ slice(s) is/are left.

㉜ Jill invited _____ friends to her party. 5 of them were boys. How many were girls?

_____ ◯ _____ = _____

_____ were girls.

ISBN: 978-1-897164-11-2

8 Numbers to 100

Maxine Mouse is looking for a box of crackers that has exactly 42 crackers in it. Estimate how many crackers are in each box. Then circle every 10 crackers and count how many crackers are in each box. Answer the questions.

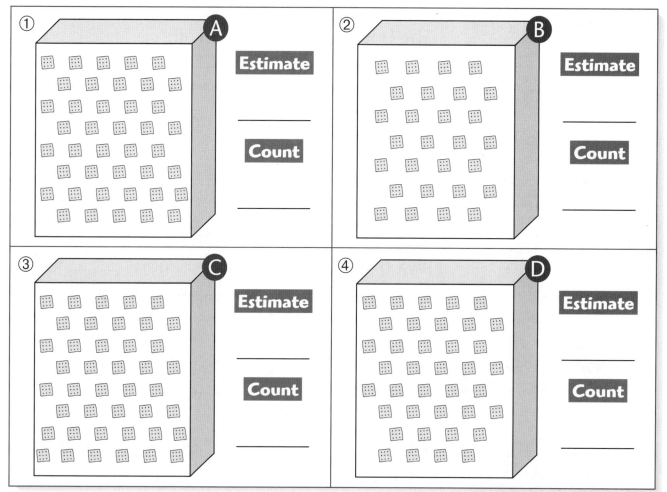

① **A** Estimate _____ Count _____

② **B** Estimate _____ Count _____

③ **C** Estimate _____ Count _____

④ **D** Estimate _____ Count _____

⑤ Which box of crackers is Maxine Mouse looking for?   Box _____

⑥ How many more crackers are in box C than in box A?   _____ cracker(s)

⑦ What is the difference between the number of crackers in box B and box D?   _____ cracker(s)

⑧ If Maxine Mouse takes 2 crackers from box C, how many crackers are still in box C?   _____ cracker(s)

Quick Tip

A fast way to count is to count by 10's.

e.g. +10 +10 +10
10 , 20 , 30 , 40 , ...

ISBN: 978-1-897164-11-2

The children are playing a card game. Read what Janice says. Then fill in the blanks.

> Each of us gets 5 cards. Each round we have to take 1 card out. We compare our cards and the one with the biggest number wins the round.

	Janice	Brenda	Lucy	Alex	Nancy	
⑨ 1st round	25	19	42	35	40	_____ wins.
⑩ 2nd round	89	48	50	37	13	_____ wins.
⑪ 3rd round	40	22	31	60	15	_____ wins.
⑫ 4th round	70	65	82	41	20	_____ wins.
⑬ 5th round	53	26	48	10	88	_____ wins.

⑭ Who is the final winner in the 5 rounds? _____

⑮ Who never wins in the 5 rounds? _____

⑯ If Alex gets a ⌊80⌋ instead of ⌊10⌋ in the 5th round and

he deals this card, will he win that round? _____

⑰ Put the numbers in the 1st round in order from the biggest to the smallest.

☐ , ☐ , ☐ , ☐ , ☐

⑱ Put the numbers in the 4th round in order from the smallest to the biggest.

☐ , ☐ , ☐ , ☐ , ☐

Count and write the number of building blocks in each group.

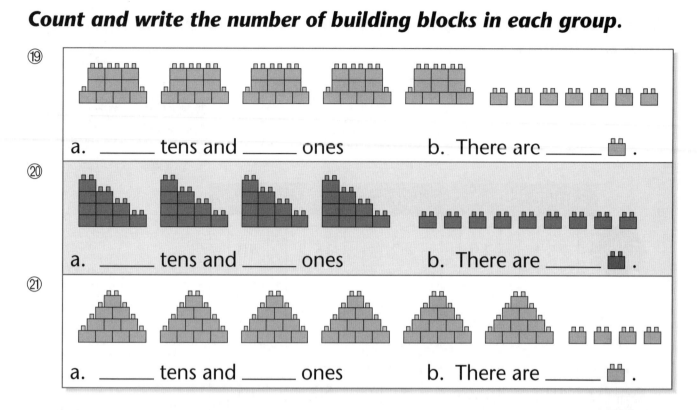

⑲

a. _____ tens and _____ ones   b. There are _____ 🧱 .

⑳

a. _____ tens and _____ ones   b. There are _____ 🧱 .

㉑

a. _____ tens and _____ ones   b. There are _____ 🧱 .

Count the building blocks by 2's or 5's to see how many building blocks are in each group.

Quick Tip

Count by 2's: Number goes up by 2 each time.

e.g. $2 \xrightarrow{+2} 4 \xrightarrow{+2} 6 \xrightarrow{+2} 8$

Count by 5's: Number goes up by 5 each time.

e.g. $5 \xrightarrow{+5} 10 \xrightarrow{+5} 15 \xrightarrow{+5} 20$

㉒

㉓

㉔

㉕

ISBN: 978-1-897164-11-2

Help the frogs jump to 50. Colour, circle or cross out ✗ the stones.

㉖ Freddie the frog jumps by 2's. Colour the stones in his route yellow.

㉗ Jenny the frog jumps by 5's. Circle the stones in her route.

㉘ Lily the frog jumps by 10's.   Cross out ✗ the stones in her route.

MIND BOGGLER

Look at the questions ㉖ to ㉘. Answer the questions.

① Do Freddie and Jenny meet on ⟨15⟩ ? _____

② Do Jenny and Lily meet on ⟨35⟩ ? _____

③ On which stones do Freddie and Lily meet? _____

④ On which stones do the 3 frogs meet? _____

ISBN: 978-1-897164-11-2

9 Addition and Subtraction

Sarah has bought some things for her birthday but she is going to buy more. Help her find out how many things she will have in all.

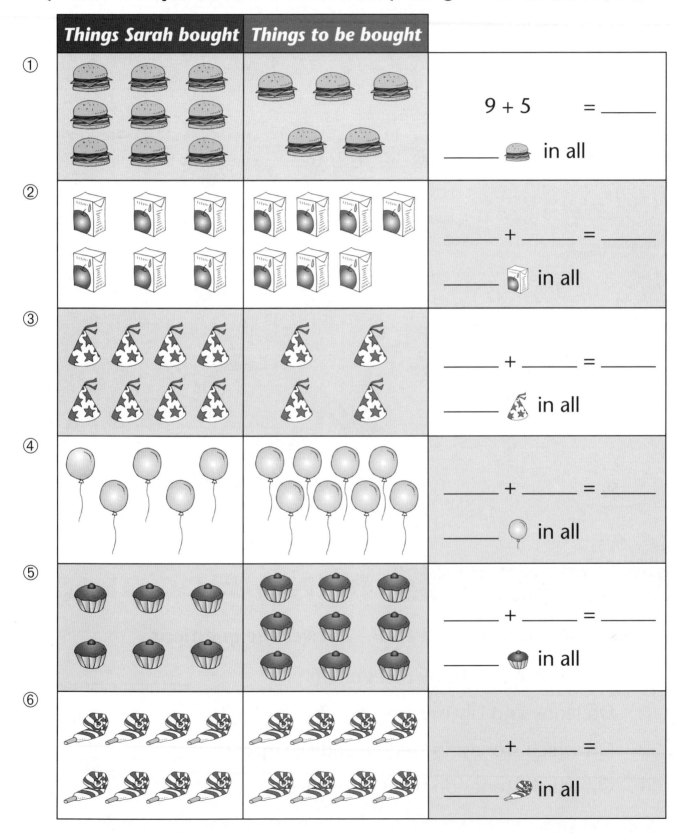

Things Sarah bought	Things to be bought	
①		$9 + 5$ = _____ _____ 🍔 in all
②		_____ + _____ = _____ _____ 📦 in all
③		_____ + _____ = _____ _____ 🎉 in all
④		_____ + _____ = _____ _____ 🎈 in all
⑤		_____ + _____ = _____ _____ 🧁 in all
⑥		_____ + _____ = _____ _____ in all

   ISBN: 978-1-897164-11-2

Cross out ✗ the exact amount of food to show how much food the children ate at Sarah's birthday party. Then find out how much food was left.

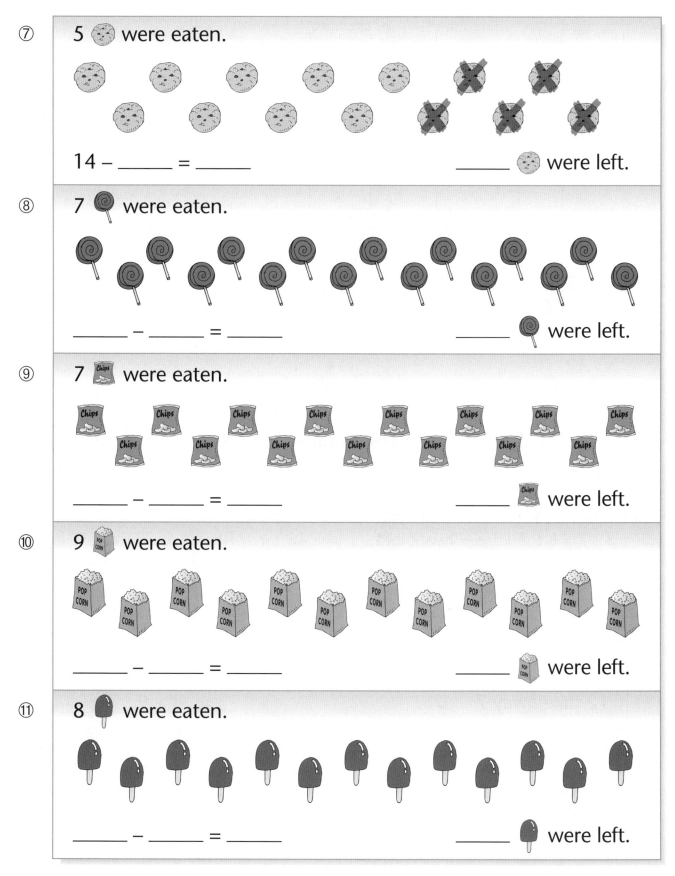

⑦ 5 🍪 were eaten.

14 – _____ = _____   _____ 🍪 were left.

⑧ 7 🍭 were eaten.

_____ – _____ = _____   _____ 🍭 were left.

⑨ 7 Chips were eaten.

_____ – _____ = _____   _____ Chips were left.

⑩ 9 Popcorn were eaten.

_____ – _____ = _____   _____ Popcorn were left.

⑪ 8 🍡 were eaten.

_____ – _____ = _____   _____ 🍡 were left.

ISBN: 978-1-897164-11-2

Add or subtract.

⑫
$$\begin{array}{r} 1\,2 \\ -\ \ 4 \\ \hline \end{array}$$

⑬
$$\begin{array}{r} 9 \\ +\ 8 \\ \hline \end{array}$$

⑭
$$\begin{array}{r} 1\,5 \\ -\ \ 6 \\ \hline \end{array}$$

⑮
$$\begin{array}{r} 7 \\ +\ 8 \\ \hline \end{array}$$

⑯
$$\begin{array}{r} 1\,1 \\ -\ \ 9 \\ \hline \end{array}$$

⑰
$$\begin{array}{r} 8 \\ +\ 5 \\ \hline \end{array}$$

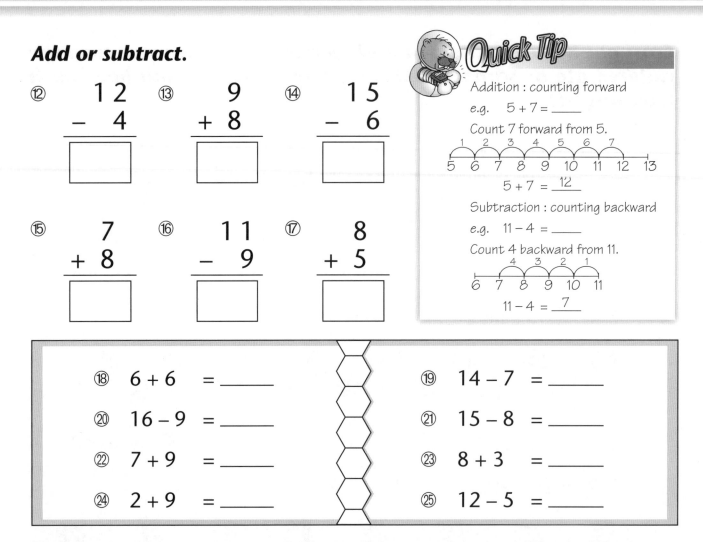

Quick Tip

Addition : counting forward

e.g. $5 + 7 =$ _____

Count 7 forward from 5.

$5 + 7 = \underline{12}$

Subtraction : counting backward

e.g. $11 - 4 =$ _____

Count 4 backward from 11.

$11 - 4 = \underline{7}$

⑱ $6 + 6$ = _____

⑲ $14 - 7$ = _____

⑳ $16 - 9$ = _____

㉑ $15 - 8$ = _____

㉒ $7 + 9$ = _____

㉓ $8 + 3$ = _____

㉔ $2 + 9$ = _____

㉕ $12 - 5$ = _____

Match the expressions with the number sentences. Then calculate.

Examples

Using tens may help you find the sum and the difference faster.

① $8 + 7 = 8 + 2 + 5$ ← Break 7 into
  $= 10 + 5$ $2 + 5.$
  $= 15$

② $12 - 4 = 10 + 2 - 4$ ← Break 12 into
   $= 10 - 4 + 2$ $10 + 2.$
   $= 6 + 2$
   $= 8$

㉖

| 15 take away 8 |
| 12 take away 7 |
| 8 plus 9 |
| 7 plus 7 |
| 16 take away 8 |

| $12 - 7$ = _____ |
| $8 + 9$ = _____ |
| $7 + 7$ = _____ |
| $15 - 8$ = _____ |
| $16 - 8$ = _____ |

ISBN: 978-1-897164-11-2

Solve the problems.

27   Aunt Doris buys 9 red apples and 5 green apples. How many apples does she buy in all?

_____ + _____ = _____

She buys _____ apples in all.

$+$

28   6 dogs and 8 cats are in a pet shop. How many dogs and cats are there in all?

_____ + _____ = _____

There are _____ dogs and cats in all.

$+$

29   Uncle Bill has 15 muffins. 6 of them are chocolate. How many are not chocolate?

_____ – _____ = _____

_____ muffins are not chocolate.

$-$

30   Melody had 12 lollipops. She ate 4 of them.   How many lollipops does she have now?

_____ – _____ = _____

She has _____ lollipops now.

$-$

MIND BOGGLER

Read what Derek says. Answer the question.

I have 11 baseball cards and my brother has 5 baseball cards. How many cards do I need to give him so that each of us has the same number of cards?

Derek needs to give _____ baseball cards to his brother.

ISBN: 978-1-897164-11-2

10 Measurement II

Look at the pictures. Put a check mark ✔ in the circle to tell which takes longer to do.

① Ⓐ eat a cookie   Ⓑ bake a cookie

② Ⓐ wash hands   Ⓑ bathe a dog

③ Ⓐ knit a sweater   Ⓑ wear a sweater

④ Ⓐ sing a song   Ⓑ ring a bell

Write morning, afternoon, evening or night to tell what time of the day John does the following things.

⑤ eats breakfast _____

⑥ goes to bed _____

⑦ eats dinner _____

⑧ goes home _____

Write one thing you will do in the following times.

⑨ Morning : _____ Afternoon : _____

Evening : _____ Night : _____

ISBN: 978-1-897164-11-2

See what Jeffrey will be doing this week. Help him fill in the blanks and answer the questions.

Sunday	Monday	Tuesday	Wednesday	Thursday	Friday	Saturday

⑩ Jeffrey is going to the [cinema] on _____ with his mom.

⑪ Jeffrey is going to have [coke burger] for lunch on _____ .

⑫ Jeffrey is going to play [bat] on _____ .

⑬ Jeffrey goes to the [library] to borrow some books on _____ .

⑭ _____ is the day Jeffrey has a [flute] lesson.

⑮ On _____ , Jeffrey will go to a [party].

⑯ How many days are there in a week? _____ days

⑰ Which day comes right after Thursday? _____

⑱ How many days will Jeffrey have [pizza] for lunch? _____ days

⑲ How many days will Jeffrey be going to play sports? _____ days

⑳ Jeffrey likes playing hockey. Which day of the week is Jeffrey's favourite day? _____

㉑ After borrowing the books, Jeffrey will return them the next day. Which day will he return the books? _____

ISBN: 978-1-897164-11-2

Match the months with the pictures. Circle the correct months.

㉒ January / **February** / December

㉓ May / July / **December**

㉔ July / September / **October**

㉕ March / **July** / November

㉖ February / June / **October**

㉗ **January** / August / April

Circle the correct answers to complete the sentences.

㉘ There are 11 / 12 / 13 months and 2 / 3 / 4 seasons in a year.

㉙ July / June / November comes just after May.

㉚ August is in spring / summer and October is in fall / winter .

㉛ Winter / Spring is the coldest season and fall / summer is the hottest season.

Look at the calendar. Answer the questions.

May

Sun	Mon	Tues	Wed	Thu	Fri	Sat
			1	2	3	4
5	6	7	8	9	10	11
12	13	14	15	16	17	18
19	20	21	22	23	24	25
26	27	28	29	30	31	

Quick Tip

The way to read a calendar :
first day of the month — month
Aug 18, on Sunday — days of a week
last day of the month

㉜ Which month comes just after this month? _____

㉝ Which day of the week is May 3? _____

㉞ Which day of the week is the first day of May? _____

㉟ Mother's day is on the 2nd Sunday. What is the date? _____

㊱ John's birthday is on the 3rd Wednesday. What is the date? _____

ISBN: 978-1-897164-11-2

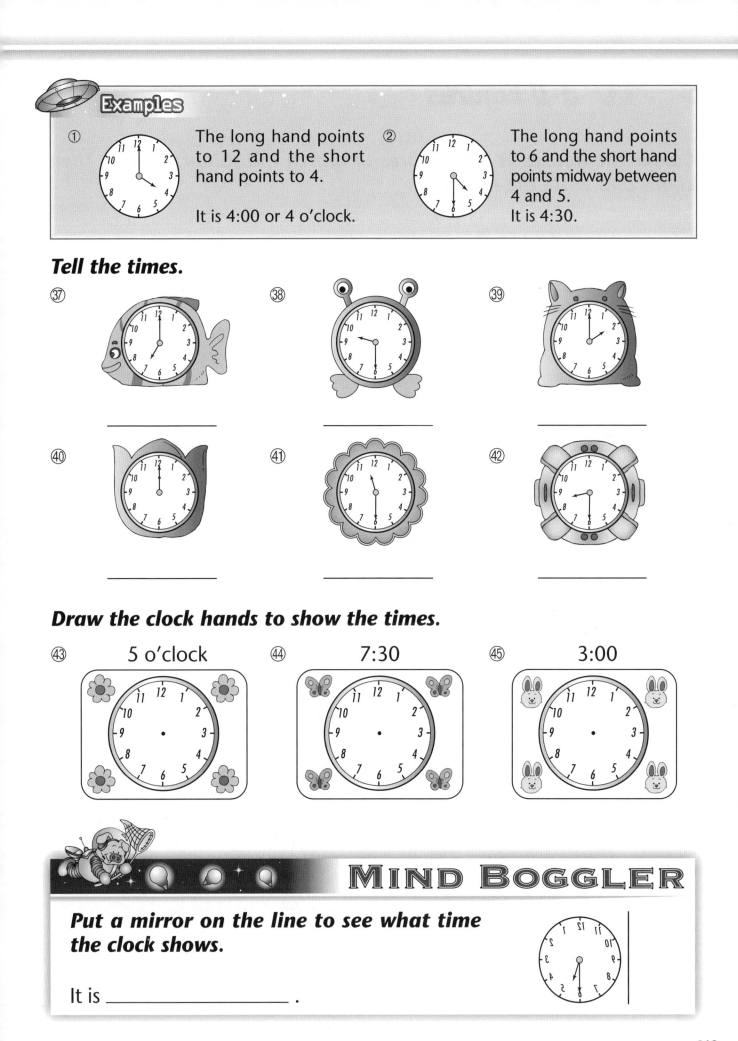

Examples

① The long hand points to 12 and the short hand points to 4.

It is 4:00 or 4 o'clock.

② The long hand points to 6 and the short hand points midway between 4 and 5.
It is 4:30.

Tell the times.

③⑦ _____

③⑧ _____

③⑨ _____

④⓪ _____

④① _____

④② _____

Draw the clock hands to show the times.

④③ 5 o'clock

④④ 7:30

④⑤ 3:00

MIND BOGGLER

Put a mirror on the line to see what time the clock shows.

It is _____ .

ISBN: 978-1-897164-11-2

Colour the figures in the pictures to match the colours given. Then count and write the numbers.

red   yellow   blue   green   orange   brown

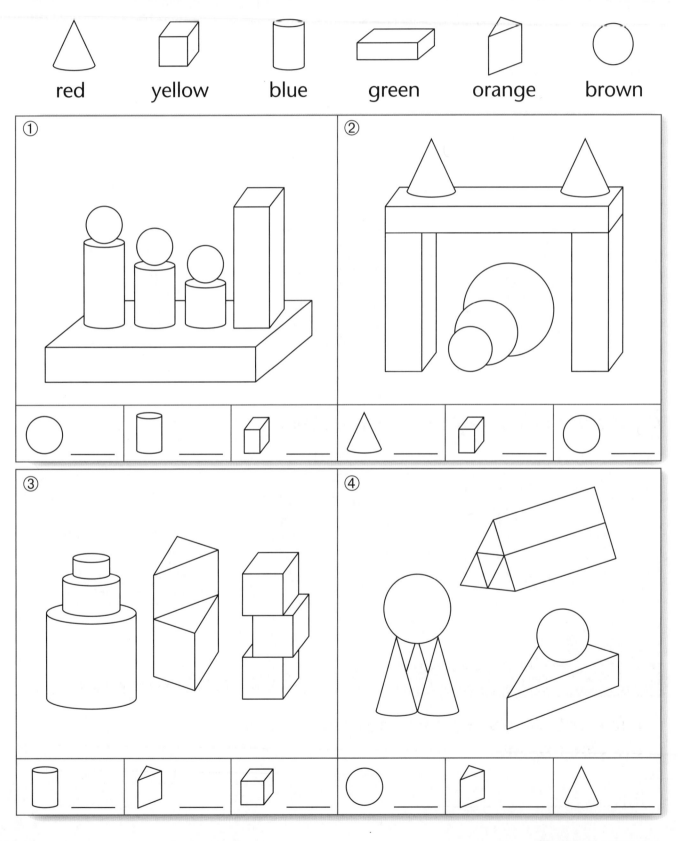

Look at each group of solids. Cross out ✗ the one that does not belong.

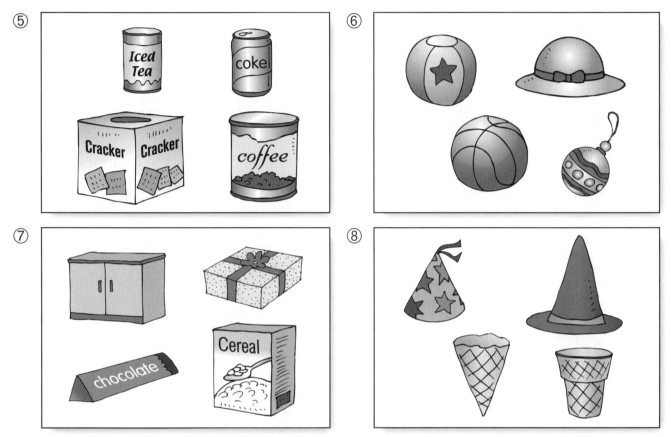

⑤

⑥

⑦

⑧

Match and write the names of the solids.

Cylinder   Cone   Cube   Sphere   Triangular prism

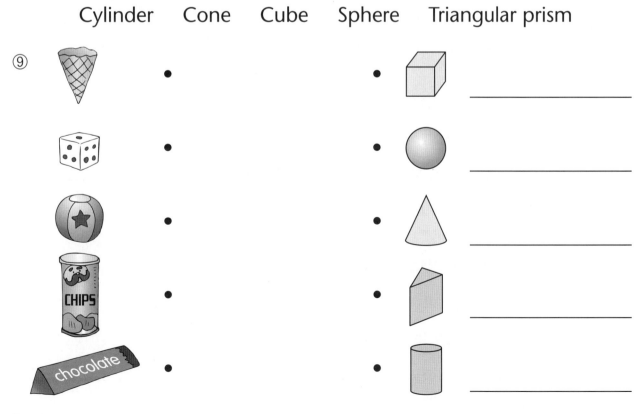

⑨

Look at the figures. Answer the questions.

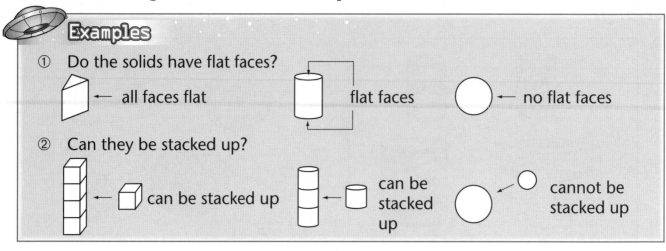

Examples

① Do the solids have flat faces?

← all faces flat   flat faces   ← no flat faces

② Can they be stacked up?

← can be stacked up   can be stacked up   cannot be stacked up

---

⑩
a. What is the name of this solid?   _____

b. Can it slide?   _____

c. Can it roll?   _____

d. Does it have flat faces?   _____

---

⑪
a. What is the name of this solid?   _____

b. Can it slide?   _____

c. Can it be stacked on top of another one?   _____

d. Does it have flat faces?   _____

---

⑫
a. What is the name of this solid?   _____

b. Can it roll?   _____

c. Can it be stacked on top of another one?   _____

d. Does it have curved faces?   _____

---

⑬
a. What is the name of this solid?   _____

b. Can it roll?   _____

c. Can it slide?   _____

d. Does it have curved faces?   _____

ISBN: 978-1-897164-11-2

Jimmy puts the solids in different groups. Find out his sorting rules and check ✔ the correct answers.

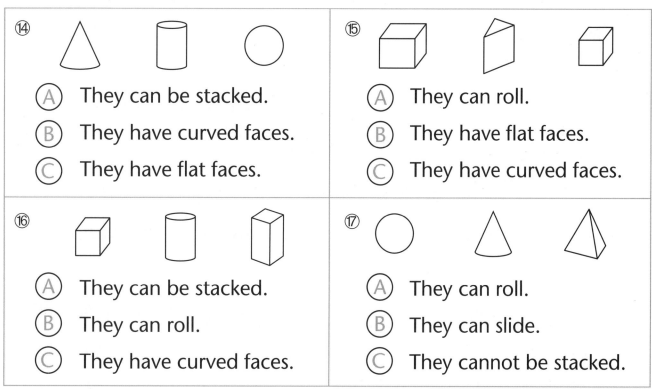

⑭
- Ⓐ They can be stacked.
- Ⓑ They have curved faces.
- Ⓒ They have flat faces.

⑮
- Ⓐ They can roll.
- Ⓑ They have flat faces.
- Ⓒ They have curved faces.

⑯
- Ⓐ They can be stacked.
- Ⓑ They can roll.
- Ⓒ They have curved faces.

⑰
- Ⓐ They can roll.
- Ⓑ They can slide.
- Ⓒ They cannot be stacked.

Look at the pictures. Fill in the blanks with numbers in words.

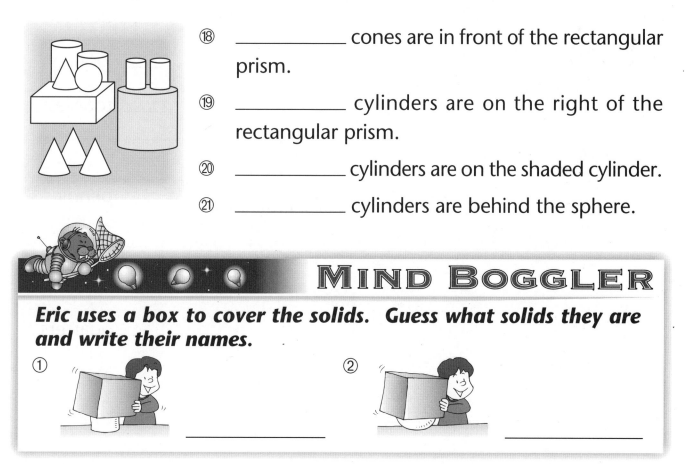

⑱ _____ cones are in front of the rectangular prism.

⑲ _____ cylinders are on the right of the rectangular prism.

⑳ _____ cylinders are on the shaded cylinder.

㉑ _____ cylinders are behind the sphere.

MIND BOGGLER

Eric uses a box to cover the solids. Guess what solids they are and write their names.

① _____

② _____

ISBN: 978-1-897164-11-2

12 Money

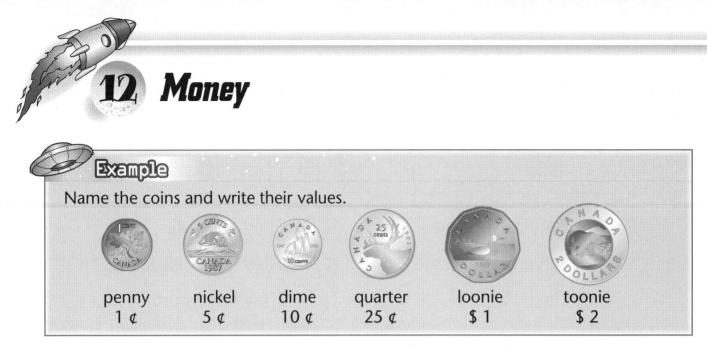

Example

Name the coins and write their values.

penny	nickel	dime	quarter	loonie	toonie
1 ¢	5 ¢	10 ¢	25 ¢	$ 1	$ 2

Look at the coins each child has. Count and write the numbers.

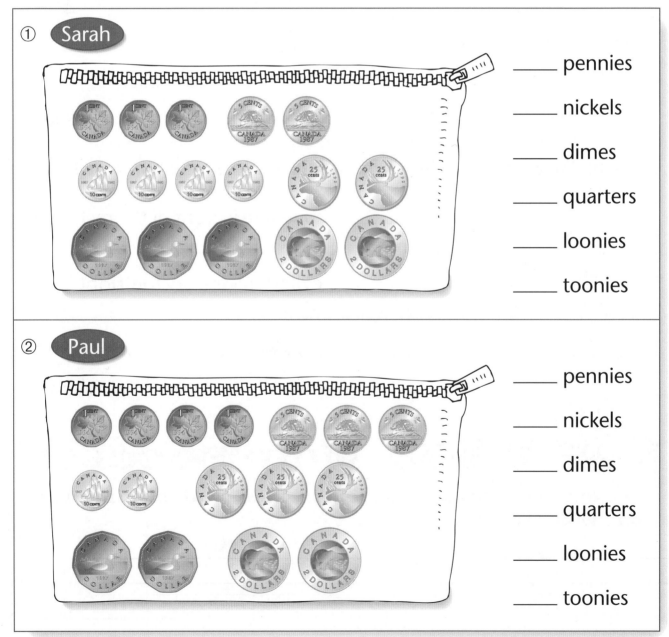

① **Sarah**

_____ pennies

_____ nickels

_____ dimes

_____ quarters

_____ loonies

_____ toonies

② **Paul**

_____ pennies

_____ nickels

_____ dimes

_____ quarters

_____ loonies

_____ toonies

Check ✔ the coins in each group to match the value on the left.

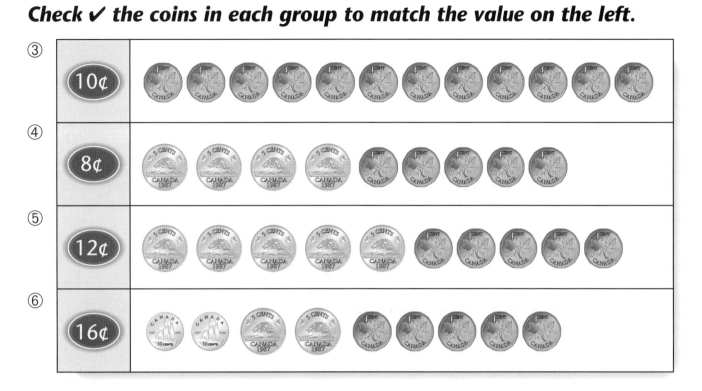

See how much money each child has. Write the amount and answer the questions.

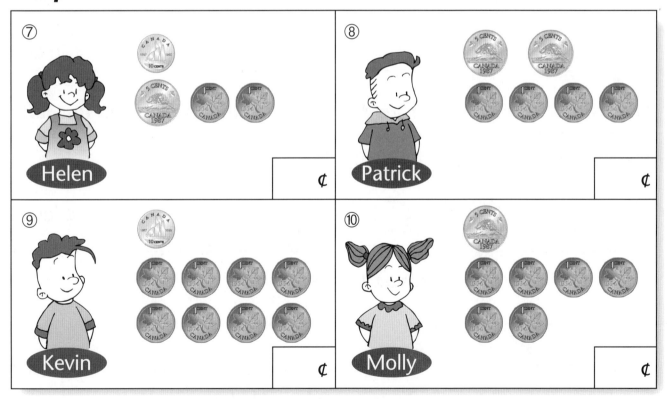

⑦ Helen _____ ¢

⑧ Patrick _____ ¢

⑨ Kevin _____ ¢

⑩ Molly _____ ¢

⑪ Which child has the fewest coins? _____

⑫ Which child has the most money? _____

Find how much money the children have in all.

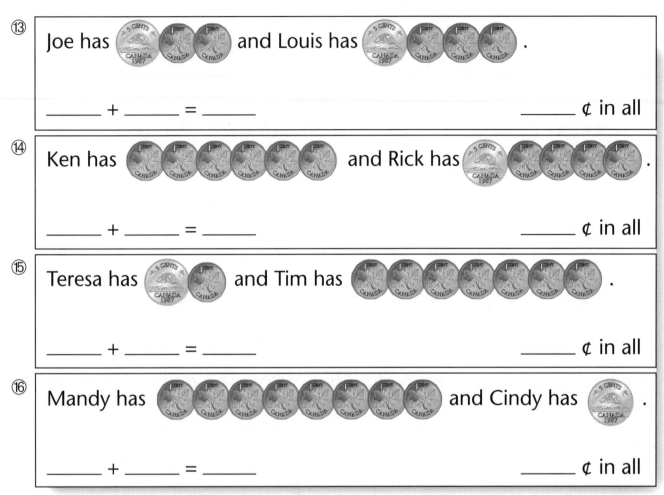

⑬ Joe has ▢▢▢ and Louis has ▢▢▢▢ .

_____ + _____ = _____   _____ ¢ in all

⑭ Ken has ▢▢▢▢▢▢ and Rick has ▢▢▢▢▢ .

_____ + _____ = _____   _____ ¢ in all

⑮ Teresa has ▢▢ and Tim has ▢▢▢▢▢▢▢▢ .

_____ + _____ = _____   _____ ¢ in all

⑯ Mandy has ▢▢▢▢▢▢▢ and Cindy has ▢ .

_____ + _____ = _____   _____ ¢ in all

Cross out ✗ some coins to see how much money each child has left.

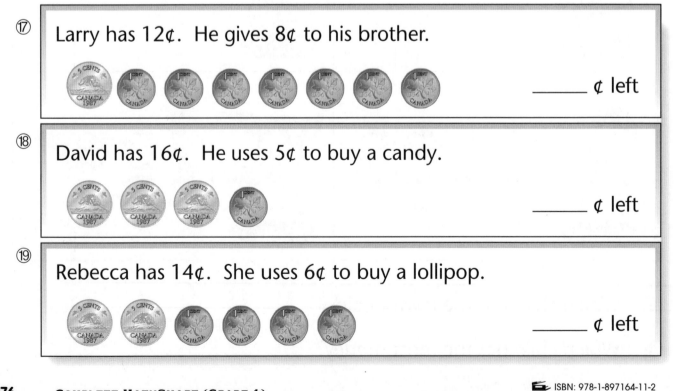

⑰ Larry has 12¢. He gives 8¢ to his brother.

_____ ¢ left

⑱ David has 16¢. He uses 5¢ to buy a candy.

_____ ¢ left

⑲ Rebecca has 14¢. She uses 6¢ to buy a lollipop.

_____ ¢ left

ISBN: 978-1-897164-11-2

See what the children are going to buy. Help them solve the problems.

5¢   7¢   6¢   4¢   8¢

⑳

a.

_____ + _____ = _____

They cost _____ ¢.

b. Sally has

_____ – _____ = _____

She has _____ ¢ left.

㉑

a.

_____ + _____ = _____

They cost _____ ¢.

b. Robert has

_____ – _____ = _____

He has _____ ¢ left.

㉒

a.

_____ + _____ = _____

They cost _____ ¢.

b. Linda has

_____ – _____ = _____

She has _____ ¢ left.

MIND BOGGLER

Edward had a 25 cents *. He bought 3 different items from the above and has* 5 cents *left. Colour the 3 items he bought.*

(A)   (B)   (C) HAPPY BIRTHDAY   (D)   (E)

ISBN: 978-1-897164-11-2

13 Graphs

Mrs. Minden asked her Grade 1 students their favourite pets. Look at the graph and answer the questions.

Favourite Pets

① How many students like 🐕 best? _____ students

② How many students like 🐈 best? _____ students

③ How many students like 🐁 best? _____ students

④ How many more students like 🐟 than 🐢 ? _____ more students

⑤ How many students are there in Mrs. Minden's class? _____ students

⑥ Which pet is the least popular? Colour it.

⑦ Which pet is the most popular? Colour it.

Mr. White asked the children their favourite movies. Look at the graph and answer the questions.

⑧ How many 😊 like 🎬Amazing Day ? ____ 😊

⑨ How many 👧 like 🎬Princess Elaine ? ____ 👧

⑩ How many children like 🎬On the way ? ____ children

⑪ How many more children like 🎬Princess Elaine than 🎬Monster ? ____ more children

⑫ How many 😊 are there? ____ 😊

⑬ How many 👧 are there? ____ 👧

⑭ How many children are there? ____ children

⑮ Colour the most popular movie blue and the least one yellow.

ISBN: 978-1-897164-11-2

Count the toys Tim has and write the numbers. Then colour the graph to show his toys and answer the questions.

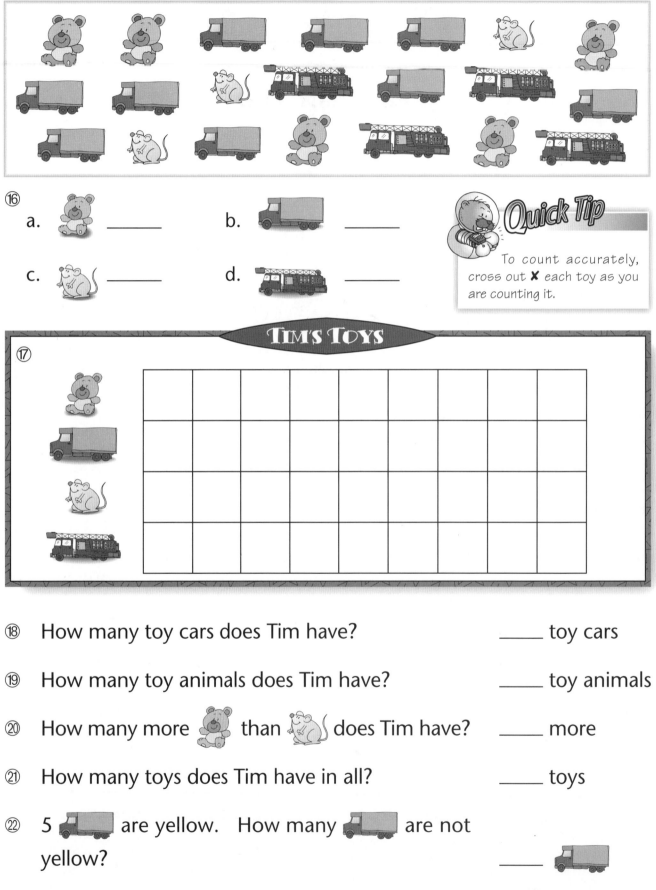

⑯
a. _____ b. _____

c. _____ d. _____

Quick Tip

To count accurately, cross out ✘ each toy as you are counting it.

TIM'S TOYS

⑰

⑱ How many toy cars does Tim have? _____ toy cars

⑲ How many toy animals does Tim have? _____ toy animals

⑳ How many more 🧸 than 🐭 does Tim have? _____ more

㉑ How many toys does Tim have in all? _____ toys

㉒ 5 🚚 are yellow. How many 🚚 are not yellow? _____ 🚚

ISBN: 978-1-897164-11-2

Each child in Ms. Gibbon's class drew his or her favourite fast food on the board. Colour the graph to show their preferences and circle the correct answers.

Our Favourite Fast Foods

㉓

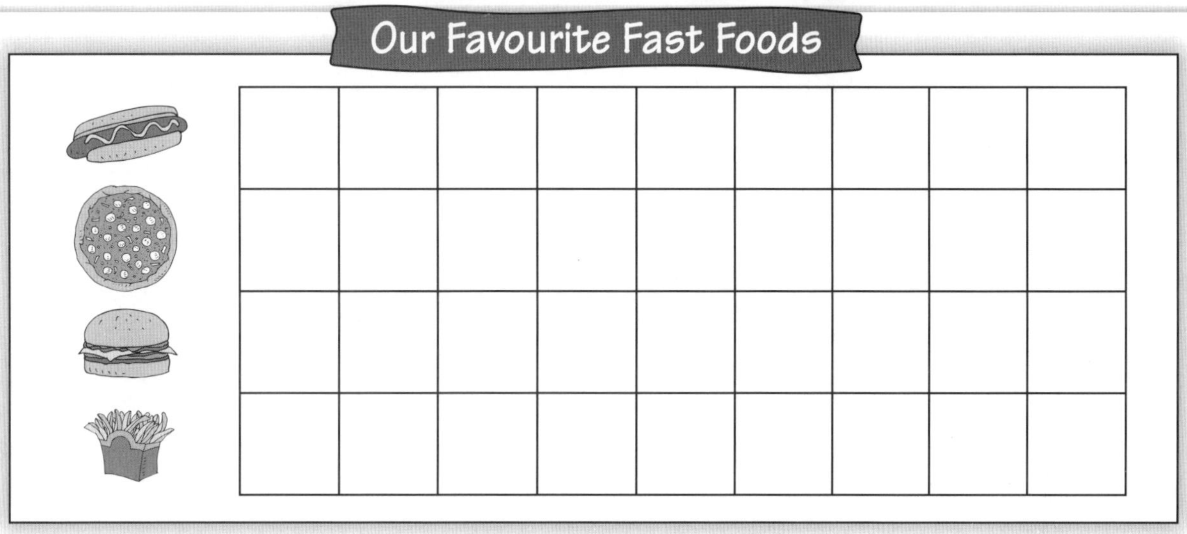

㉔ How many children are in Ms. Gibbon's class?   21   22   23

㉕ How many children like 🌭 best?   2   6   7

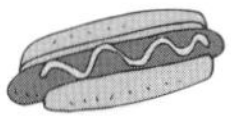

㉖ How many children like 🍕 best?   5   6   7

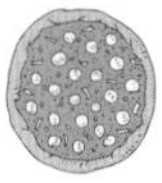

㉗ Which fast food do most children like?

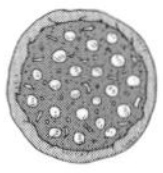

MIND BOGGLER

Look at the graph above. Answer the questions.

① How many kinds of fast foods do the children like?

_____ kinds

② Ms. Gibbon wants to buy one kind of fast food to treat her students. What should she buy? Give the reason.

_____

ISBN: 978-1-897164-11-2

14 Probability

Decide if the following are likely or unlikely to occur. Circle 'Yes' or 'No'.

① Yes / No
② Yes / No
③ Yes / No
④ Yes / No
⑤ Yes / No
⑥ Yes / No
⑦ Yes / No
⑧ Yes / No
⑨ Yes / No
⑩ Yes / No

ISBN: 978-1-897164-11-2

Look at the picture stories. Circle 'Yes' if they are likely to happen or 'No' if they are not.

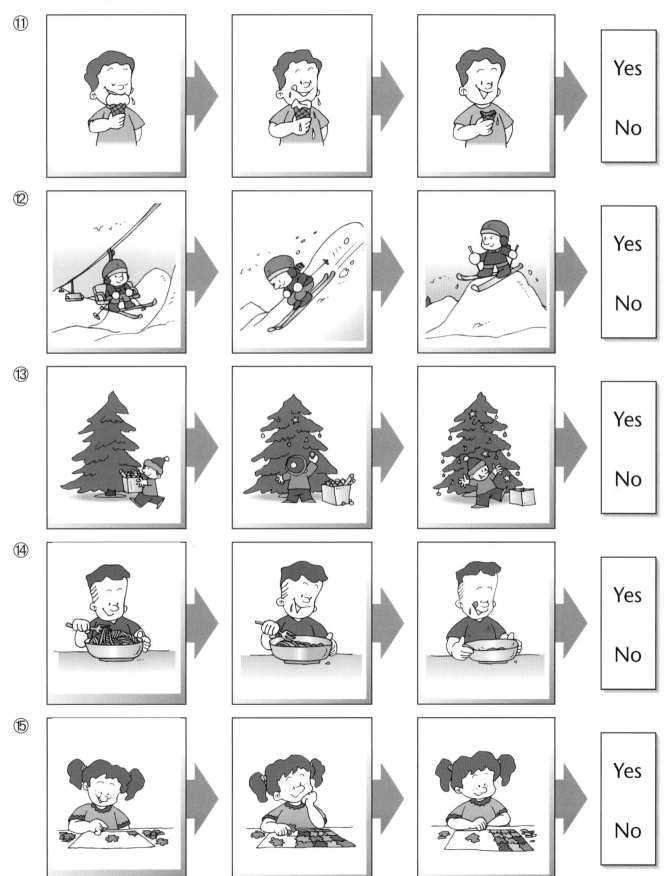

⑪ Yes / No

⑫ Yes / No

⑬ Yes / No

⑭ Yes / No

⑮ Yes / No

ISBN: 978-1-897164-11-2

Each child can spin the arrow once and get the food that the arrow lands on. Read and help the children check ✔ the correct spinners.

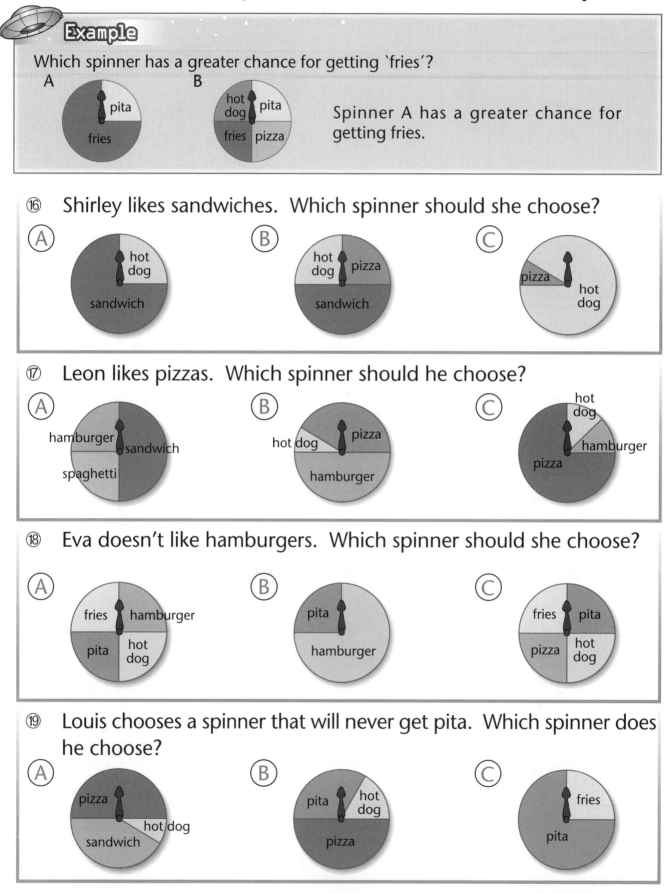

Example

Which spinner has a greater chance for getting 'fries'?

A   B

Spinner A has a greater chance for getting fries.

⑯ Shirley likes sandwiches. Which spinner should she choose?

Ⓐ   Ⓑ   Ⓒ

⑰ Leon likes pizzas. Which spinner should he choose?

Ⓐ   Ⓑ   Ⓒ

⑱ Eva doesn't like hamburgers. Which spinner should she choose?

Ⓐ   Ⓑ   Ⓒ

⑲ Louis chooses a spinner that will never get pita. Which spinner does he choose?

Ⓐ   Ⓑ   Ⓒ

ISBN: 978-1-897164-11-2

Use the words given to describe the chances.

never   **sometimes**   **often**

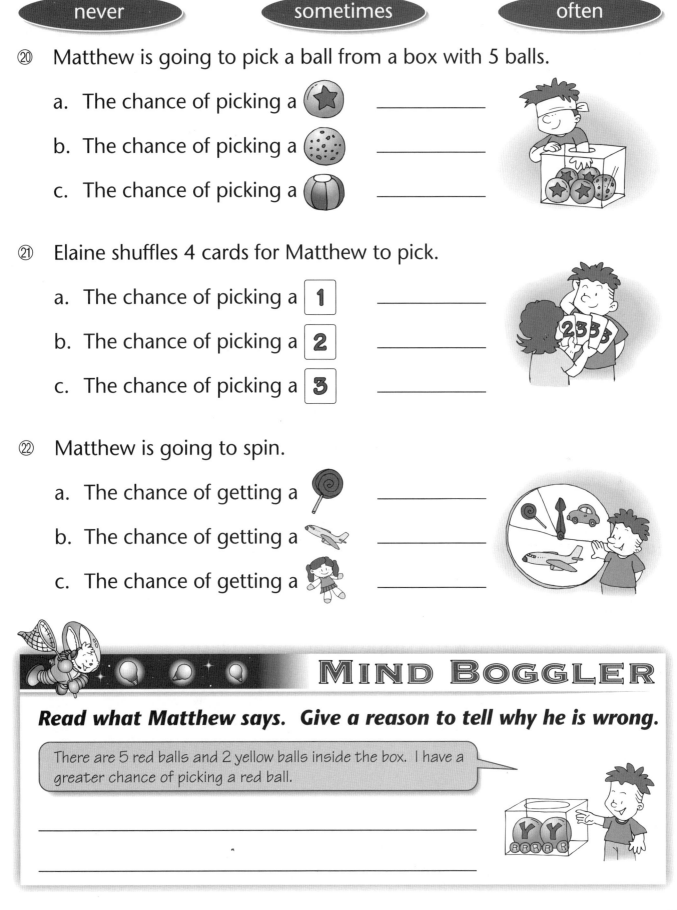

⑳ Matthew is going to pick a ball from a box with 5 balls.

 a. The chance of picking a ⭐ _____

 b. The chance of picking a 🍪 _____

 c. The chance of picking a 🔵 _____

㉑ Elaine shuffles 4 cards for Matthew to pick.

 a. The chance of picking a **1** _____

 b. The chance of picking a **2** _____

 c. The chance of picking a **3** _____

㉒ Matthew is going to spin.

 a. The chance of getting a 🍭 _____

 b. The chance of getting a ✈️ _____

 c. The chance of getting a 🧍 _____

MIND BOGGLER

Read what Matthew says. Give a reason to tell why he is wrong.

> There are 5 red balls and 2 yellow balls inside the box. I have a greater chance of picking a red ball.

_____

_____

Find out how many shapes will cover each picture. Answer the questions.

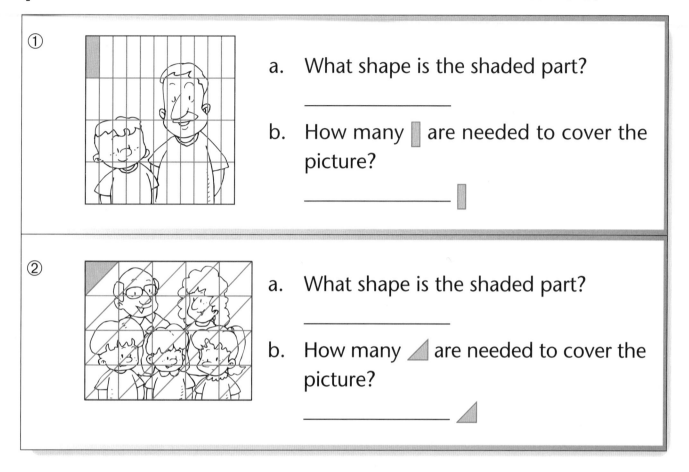

①   a.   What shape is the shaded part?

     _____

     b.   How many ▊ are needed to cover the picture?

     _____ ▊

②   a.   What shape is the shaded part?

     _____

     b.   How many ◸ are needed to cover the picture?

     _____ ◸

Joyce coloured one face of each solid. Help her answer the questions.

③   a.   What is the name of the solid?   _____

     b.   What is the shape of the shaded face?   _____

④   a.   What is the shape of the shaded face?   _____

     b.   What is the shape of the spotted face?   _____

⑤   a.   What is the name of the solid?   _____

     b.   What is the shape of the shaded face?   _____

Extend the patterns.

⑥ A B B C A B B C A B B C ___ ___ ___

⑦ 4 4 2 2 1 4 4 2 2 1 4 4 ___ ___ ___ ___

⑧ △ △ ○ ▼ △ △ ○ ▼ △ △ ___ ___ ___ ___

⑨ 1 3 2 1 1 3 2 1 1 3 2 1 ___ ___ ___ ___

Circle 'Yes' or 'No' to show if the following are likely or unlikely to happen.

⑩	Snow in winter	Yes	No
⑪	School in September	Yes	No
⑫	Swimming in a lake in January	Yes	No
⑬	Ice-skating on a lake in July	Yes	No
⑭	Butterflies flying in the sea	Yes	No
⑮	Going to see a movie on Monday	Yes	No

Jane wants to share her snacks with her brother. Help her divide the snacks into 2 equal halves with a line.

⑯ ⑰ ⑱ ⑲

ISBN: 978-1-897164-11-2

Look at Melody's calendar. Answer the questions and solve the problems.

Swimming lesson Start	March							Drama contest Start
	Sunday	Monday	Tuesday	Wednesday	Thursday	Friday	Saturday	
			1	2	3	4	5	
	6	7	8	9	10	11	12	01:30
Baseball match Start	13	14	15	16	17	18	19	
12:00	20	21	22	23	24	25	26	
	27	28	29	30	31			

⑳ How many days are there in a week?　　　　_____

㉑ Which month comes just after this month?　　_____

㉒ Which day of a week is March 15?　　　　　_____

㉓ Melody has a swimming lesson in March. What is the date?　　　　　　　　　　　　　　　_____

㉔ Melody has a baseball match in March. At what time does the match start?　　　　　　　　_____

㉕ How many days will the drama contest be held? What are the dates?　　　　　　　　　　　_____

㉖ Each drama contest lasts 2 hours. At what time does the drama contest end?　　　　　　　_____

㉗ The swimming lesson ends at 3:00 and the baseball match ends at 1:30. Draw the clock hands to show the times.

a. Swimming lesson　　　　　b. Baseball match

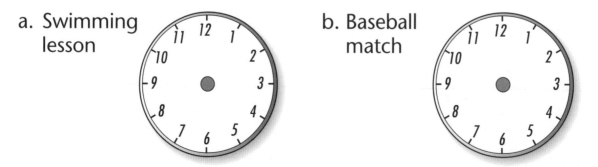

Add or subtract.

㉘ 5 + 3 ☐	㉙ 4 + 6 ☐	㉚ 9 − 5 ☐	㉛ 7 − 2 ☐
㉜ 1 2 − 4 ☐	㉝ 5 + 6 ☐	㉞ 8 + 8 ☐	㉟ 1 4 − 9 ☐

㊱ $10 - 8 =$ _____   ㊲ $3 + 6 \ =$ _____

㊳ $5 + 9 \ =$ _____   ㊴ $11 - 8 =$ _____

㊵ $9 + 9 \ =$ _____   ㊶ $16 - 7 =$ _____

Solve the problems.

㊷   There are 15 fish in the fish tank. Aunt Sabrina takes away 6 fish. How many fish are left in the fish tank?

_____ ◯ _____ = _____   _____ fish

㊸   Tim has 8 stamps. Uncle Bill gives Tim 5 more. How many stamps does Tim have in all?

_____ ◯ _____ = _____   _____ stamps in all

㊹   Ray has 9 storybooks in French and 6 storybooks in English. How many storybooks does Ray have in all?

_____ ◯ _____ = _____   _____ storybooks in all

㊺   Aunt Mary has 11 hamburgers. She gives 2 hamburgers to her son. How many hamburgers are left?

_____ ◯ _____ = _____   _____ hamburgers

ISBN: 978-1-897164-11-2

Count the blocks and pennies Sam uses to measure the paper. Write the numbers.

㊻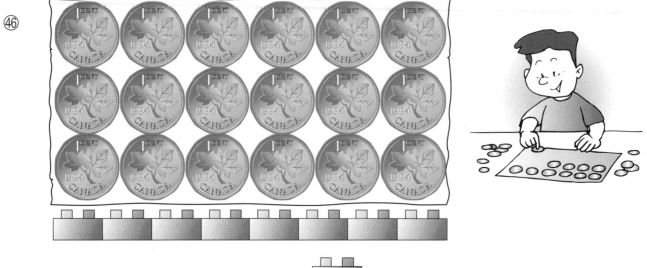

a. The paper is as long as _____ [blocks] .

b. _____ pennies are needed to cover the paper.

Count by 2's, 5's or 10's to find the number of hairpins in each group. Then answer the questions.

㊼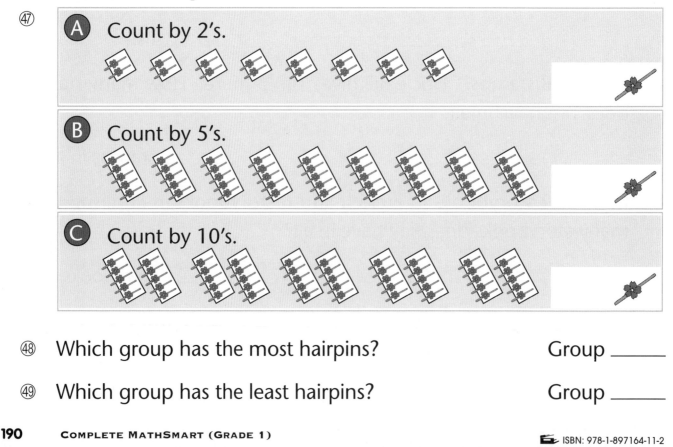

A Count by 2's.

B Count by 5's.

C Count by 10's.

㊽ Which group has the most hairpins? Group _____

㊾ Which group has the least hairpins? Group _____

ISBN: 978-1-897164-11-2

Look at the prices of the treats. Solve the problems.

 2¢    5¢   6¢   8¢   3¢

50 Check ✔ the coins to show the values of the treats.

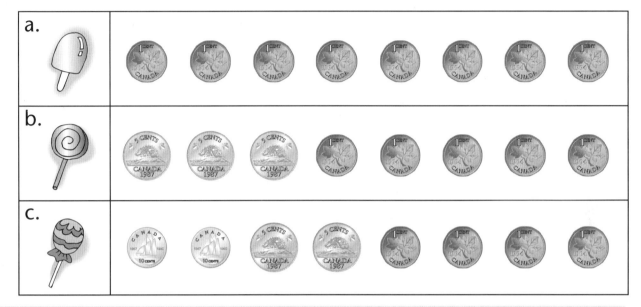

51 Sally wants to buy a and a . How much does she need to pay?

_____ + _____ = _____   _____ ¢

52 Ray wants to buy a and a . How much does he need to pay?

_____ + _____ = _____   _____ ¢

53 Sarah had 10¢. She bought a . How much does she have now?

_____ – _____ = _____   _____ ¢

54 Tom had 15¢. He bought a . How much does he have now?

_____ – _____ = _____   _____ ¢

55 Peter bought a and had 5¢ left. How much had he got at first?

_____ + _____ = _____   _____ ¢

Ms. Shim asked her Grade 1 students their favourite footwear. Look at the graph and answer the questions.

⑤⑥ How many students like to wear running shoes? _____

⑤⑦ How many students like to wear boots? _____

⑤⑧ How many boys like to wear slippers? _____

⑤⑨ How many girls like to wear dress shoes? _____

⑥⓪ How many more students like to wear running shoes than boots? _____

⑥① How many students like to wear dress shoes and slippers? _____

⑥② Which is the most popular footwear? _____

⑥③ Which is the least popular footwear? _____

⑥④ Today all the children wear their favourite shoes except those who like slippers. The boys who like slippers wear running shoes and the girls who like slippers wear dress shoes.

　　a. How many students wear running shoes? _____

　　b. How many students wear dress shoes? _____

 ISBN: 978-1-897164-11-2

Overview

In Section III, children were introduced to the five major areas of mathematics: Number Sense and Numeration, Measurement, Geometry and Spatial Sense, Patterning and Algebra, and Data Management and Probability.

In this section, concepts of shape, money, measurement, graph, addition and subtraction are further developed and practised in integrated exercises.

Solving "story problems" provides children with practice in reading as well as translating words into mathematical terms. The exercises describe everyday situations to provide context and interest for the Grade 1 students.

ISBN: 978-1-897164-11-2

Use the pictures to answer the questions.

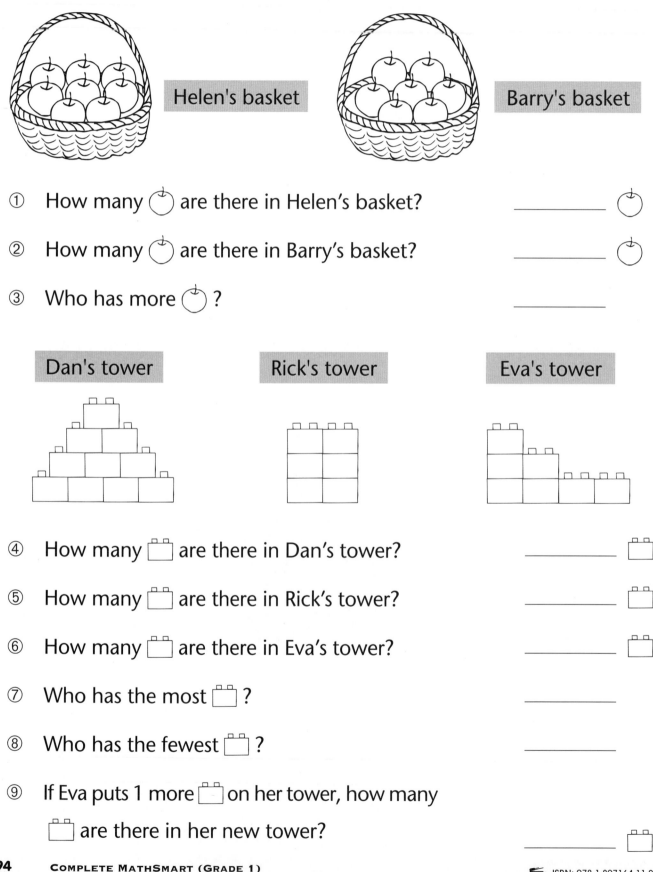

① How many 🍎 are there in Helen's basket? _____ 🍎

② How many 🍎 are there in Barry's basket? _____ 🍎

③ Who has more 🍎 ? _____

④ How many ▭ are there in Dan's tower? _____ ▭

⑤ How many ▭ are there in Rick's tower? _____ ▭

⑥ How many ▭ are there in Eva's tower? _____ ▭

⑦ Who has the most ▭ ? _____

⑧ Who has the fewest ▭ ? _____

⑨ If Eva puts 1 more ▭ on her tower, how many ▭ are there in her new tower? _____ ▭

ISBN: 978-1-897164-11-2

Jamie's cookies	Carmen's cookies	Lucy's cookies

⑩ How many 🍪 does Jamie have? _____ 🍪

⑪ How many 🍪 does Carmen have? _____ 🍪

⑫ How many 🍪 does Lucy have? _____ 🍪

⑬ How many 🍪 could Jamie give to his friends if he ate one himself? _____ 🍪

⑭ How many 🍪 would Lucy have if she got one from Jamie? _____ 🍪

Fill in the blanks.

⑮ How many boys are there? _____ boys

⑯ How many girls are there? _____ girls

⑰ How many children are there? _____ children

⑱ Who is the 1st in the line? _____

⑲ Who is the 3rd in the line? _____

See how many stickers each child has. Answer the questions.

① Ann has _____ 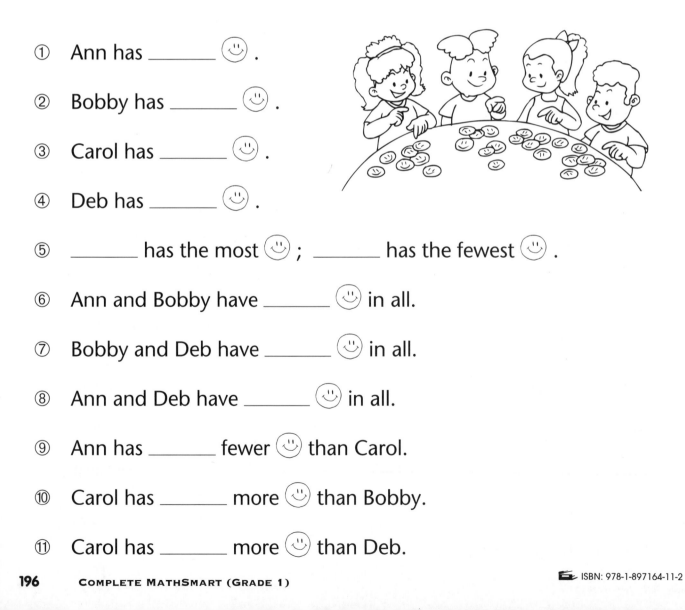 .

② Bobby has _____ ☺ .

③ Carol has _____ ☺ .

④ Deb has _____ ☺ .

⑤ _____ has the most ☺ ; _____ has the fewest ☺ .

⑥ Ann and Bobby have _____ ☺ in all.

⑦ Bobby and Deb have _____ ☺ in all.

⑧ Ann and Deb have _____ ☺ in all.

⑨ Ann has _____ fewer ☺ than Carol.

⑩ Carol has _____ more ☺ than Bobby.

⑪ Carol has _____ more ☺ than Deb.

ISBN: 978-1-897164-11-2

Use the pictures to answer the questions.

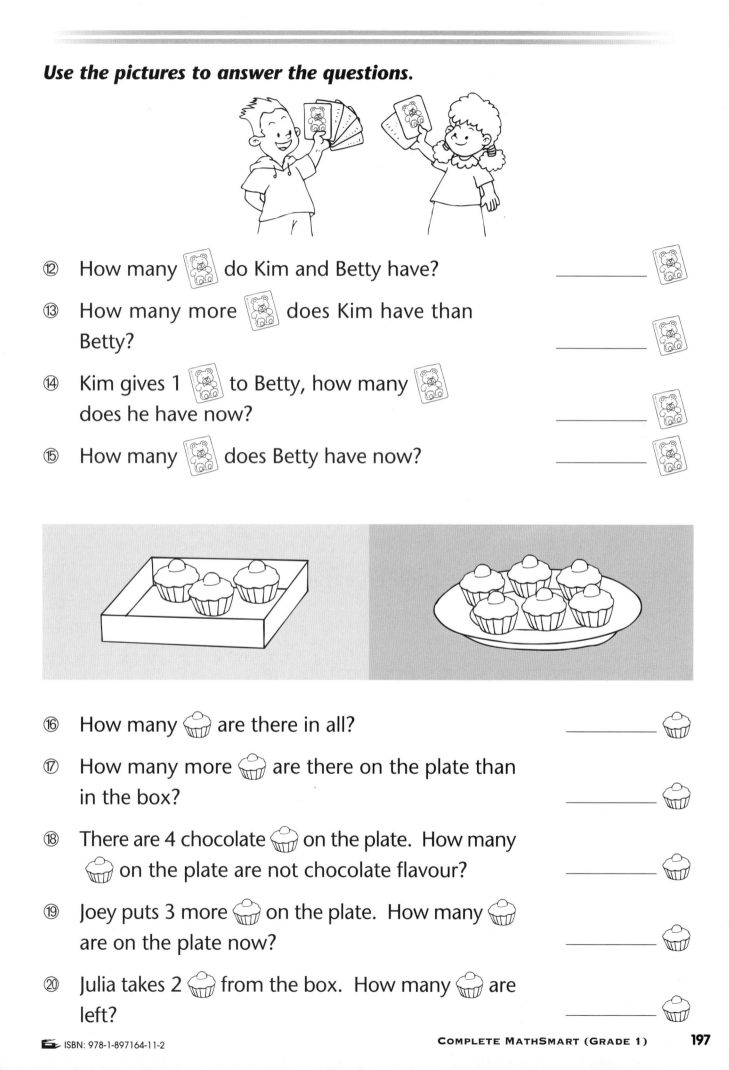

⑫ How many 🐻 do Kim and Betty have? _____ 🐻

⑬ How many more 🐻 does Kim have than Betty? _____ 🐻

⑭ Kim gives 1 🐻 to Betty, how many 🐻 does he have now? _____ 🐻

⑮ How many 🐻 does Betty have now? _____ 🐻

⑯ How many 🧁 are there in all? _____ 🧁

⑰ How many more 🧁 are there on the plate than in the box? _____ 🧁

⑱ There are 4 chocolate 🧁 on the plate. How many 🧁 on the plate are not chocolate flavour? _____ 🧁

⑲ Joey puts 3 more 🧁 on the plate. How many 🧁 are on the plate now? _____ 🧁

⑳ Julia takes 2 🧁 from the box. How many 🧁 are left? _____ 🧁

ISBN: 978-1-897164-11-2

See how many biscuits each child ate yesterday. Then answer the questions.

	Brian	Dave	Beth
Morning	🍘🍘	🍘🍘🍘	🍘🍘🍘 🍘🍘
Afternoon	🍘🍘🍘🍘	🍘🍘🍘🍘 🍘🍘🍘	🍘🍘

㉑ How many 🍘 did Brian eat in all? _____ 🍘

㉒ How many 🍘 did Dave eat in all? _____ 🍘

㉓ How many 🍘 did Beth eat in all? _____ 🍘

㉔ How many 🍘 did the children eat in the morning? _____ 🍘

㉕ How many more 🍘 did Brian eat in the afternoon than in the morning? _____ 🍘

㉖ How many fewer 🍘 did Dave eat in the morning than in the afternoon? _____ 🍘

㉗ How many fewer 🍘 did Beth eat in the afternoon than in the morning? _____ 🍘

㉘ If Beth ate 3 more 🍘 in the afternoon, how many 🍘 did he eat the whole day? _____ 🍘

ISBN: 978-1-897164-11-2

See what Jack has for his birthday party. Then write the numbers.

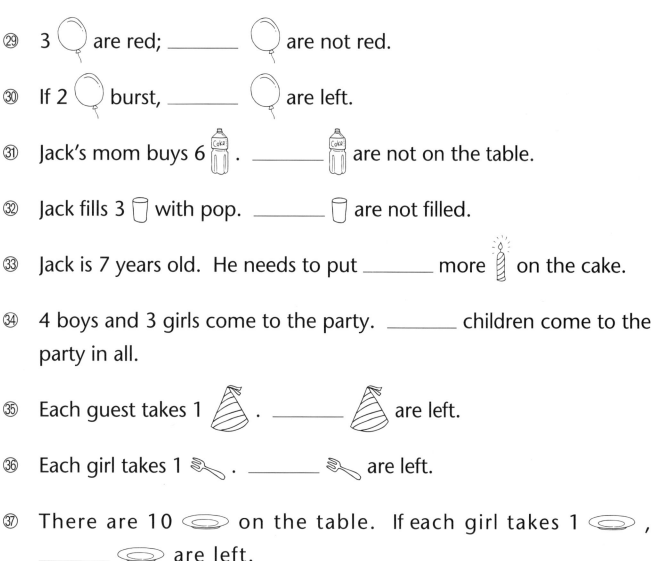

㉙ 3  are red; _____ are not red.

㉚ If 2 burst, _____ are left.

㉛ Jack's mom buys 6 . _____ are not on the table.

㉜ Jack fills 3 with pop. _____ are not filled.

㉝ Jack is 7 years old. He needs to put _____ more on the cake.

㉞ 4 boys and 3 girls come to the party. _____ children come to the party in all.

㉟ Each guest takes 1 . _____ are left.

㊱ Each girl takes 1 . _____ are left.

㊲ There are 10 on the table. If each girl takes 1 , _____ are left.

ISBN: 978-1-897164-11-2

See how many candies each child collected at Halloween. Count and write the numbers. Then answer the questions.

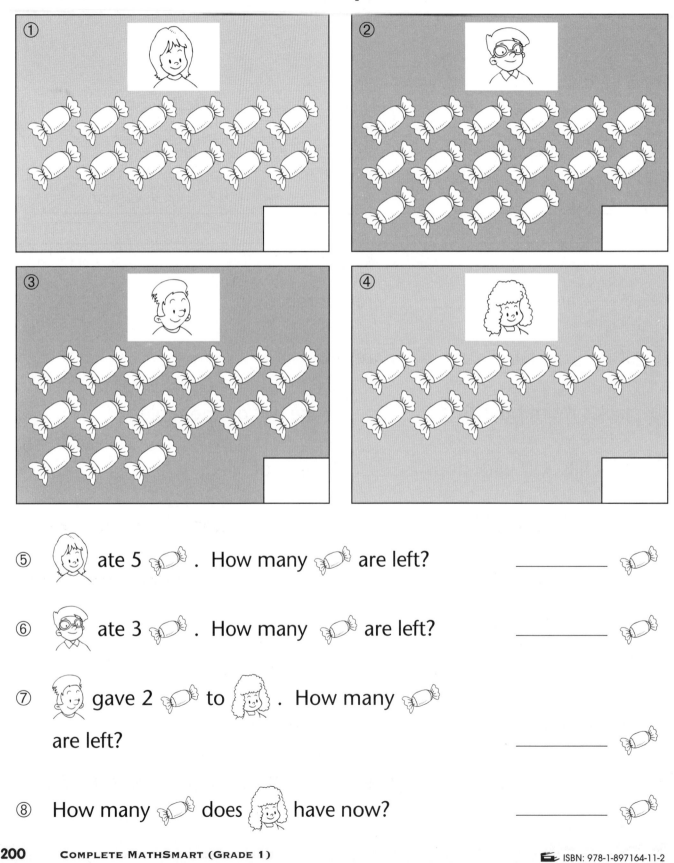

⑤ [girl] ate 5 🍬 . How many 🍬 are left? _____ 🍬

⑥ [boy] ate 3 🍬 . How many 🍬 are left? _____ 🍬

⑦ [boy] gave 2 🍬 to [girl] . How many 🍬 are left? _____ 🍬

⑧ How many 🍬 does [girl] have now? _____ 🍬

ISBN: 978-1-897164-11-2

Look at the fruits Brad's mom bought. Count and write the numbers. Then answer the questions.

⑨

⑩

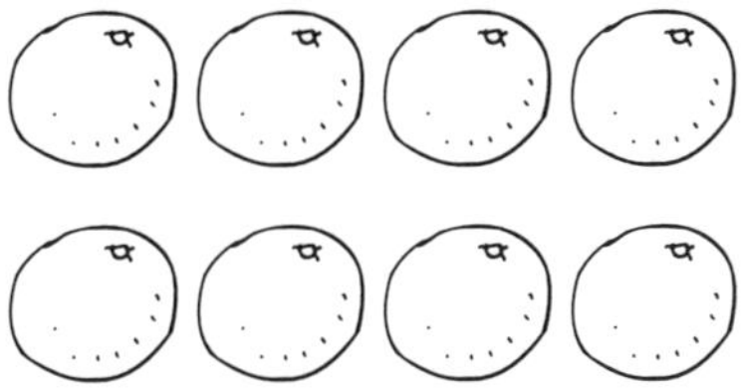

⑪

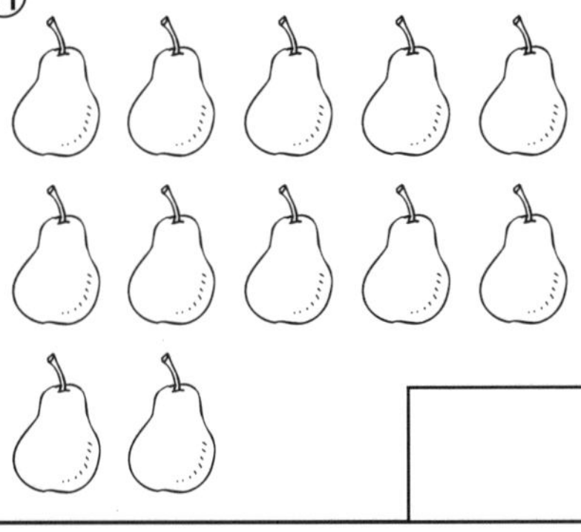

⑫	How many 🍎 and 🍊 did Brad's mom buy in all? _____ 🍎 🍊 in all	$\begin{array}{r} 6 \\ +\ \ 8 \\ \hline \end{array}$
⑬	How many 🍊 and 🍐 did Brad's mom buy in all? _____ 🍊 🍐 in all	
⑭	How many more 🍐 are there than 🍎 ? _____ more 🍐	
⑮	How many more 🍐 are there than 🍊 ? _____ more 🍐	
⑯	Brad's mom gives 5 🍐 to a friend. How many 🍐 are left? _____ 🍐 left	

ISBN: 978-1-897164-11-2

Answer the questions.

⑰ Ann has 7 🌼 ; Grace has 11 🌼 . How many 🌼 do they have in all?

<u>   7 + 11   </u> = _____   _____ 🌼 in all

⑱ How many more 🌼 does Grace have than Ann?

_____ = _____   _____ more 🌼

⑲ In Mrs Ling's class, there are 17 😊 👧 . 5 are 👧 . How many 😊 are there?

_____ = _____   _____ 😊

⑳ How many more 😊 are there than 👧 ?

_____ = _____   _____ more 😊

㉑ Tim has 13 🍫 ; Rick has 7 🍫 . How many 🍫 do they have in all?

_____ = _____   _____ 🍫 in all

㉒ How many more 🍫 does Tim have than Rick?

_____ = _____   _____ more 🍫

ISBN: 978-1-897164-11-2

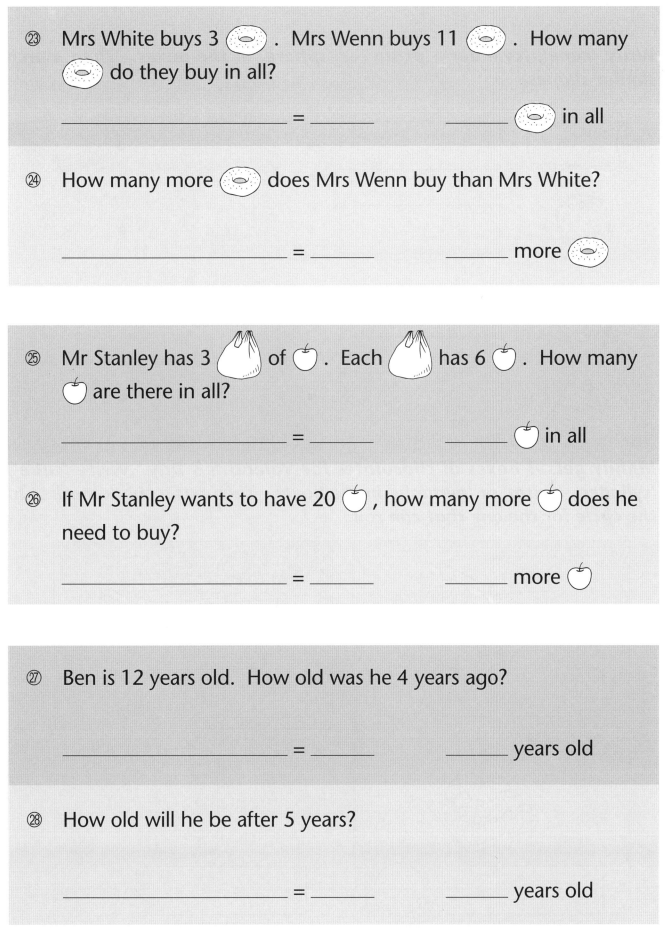

㉓ Mrs White buys 3 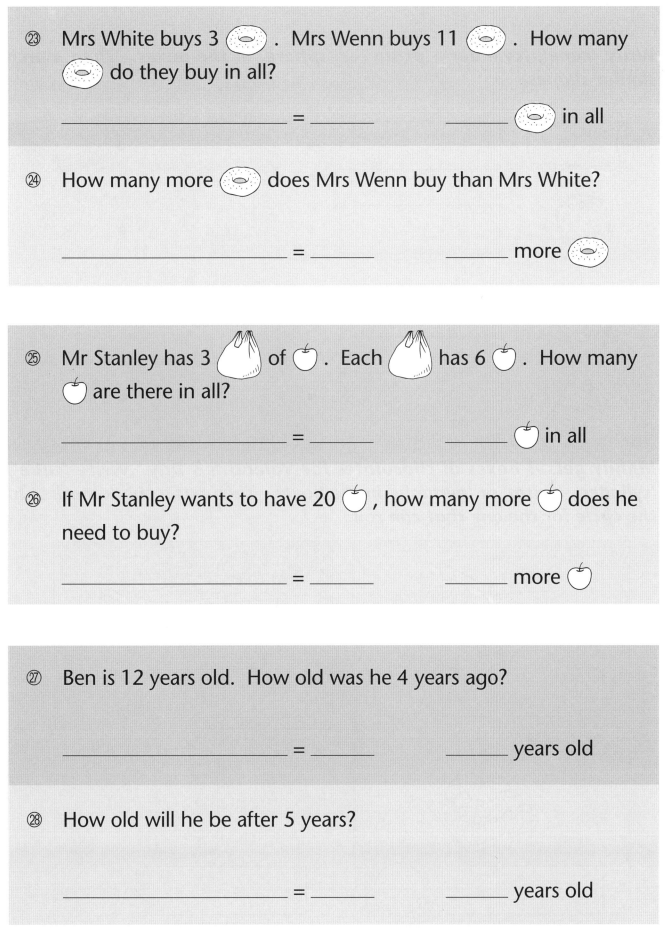. Mrs Wenn buys 11 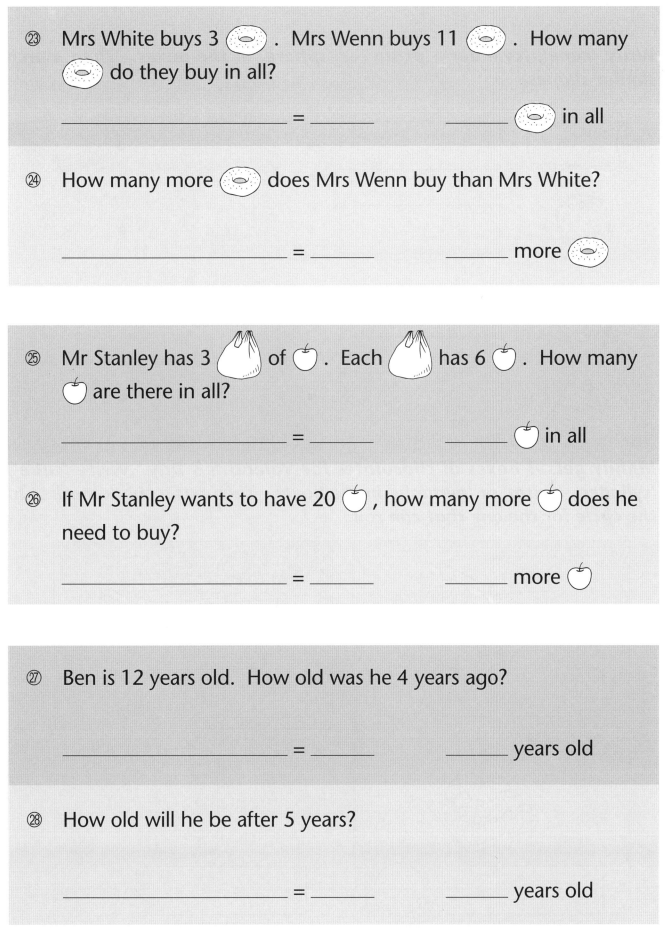. How many do they buy in all?

_____ = _____   _____ in all

㉔ How many more does Mrs Wenn buy than Mrs White?

_____ = _____   _____ more

㉕ Mr Stanley has 3 of . Each has 6 . How many are there in all?

_____ = _____   _____ in all

㉖ If Mr Stanley wants to have 20 , how many more does he need to buy?

_____ = _____   _____ more

㉗ Ben is 12 years old. How old was he 4 years ago?

_____ = _____   _____ years old

㉘ How old will he be after 5 years?

_____ = _____   _____ years old

ISBN: 978-1-897164-11-2

Write 'cone', 'cylinder', 'prism' or 'sphere' in the boxes. Then match similar shapes.

①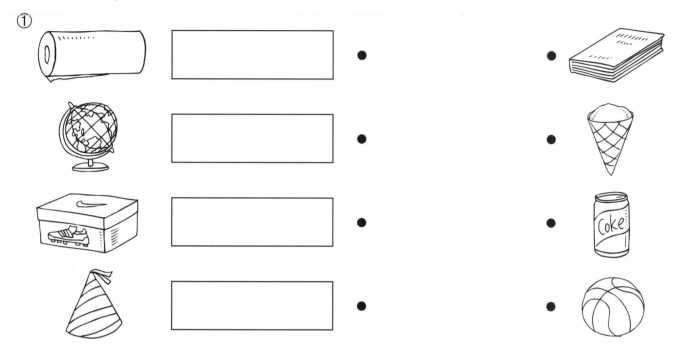

Mandy gets 4 boxes of chocolates for Valentine's Day. Write 'cube', 'cylinder', 'prism' or 'pyramid' in the boxes. Then put a check mark ✔ in the circle for the one that can roll.

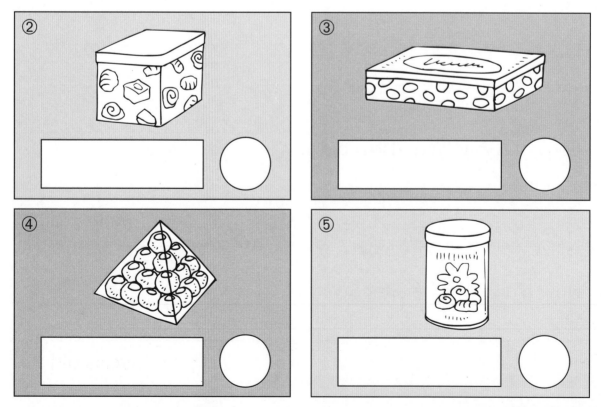

ISBN: 978-1-897164-11-2

Check ✔ the correct sentences and cross out ✗ the wrong ones.

⑥ A prism can slide. ◯

⑦ A cylinder can slide and roll. ◯

⑧ A sphere can roll but not slide. ◯

⑨ A cube can roll and slide. ◯

⑩ A pyramid can roll. ◯

See how many blocks are needed to build each tower. Then answer the questions.

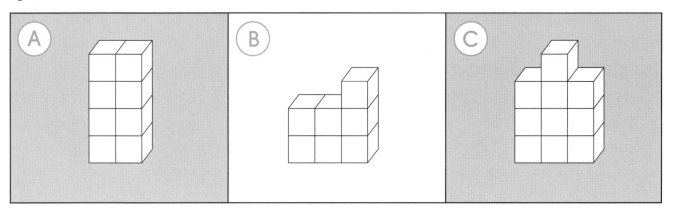

⑪ How many blocks are needed to build tower A? _____ blocks

⑫ How many blocks are needed to build tower B? _____ blocks

⑬ How many blocks are needed to build tower C? _____ blocks

⑭ Which of the towers is a prism? Tower _____

⑮ What is the fewest number of blocks you need to add on tower B to make it a prism? _____

ISBN: 978-1-897164-11-2

Look at the shaded part of each flag. Then name the shape.

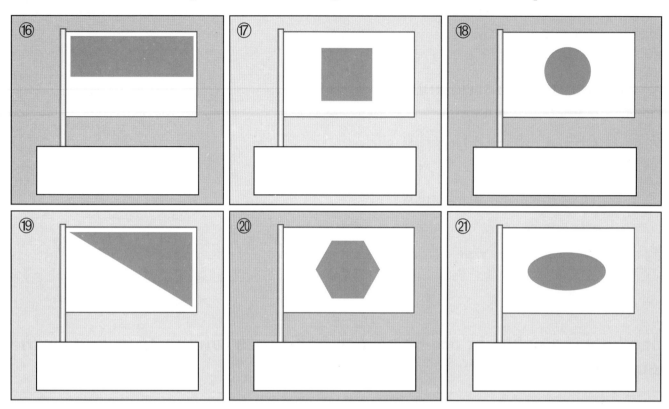

Look at the shapes and complete the table.

	㉒	㉓	㉔	㉕
Number of sides				
Number of corners				

Draw a line to cut each shape into two matching parts.

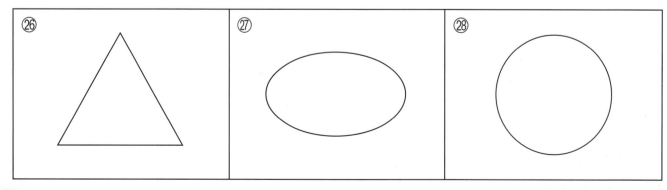

ISBN: 978-1-897164-11-2

Draw the matching part of each shape from the dotted line.

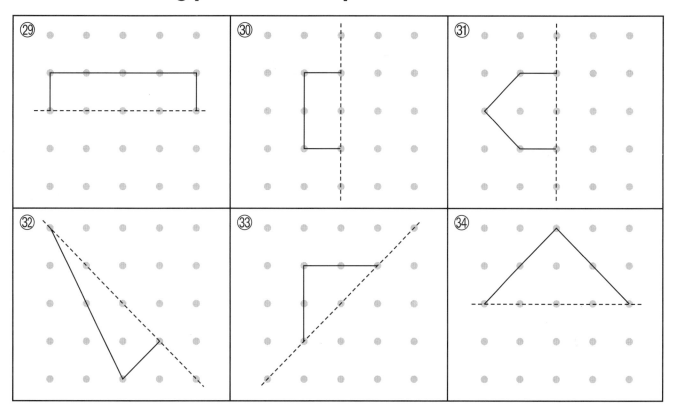

See how many books Uncle Bill uses to cover each board. Estimate and count. Write the numbers.

③⑤ Estimate: _____ Count: _____

③⑥ Estimate: _____ Count: _____

③⑦ Estimate: _____ Count: _____

③⑧ Estimate: _____ Count: _____

ISBN: 978-1-897164-11-2

Solid Column Graphs

The graph shows which sports the students like best. Check ✔ the correct answers.

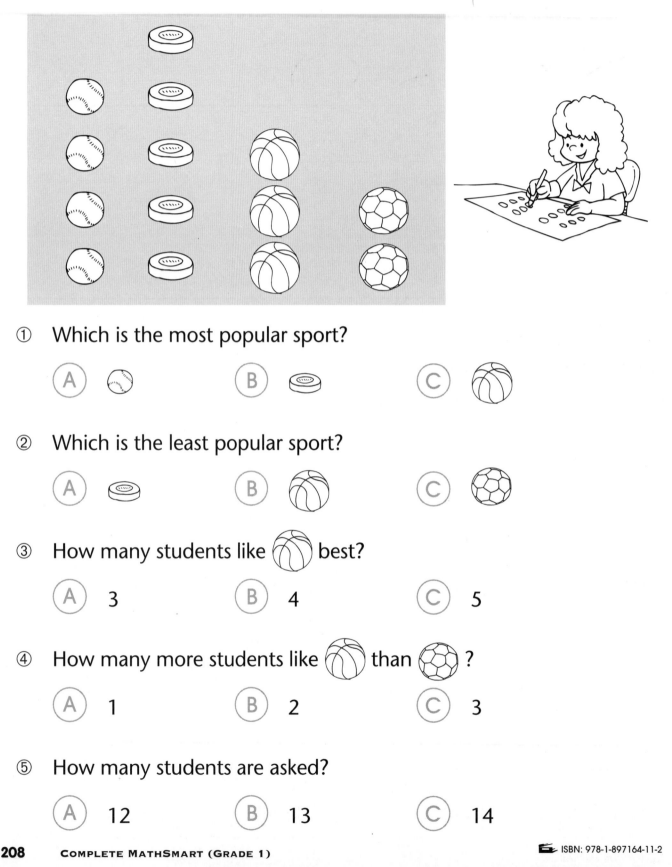

① Which is the most popular sport?

Ⓐ 🔵   Ⓑ ⬭   Ⓒ 🏀

② Which is the least popular sport?

Ⓐ ⬭   Ⓑ 🏀   Ⓒ ⚽

③ How many students like 🏀 best?

Ⓐ 3   Ⓑ 4   Ⓒ 5

④ How many more students like 🏀 than ⚽ ?

Ⓐ 1   Ⓑ 2   Ⓒ 3

⑤ How many students are asked?

Ⓐ 12   Ⓑ 13   Ⓒ 14

ISBN: 978-1-897164-11-2

Kay, Kim and Karen are collecting stickers. See how many stickers they have and answer the questions.

⑥ Who has the most ⭐ ?

Karen

⑦ Who has the fewest ⭐ ?

Kim

⑧ How many ⭐ does Kay have?

7 ⭐

⑨ How many ⭐ does Kim have?

5 ⭐

⑩ How many ⭐ does Karen have?

8 ⭐

⑪ How many ⭐ do Kay and Kim have?

12 ⭐

⑫ How many more ⭐ does Karen have than Kim?

3 ⭐

⑬ How many ⭐ do they have in all?

20 ⭐

⑭ If Kay collects 5 more ⭐ , how many does he have in all?

12 ⭐

Count the fish in the tank. Then answer the questions and colour the pictures to complete the graph.

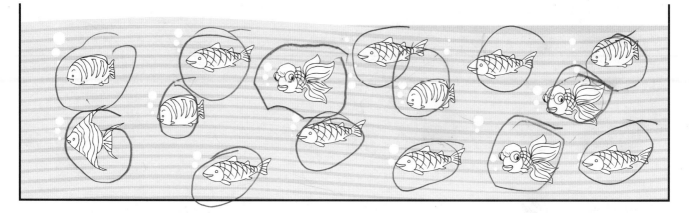

⑮ How many 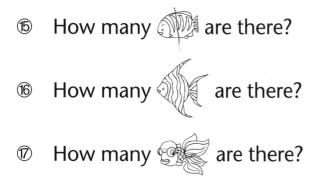 are there?   4

⑯ How many 🐟 are there?   1

⑰ How many 🐠 are there?   3

⑱ How many 🐡 are there?   7

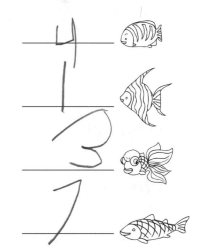

⑲

Fish in the Tank

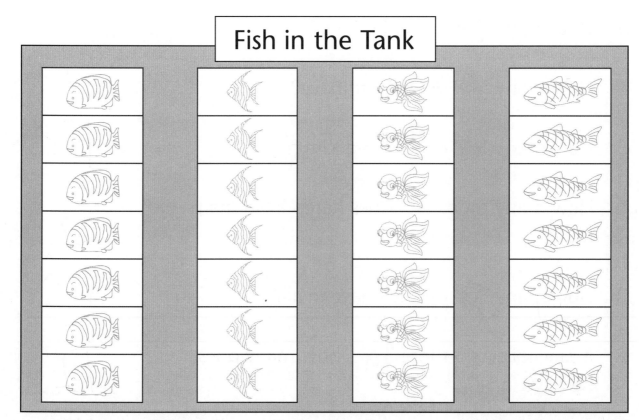

Count the animals in the pet shop. Then answer the questions and colour the pictures to complete the graph.

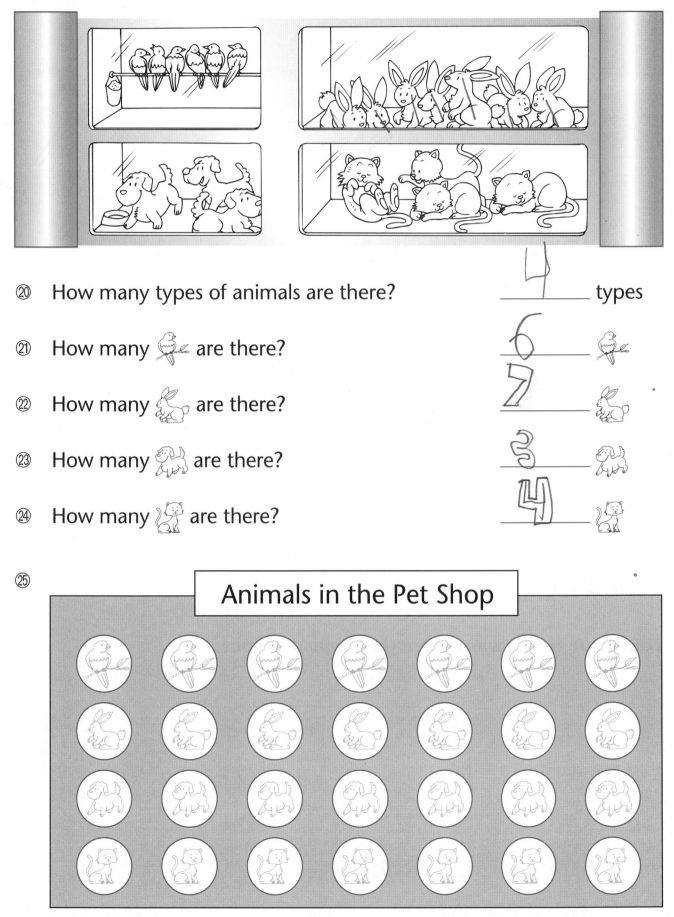

20 How many types of animals are there? _____ types

21 How many are there?   6

22 How many are there?   7

23 How many are there?   3

24 How many are there?   4

25

Animals in the Pet Shop

ISBN: 978-1-897164-11-2

Count the ice cubes each child has. Then answer the questions.

Greg

Pat

Sam

① How many 🧊 does Greg have? _____ 🧊

② How many 🧊 does Pat have? _____ 🧊

③ How many 🧊 does Sam have? _____ 🧊

④ How many more 🧊 does Grey have than Sam? _____ 🧊

⑤ If Greg gives Pat 2 🧊 , how many 🧊 does Pat have in all? _____ 🧊

⑥ If 3 of Sam's 🧊 melted, how many 🧊 would be left? _____ 🧊

Colour the things which have the shape of a sphere.

⑦

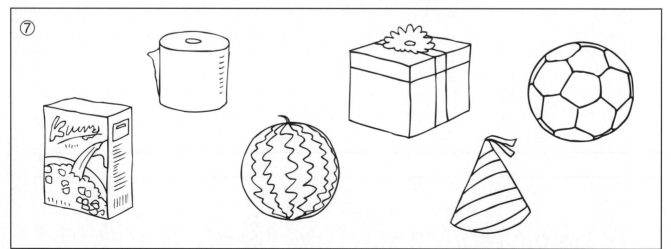

    ISBN: 978-1-897164-11-2

The pictures show how many glasses of milk the children drink in a week. Use the pictures to answer the questions.

Sue	Mabel	Paul	Sam

⑧ Sue drinks _____ 🥛 in a week.

⑨ Mabel drinks _____ 🥛 in a week.

⑩ Paul drinks _____ 🥛 in a week.

⑪ Sam drinks _____ 🥛 in a week.

⑫ Sue and Paul drink _____ 🥛 in all.

⑬ Mabel and Sam drink _____ 🥛 in all.

⑭ Mabel drinks _____ more 🥛 than Paul.

⑮ The girls drink _____ 🥛 in all.

⑯ The boys drink _____ 🥛 in all.

⑰ The boys drink _____ 🥛 fewer than the girls.

⑱ If Paul drinks 7 more 🥛 , he would drink _____ 🥛 in a week.

Look at the shapes of Judy's containers. Check ✔ the correct answers and colour the pictures to complete the graph.

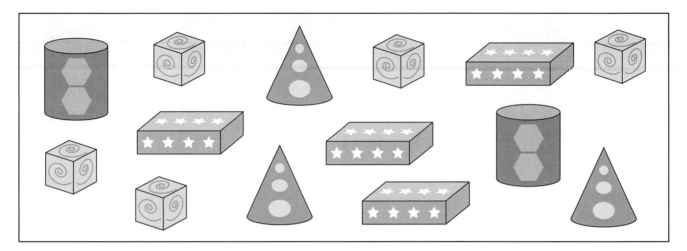

⑲ How many types of shapes are in Judy's collection?

Ⓐ 2   Ⓑ 3   Ⓒ 4

⑳ Which shape does Judy have the most?

Ⓐ cylinder   Ⓑ cube   Ⓒ prism

㉑ How many cones does Judy have?

Ⓐ 2   Ⓑ 3   Ⓒ 4

㉒ How many cubes and cylinders does Judy have in all?

Ⓐ 6   Ⓑ 7   Ⓒ 8

㉓ How many more cubes are there than cones?

Ⓐ 2   Ⓑ 3   Ⓒ 4

㉔ How many containers does Judy have in all?

Ⓐ 12   Ⓑ 13   Ⓒ 14

ISBN: 978-1-897164-11-2

㉕

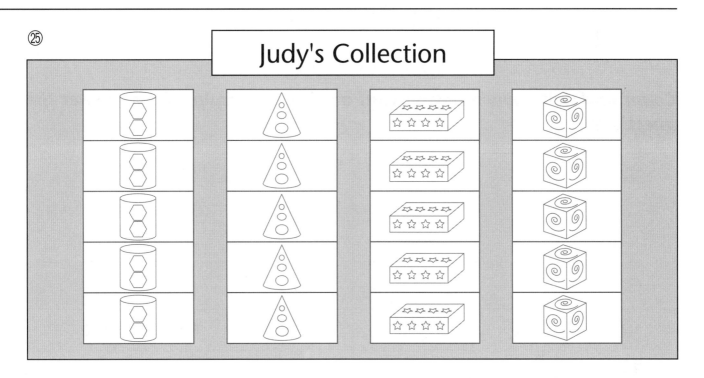

| Judy's Collection |

Lucy traces the shapes on the paper. Match the containers with the shapes and write the names of the shapes.

㉖

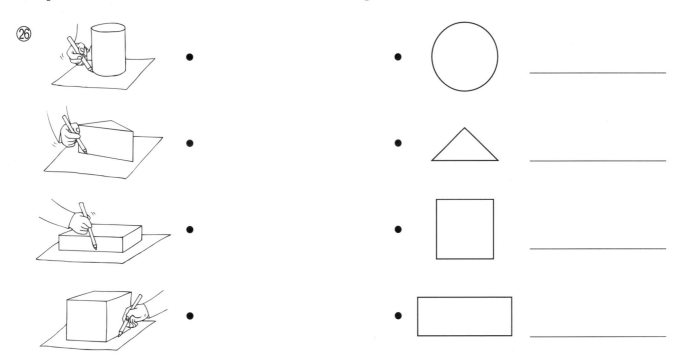

Draw a line to cut each shape into two matching parts.

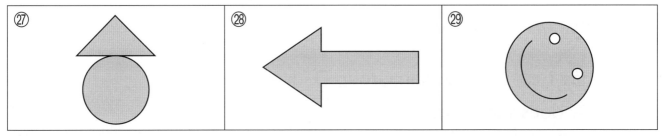

㉗   ㉘   ㉙

ISBN: 978-1-897164-11-2   **COMPLETE MATHSMART (GRADE 1)**   **215**

Count and write how many crayons are in each group. Then answer the questions.

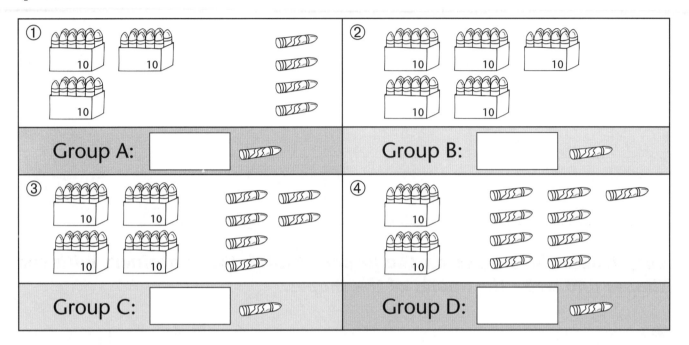

⑤ Which group has the most ?   Group _____

⑥ Which group has the fewest ?   Group _____

⑦ Put the groups in order from the one that has the most to the one that has the fewest.

Group _____ , Group _____ , Group _____ , Group _____

⑧ If Wayne puts 10 more in Group B, how many are there in all?   _____

⑨ If George takes 10 away from Group C, how many will be left?   _____

⑩ Jill has 1 more than Group D. How many does she have?   _____

The children put the pennies in piles of 10. Write how many pennies each child has. Then answer the questions.

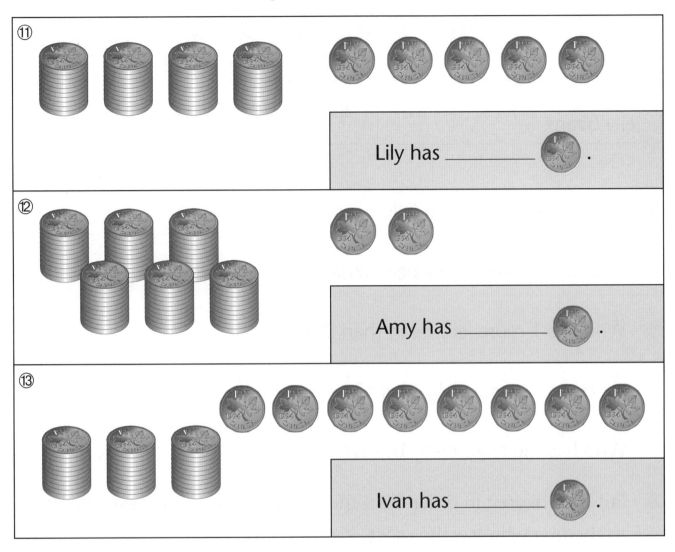

⑪ Lily has _____ .

⑫ Amy has _____ .

⑬ Ivan has _____ .

⑭ _____ has the most money.

⑮ _____ has the least money.

⑯ Put the children in order from the one who has the most money to the one who has the least.

_____ , _____ , _____

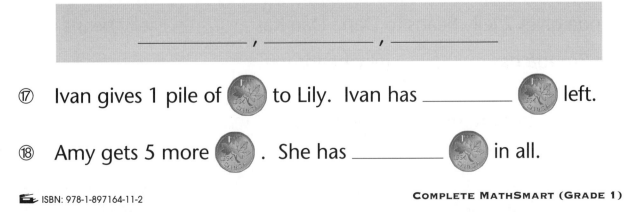

⑰ Ivan gives 1 pile of to Lily. Ivan has _____ left.

⑱ Amy gets 5 more . She has _____ in all.

ISBN: 978-1-897164-11-2

See how many jelly beans each child has. Use the table to answer the questions.

	Brenda	Derek	Mike	Dan
Number of jelly beans	79	52	69	78

⑲ Who has seventy-eight jelly beans? _____

⑳ Who has 10 fewer jelly beans than Brenda? _____

㉑ Who has 1 more jelly bean than Dan? _____

㉒ Who has the most jelly beans? _____

㉓ Who has the fewest jelly beans? _____

㉔ Put the children in order from the one who has the fewest jelly beans to the one who has the most.

_____ , _____ , _____ , _____

㉕ Mike gives 1 jelly bean to Derek. Mike has _____ jelly beans left and Derek has _____ jelly beans in all.

㉖ Brenda gives 2 jelly beans to Dan. Dan has _____ jelly beans in all and Brenda has _____ jelly beans left.

㉗ _____ has the most jelly beans now.

ISBN: 978-1-897164-11-2

Read what the children say. Then write the numbers on the fence.

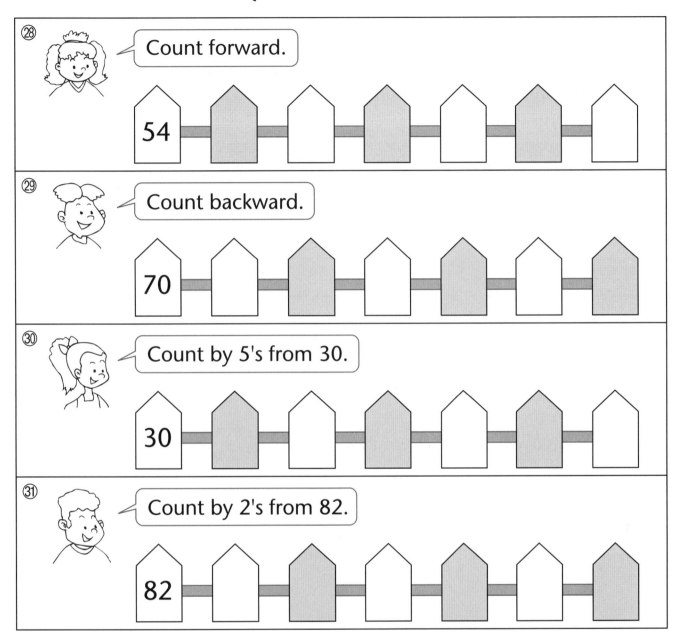

㉘ Count forward.

54

㉙ Count backward.

70

㉚ Count by 5's from 30.

30

㉛ Count by 2's from 82.

82

Answer the questions.

㉜ Jim has 68 🍩 ; Mary has 72 🍩 . Who has more 🍩 ? _____

㉝ William has 48 🍭 ; Stephen has 51 🍭 . Who has fewer 🍭 ? _____

㉞ Alvin has 25 🍬 ; Louis has 20 more 🍬 than Alvin. How many 🍬 does Louis have? _____

ISBN: 978-1-897164-11-2

Addition and Subtraction to 50

Calculators may be used to calculate or check answers. Count and write how many boys and girls are in each group. Then use the pictures to answer the questions.

① Group A	② Group B
(pictures of boys)	(pictures of boys)
(pictures of girls)	(pictures of girls)

③ How many boys are there in all?

_____ = _____   _____ boys

④ How many girls are there in all?

_____ = _____   _____ girls

⑤ How many children are in Group A?

_____ = _____   _____ children

⑥ How many children are in Group B?

_____ = _____   _____ children

⑦ How many children are there in all?

_____ = _____   _____ children

ISBN: 978-1-897164-11-2

See how many pins are in each pincushion. Use the pictures to answer the questions.

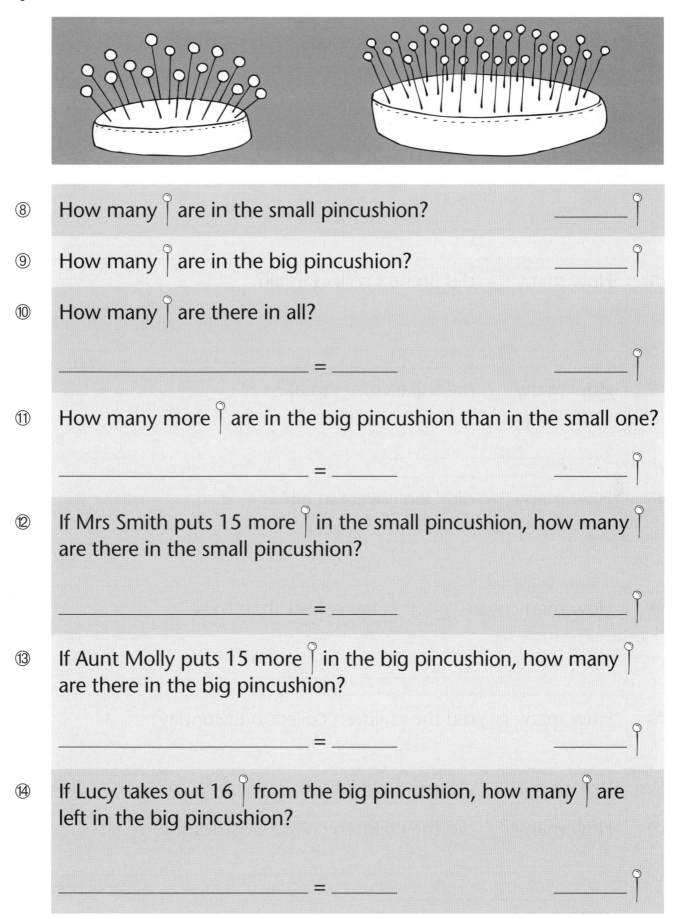

⑧ How many are in the small pincushion? _____

⑨ How many are in the big pincushion? _____

⑩ How many are there in all?

_____ = _____   _____

⑪ How many more are in the big pincushion than in the small one?

_____ = _____   _____

⑫ If Mrs Smith puts 15 more in the small pincushion, how many are there in the small pincushion?

_____ = _____   _____

⑬ If Aunt Molly puts 15 more in the big pincushion, how many are there in the big pincushion?

_____ = _____   _____

⑭ If Lucy takes out 16 from the big pincushion, how many are left in the big pincushion?

_____ = _____

ISBN: 978-1-897164-11-2

Brenda, Mike and Dan collected some shells on Monday and Tuesday. Look at the record and answer the questions.

	Monday	Tuesday
Brenda	15	17
Mike	11	14
Dan	18	19

⑮ How many 🐚 did Brenda collect in all?

_____ = _____   _____ 🐚

⑯ How many 🐚 did Mike collect in all?

_____ = _____   _____ 🐚

⑰ How many 🐚 did Dan collect in all?

_____ = _____   _____ 🐚

⑱ How many more 🐚 did Dan collect than Mike?

_____ = _____   _____ 🐚

⑲ How many 🐚 did the children collect on Monday?

_____ = _____   _____ 🐚

⑳ How many 🐚 did the children collect on Tuesday?

_____ = _____   _____ 🐚

ISBN: 978-1-897164-11-2

Look at the record showing the loaves of bread baked and sold in the past 3 days. Then answer the questions.

	Thursday	Friday	Saturday
Number of 🍞 baked	21	24	28
Number of 🍞 sold	17	18	19

㉑ How many 🍞 were left on Thursday?

_____ = _____   _____ 🍞

㉒ How many 🍞 were left on Friday?

_____ = _____   _____ 🍞

㉓ How many 🍞 were left on Saturday?

_____ = _____   _____ 🍞

㉔ How many 🍞 did the baker bake on Thursday and Friday?

_____ = _____   _____ 🍞

㉕ How many 🍞 did the baker bake on Thursday and Saturday?

_____ = _____   _____ 🍞

㉖ How many 🍞 were sold on Friday and Saturday?

_____ = _____   _____ 🍞

ISBN: 978-1-897164-11-2

Addition and Subtraction to 100

Calculators can be used to calculate or check answers. Count and write how many shells each child collected. Then answer the questions.

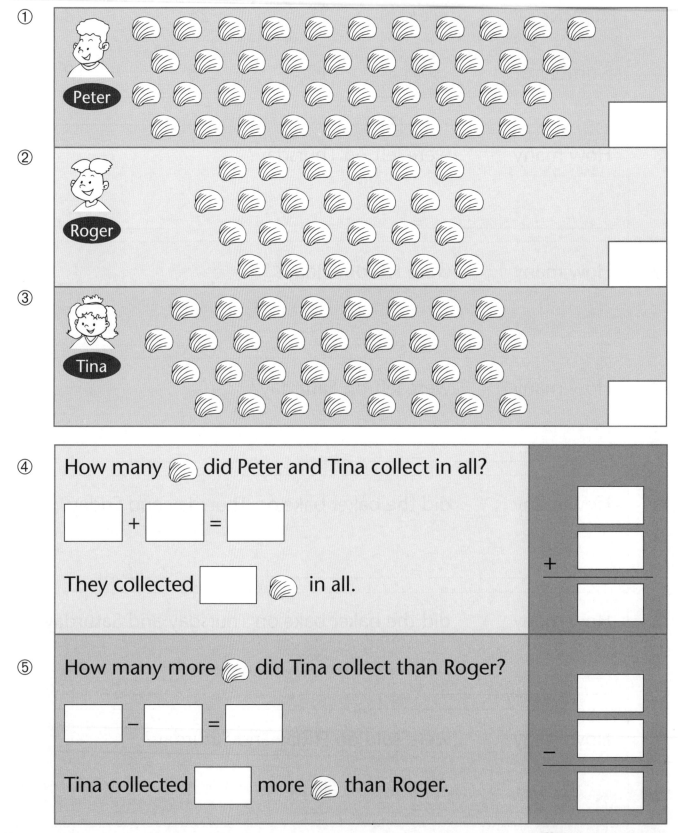

④ How many 🐚 did Peter and Tina collect in all?

[ ] + [ ] = [ ]

They collected [ ] 🐚 in all.

⑤ How many more 🐚 did Tina collect than Roger?

[ ] – [ ] = [ ]

Tina collected [ ] more 🐚 than Roger.

ISBN: 978-1-897164-11-2

⑥ How many 🐚 did the boys collect in all?

[ ] + [ ] = [ ]

They collected [ ] 🐚 in all.

+ [ ]
  [ ]
──
  [ ]

⑦ How many more 🐚 did Peter collect than Tina?

[ ] – [ ] = [ ]

Peter collected [ ] more 🐚 than Tina.

− [ ]
  [ ]
──
  [ ]

⑧ Tina's goal was to collect 60 🐚 . How many more 🐚 must she collect to meet her goal?

[ ] – [ ] = [ ]

She must collect [ ] more 🐚 .

− [ ]
  [ ]
──
  [ ]

⑨ Peter's goal was to collect 35 🐚 . How many more 🐚 had he collected ?

[ ] – [ ] = [ ]

He had collected [ ] more 🐚 .

− [ ]
  [ ]
──
  [ ]

⑩ How many 🐚 did the children collect in all?

[ ] + [ ] + [ ] = [ ]

They collected [ ] 🐚 in all.

+ [ ]
  [ ]
  [ ]
──
  [ ]

ISBN: 978-1-897164-11-2

See how many animals are on each farm. Then use the table to answer the questions.

	Fred's Farm	Roy's Farm	Andy's Farm
🐔	37	29	27
🐄	16	28	23
🐴	15	16	49

⑪ Whose farm has the most 🐔 ? _____'s farm

⑫ Whose farm has the most 🐄 ? _____'s farm

⑬ Whose farm has the fewest 🐴 ? _____'s farm

⑭ How many animals are there on Fred's farm?

_____ = _____ _____ animals

⑮ How many animals are there on Roy's farm?

_____ = _____ _____ animals

⑯ How many animals are there on Andy's farm?

_____ = _____ _____ animals

⑰ How many 🐔 are on these three farms?

_____ = _____ _____ 🐔

ISBN: 978-1-897164-11-2

⑱ How many 🐄 are on these three farms?

_____ = _____   _____ 🐄

⑲ How many 🐴 are on these three farms?

_____ = _____   _____ 🐴

⑳ How many 4-legged animals are on Fred's farm?

_____ = _____   _____ animals

㉑ If Fred gives 12 🐔 to Roy, how many 🐔 are left?

_____ = _____   _____ 🐔

㉒ If Roy gets 12 🐔 from Fred, how many 🐔 does he have in all?

_____ = _____   _____ 🐔

㉓ If Andy buys 18 more 🐄 , how many 🐄 does he have in all?

_____ = _____   _____ 🐄

㉔ On Andy's farm, there are 16 white 🐴 . How many 🐴 on Andy's farm are not white?

_____ = _____   _____ 🐴

㉕ On Andy's farm, there are 13 cocks. How many hens are there?

_____ = _____   _____ hens

Write how much each item costs. Then answer the questions.

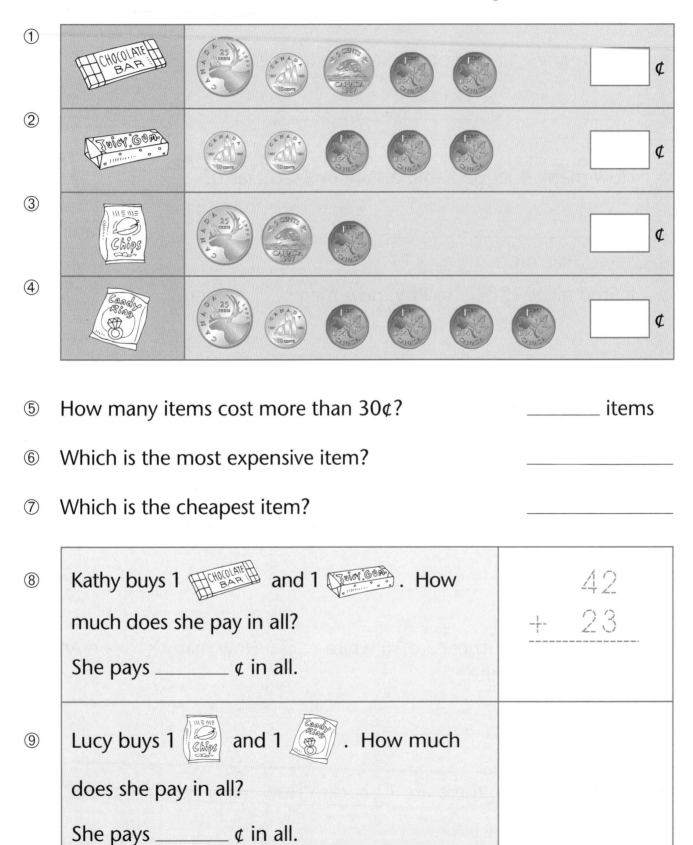

⑤ How many items cost more than 30¢?   _____ items

⑥ Which is the most expensive item?   _____

⑦ Which is the cheapest item?   _____

⑧ Kathy buys 1 CHOCOLATE BAR and 1 Juicy Gum. How much does she pay in all?

She pays _____ ¢ in all.

$$42 + 23$$

⑨ Lucy buys 1 Chips and 1 Candy Ring. How much does she pay in all?

She pays _____ ¢ in all.

ISBN: 978-1-897164-11-2

⑩ Sean buys 1 [Chips] . How much change does he get from 50¢?

He gets _____ ¢ change.

⑪ Kim buys 1 [Candy Ring] . Sandy buys 1 [Juicy Gum] .

How much more does Kim pay?

Kim pays _____ ¢ more.

⑫ Jack buys 2 [CHOCOLATE BAR] . How much does he pay in all?

He pays _____ ¢ in all.

⑬ The [Chips] is on sale. It costs 7¢ less. How much does it cost now?

It costs _____ ¢ now.

⑭ Cliff has 18¢. He wants to buy 1 [Juicy Gum] .

How much more money does he need?

He needs _____ ¢ more.

⑮ Amy has 24¢ and Brian has 18¢. They want to buy 1 item together. Which item with the highest price can they buy?

They can buy a _____ .

See how much each toy costs. Then complete the tables and answer the questions.

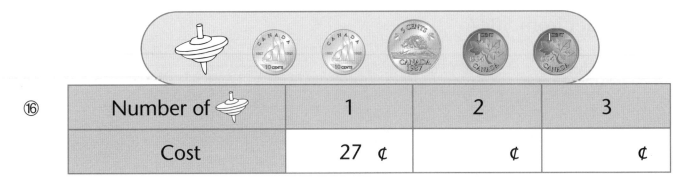

⑯	Number of 🪀	1	2	3
	Cost	27 ¢	¢	¢

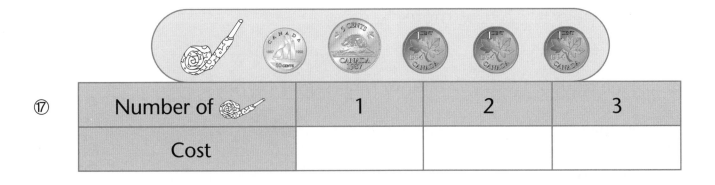

⑰	Number of 🎉	1	2	3
	Cost			

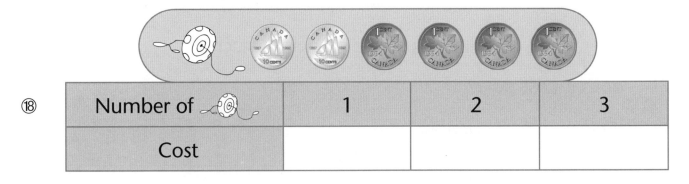

⑱	Number of 🪀	1	2	3
	Cost			

⑲ Jane buys a 🪀 and a 🎉 . How much does she pay in all?

_____ = _____   _____ ¢ in all

⑳ Alexander buys a 🎉 and a 🪀 . How much does he pay in all?

_____ = _____   _____ ¢ in all

㉑ Raymond pays 50¢ for a 🪀 . How much change does he get?

_____ = _____   _____ ¢ change

ISBN: 978-1-897164-11-2

Look at the toys on the previous page. Then answer the questions and check ✔ the fewest coins to match the answers.

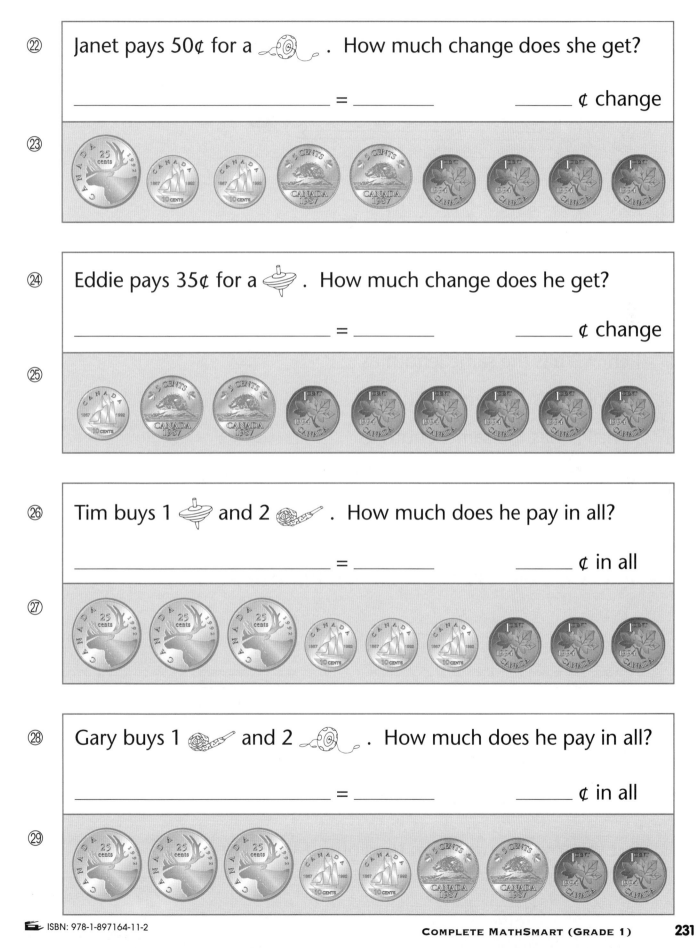

㉒ Janet pays 50¢ for a 🪀. How much change does she get?

_____ = _____   _____ ¢ change

㉓

㉔ Eddie pays 35¢ for a 🪀. How much change does he get?

_____ = _____   _____ ¢ change

㉕

㉖ Tim buys 1 🪀 and 2 🎺. How much does he pay in all?

_____ = _____   _____ ¢ in all

㉗

㉘ Gary buys 1 🎺 and 2 🪀. How much does he pay in all?

_____ = _____   _____ ¢ in all

㉙

ISBN: 978-1-897164-11-2

See how long each pencil is. Then fill in the blanks.

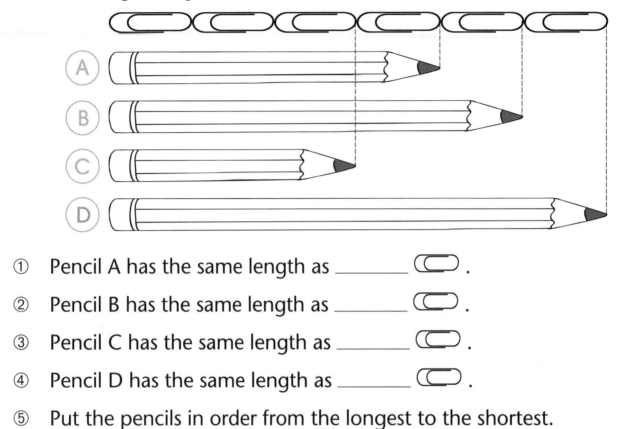

① Pencil A has the same length as _____ 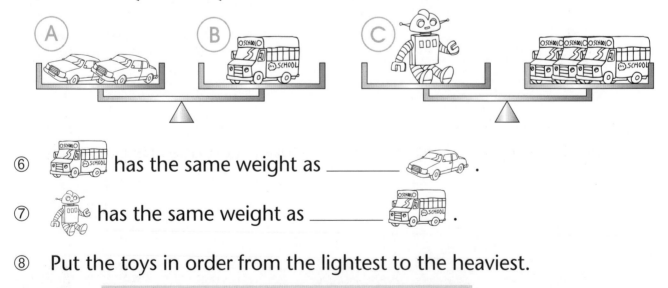.

② Pencil B has the same length as _____ .

③ Pencil C has the same length as _____ .

④ Pencil D has the same length as _____ .

⑤ Put the pencils in order from the longest to the shortest.

_____ , _____ , _____ , _____

See how heavy each toy is. Then fill in the blanks.

⑥ has the same weight as _____ .

⑦ has the same weight as _____ .

⑧ Put the toys in order from the lightest to the heaviest.

_____ , _____ , _____

ISBN: 978-1-897164-11-2

Write the time or draw the clock hands to show the times. Then answer the questions.

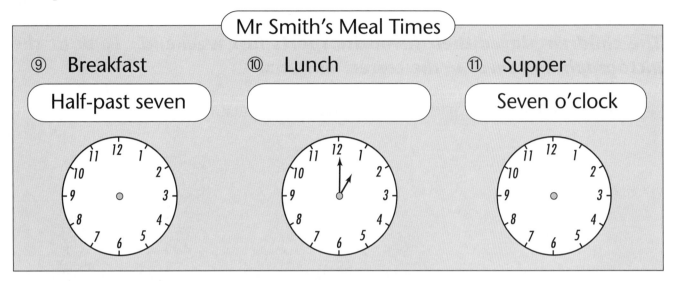

Mr Smith's Meal Times

⑨ Breakfast

Half-past seven

⑩ Lunch

⑪ Supper

Seven o'clock

⑫ Does Mr Smith eat breakfast before or after seven o'clock?

_____

⑬ Mr Smith comes home at half-past six. Is he early or late for supper?

_____

Count and write the numbers.

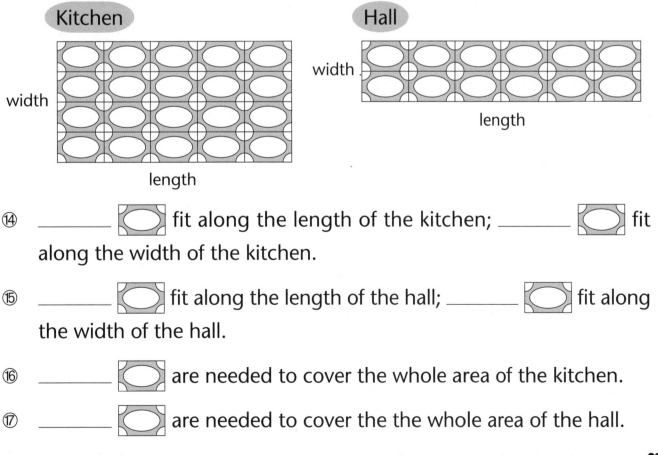

Kitchen

Hall

width

length

width

length

⑭ _____ [oval] fit along the length of the kitchen; _____ [oval] fit along the width of the kitchen.

⑮ _____ [oval] fit along the length of the hall; _____ [oval] fit along the width of the hall.

⑯ _____ [oval] are needed to cover the whole area of the kitchen.

⑰ _____ [oval] are needed to cover the the whole area of the hall.

UNIT 11 Pictographs

The children played their favourite sports last weekend. Look at the pictograph and check ✔ the correct answers.

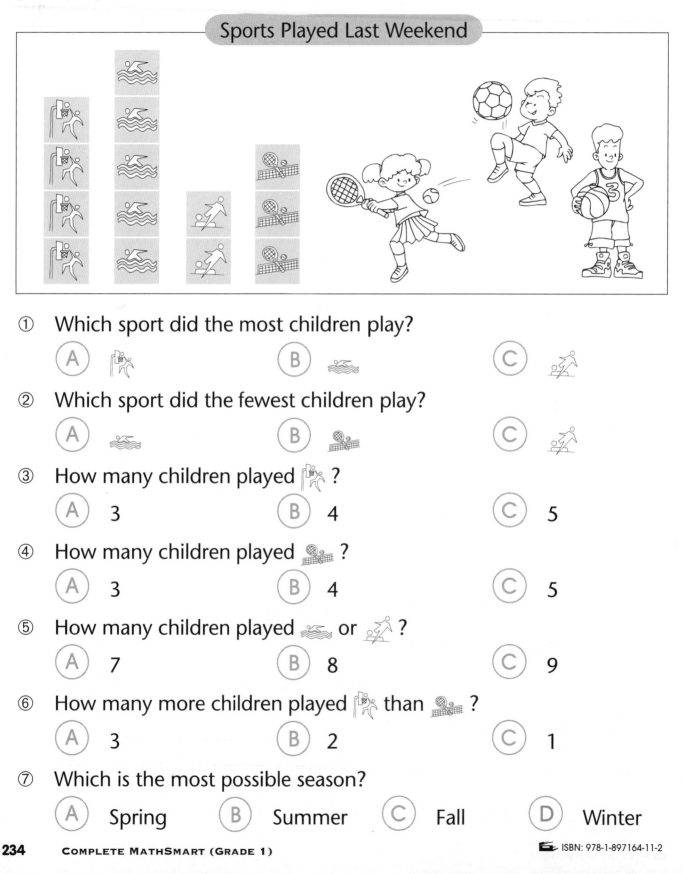

Sports Played Last Weekend

① Which sport did the most children play?

Ⓐ   Ⓑ   Ⓒ

② Which sport did the fewest children play?

Ⓐ   Ⓑ   Ⓒ

③ How many children played ？

Ⓐ 3   Ⓑ 4   Ⓒ 5

④ How many children played ？

Ⓐ 3   Ⓑ 4   Ⓒ 5

⑤ How many children played 〰 or ？

Ⓐ 7   Ⓑ 8   Ⓒ 9

⑥ How many more children played than ？

Ⓐ 3   Ⓑ 2   Ⓒ 1

⑦ Which is the most possible season?

Ⓐ Spring   Ⓑ Summer   Ⓒ Fall   Ⓓ Winter

ISBN: 978-1-897164-11-2

Read the pictograph and answer the questions.

Number of Marbles Each Child Has

Joe	🔵 🔵 🔵 🔵 🔵 🔵
Anita	🔵 🔵
Britt	🔵 🔵 🔵 🔵 🔵
Paula	🔵 🔵 🔵 🔵 🔵 🔵 🔵 🔵

⑧ Who has the most marbles? _____

⑨ Who has the fewest marbles? _____

⑩ Who has more marbles than Anita but fewer than Joe? _____

⑪ How many 🔵 do Joe and Britt have in all? _____ 🔵

⑫ How many 🔵 do Anita and Paula have in all? _____ 🔵

⑬ How many more 🔵 does Joe have than Anita? _____ 🔵

⑭ How many more 🔵 does Paula have than Britt? _____ 🔵

⑮ How many children have 6 or more marbles? _____ children

⑯ How many 🔵 do the children have in all? _____ 🔵

⑰ If Paula gives Britt 1 🔵 , how many 🔵 does Paula have now? _____ 🔵

⑱ If Britt gets 1 more 🔵 , does she have more 🔵 than Joe? _____

ISBN: 978-1-897164-11-2

Count how many toys Debbie has. Then colour the pictograph and circle the correct answers.

Debbie's Toys

⑲

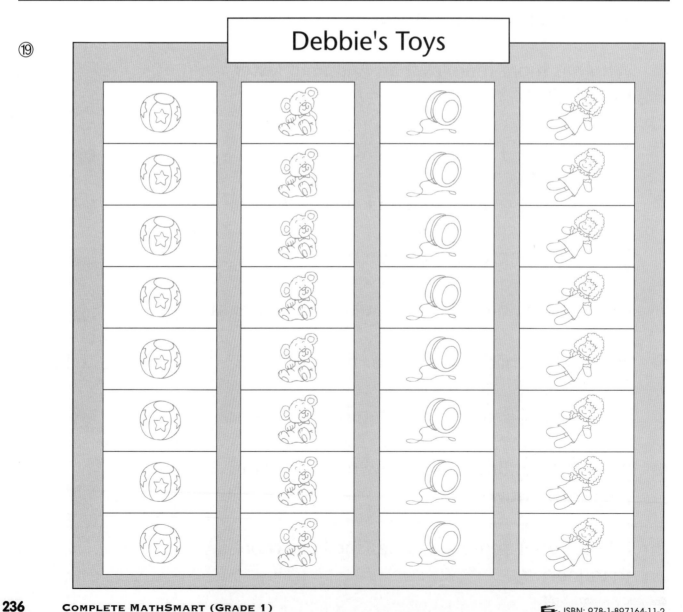

Debbie's Toys

ISBN: 978-1-897164-11-2

20. How many 🧸 does Debbie have?   6   7   8

21. How many ⚽ does Debbie have?   6   7   8

22. How many 🪆 and 🧸 does Debbie have?   12   13   14

23. How many 🪀 and ⚽ does Debbie have?   8   9   10

24. How many of Debbie's toys are not 🧸?   12   13   14

25. Which kind of toy does Debbie have the most?   🪆   🧸   🪀

26. Which kind of toy does Debbie have the fewest?   🪆   🪀   ⚽

27. How many more 🧸 than 🪆 does Debbie have?   3   4   5

28. How many toys does Debbie have in all?   19   20   21

29. On Debbie's birthday, she gets 4 more 🪆. How many 🪆 does she have now?   7   8   9

ISBN: 978-1-897164-11-2

Look at the pictures. Then check ✔ the correct answers.

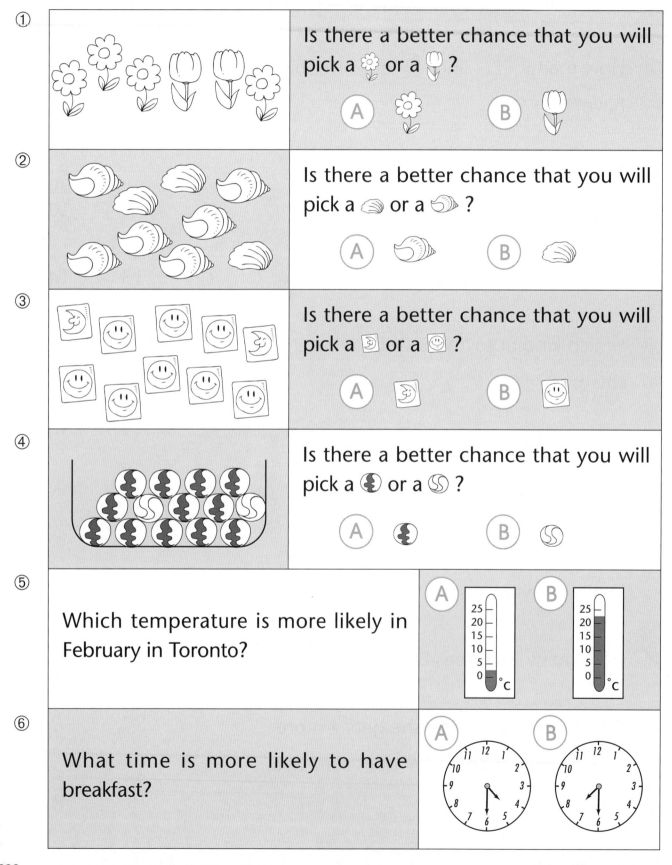

① Is there a better chance that you will pick a 🌸 or a 🌷?

    (A) 🌸   (B) 🌷

② Is there a better chance that you will pick a 🐚 or a 🐚?

    (A) 🐚   (B) 🐚

③ Is there a better chance that you will pick a 🌙 or a 🙂?

    (A) 🌙   (B) 🙂

④ Is there a better chance that you will pick a ☯ or a ☯?

    (A) ☯   (B) ☯

⑤ Which temperature is more likely in February in Toronto?

    (A)   (B)

⑥ What time is more likely to have breakfast?

    (A)   (B)

Look at the bag of marbles. Then check ✔ the correct answers.

⑦ Which word is the best to describe the chance of picking a green marble?

(A) likely   (B) unlikely   (C) never

⑧ Which word is the best to describe the chance of picking a red marble?

(A) likely   (B) unlikely   (C) never

⑨ Which word is the best to describe the chance of picking a black marble?

(A) likely   (B) unlikely   (C) never   (D) maybe

⑩ What colour are you most likely to pick from the bag?

(A) yellow   (B) green   (C) red   (D) black

Look at the spinner. Then answer the questions.

⑪

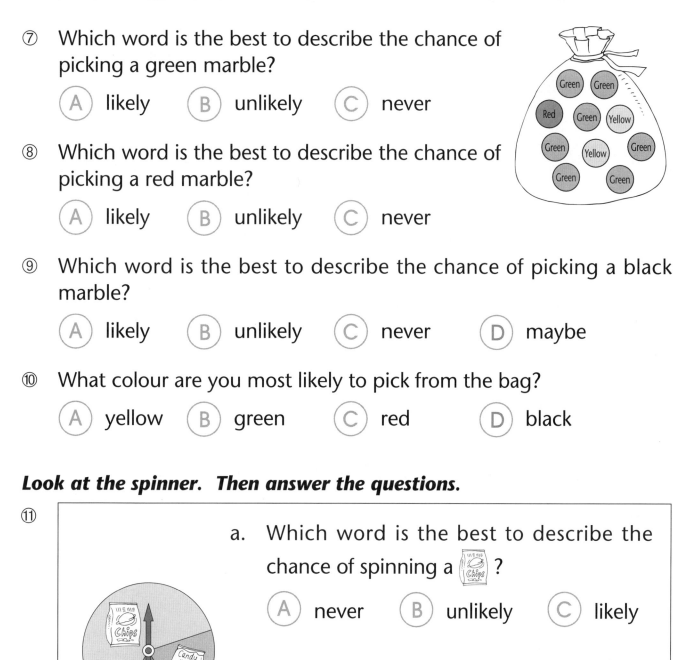

a. Which word is the best to describe the chance of spinning a [Chips] ?

(A) never   (B) unlikely   (C) likely

b. Which word is the best to describe the chance of spinning a 🍦 ?

(A) never   (B) maybe   (C) likely

c. Which word is the best to describe the chance of spinning a [CHOCOLATE BAR] ?

(A) never   (B) maybe   (C) unlikely

Count and write how much each child has. Then answer the questions.

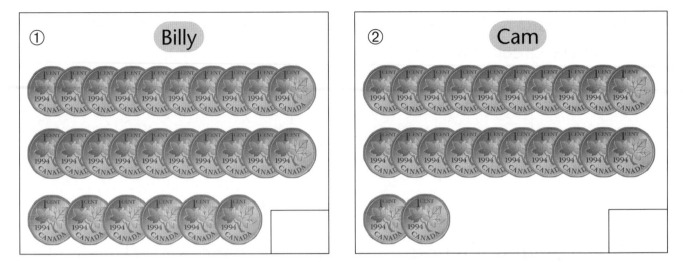

③ How much do Billy and Cam have in all?

[ ] + [ ] = [ ]

They have [ ] ¢ in all.

[ ]
+ [ ]
—
[ ]

④ How much more does Billy have than Cam?

[ ] – [ ] = [ ]

Billy has [ ] ¢ more than Cam.

[ ]
– [ ]
—
[ ]

⑤ Uncle Tom gives Billy 5¢. How much does Billy have now?

[ ] + [ ] = [ ]

Billy has [ ] ¢ now.

[ ]
+ [ ]
—
[ ]

⑥ A 🍭 costs 7¢. Cam buys a 🍭 . How much has Cam left?

[ ] – [ ] = [ ]

Cam has [ ] ¢ left.

[ ]
– [ ]
—
[ ]

ISBN: 978-1-897164-11-2

See how many pizzas Mrs Winter ordered for her class. Then answer the questions.

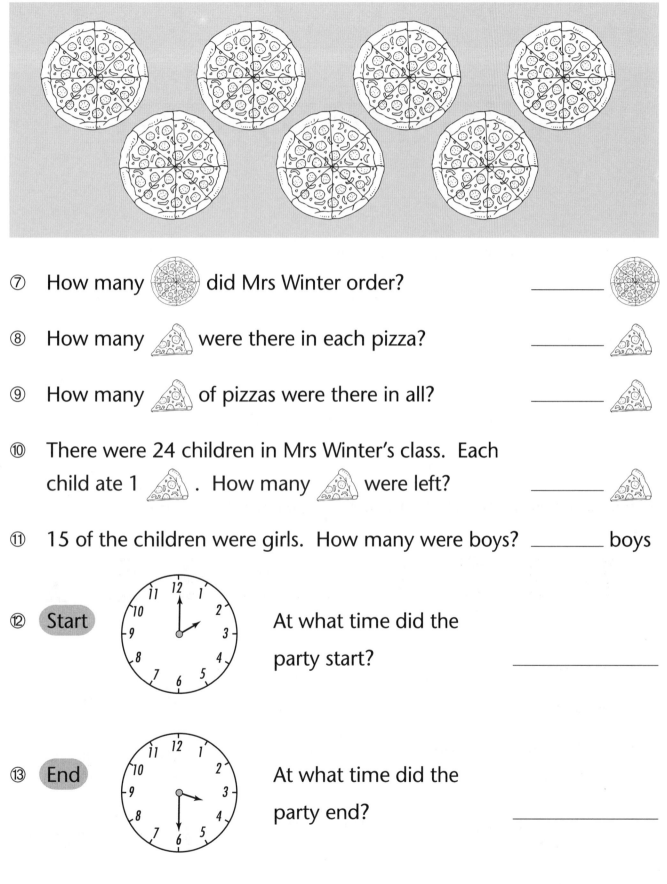

⑦ How many did Mrs Winter order? _____

⑧ How many were there in each pizza? _____

⑨ How many of pizzas were there in all? _____

⑩ There were 24 children in Mrs Winter's class. Each child ate 1 . How many were left? _____

⑪ 15 of the children were girls. How many were boys? _____ boys

⑫ Start — At what time did the party start? _____

⑬ End — At what time did the party end? _____

Look at the ribbons. Write the letters to answer the questions.

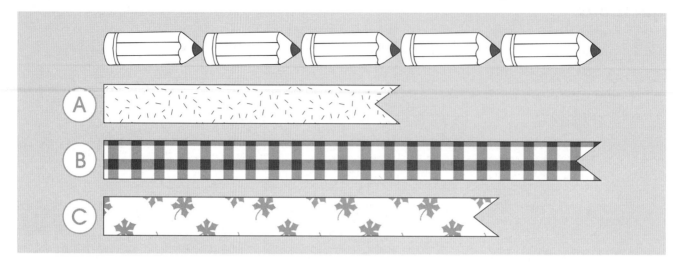

⑭ Which piece of ribbon is the longest?   Ribbon _____

⑮ Which piece of ribbon is the shortest?   Ribbon _____

⑯ Which piece of ribbon has the same length as
3 ✏️ ?   Ribbon _____

⑰ Which piece of ribbon has the same length as
4 ✏️ ?   Ribbon _____

Look at the number cards. Then circle the correct answers.

⑱ Is there a better chance that you will pick
a **1** or a **2** ?   **1**   **2**

⑲ Is there a better chance that you will pick
a **2** or a **3** ?   **2**   **3**

⑳ Which number card are you most likely
to pick?   **1**   **2**   **3**

ISBN: 978-1-897164-11-2

Look at the pictograph. Then circle the correct answers.

Favourite Snacks in Mrs Miller's Class

㉑ Which is the most popular snack?

㉒ Which is the least popular snack?

㉓ How many children like 🍬 ?   5   6   7

㉔ How many children like 🍫 ?   5   6   7

㉕ How many more children like 🍟 than 🍫 ?   1   2   3

㉖ If 3 girls like 🍟 , how many boys like 🍟 ?   2   3   4

ISBN: 978-1-897164-11-2

See how many pets are in each shop. Then answer the questions.

	🐕	🐈	🐇
ABC PETSHOP	32	16	9
Bingo PET SHOP	14	28	13

㉗ How many pets are in ABC Pet Shop?

_____ = _____ _____ pets

㉘ How many pets are in Bingo Pet Shop?

_____ = _____ _____ pets

㉙ How many more dogs are in ABC Pet Shop than Bingo Pet Shop?

_____ = _____ _____ more dogs

㉚ How many more cats are in Bingo Pet Shop than in ABC Pet Shop?

_____ = _____ _____ more cats

㉛ How many rabbits are in both pet shops?

_____ = _____ _____ rabbits

㉜ How many cats are in both pet shops?

_____ = _____ _____ cats

㉝ If there are 13 white dogs in ABC Pet Shop, how many dogs in ABC Pet Shop are not white?

_____ = _____ _____ dogs

ISBN: 978-1-897164-11-2

Parents' Guide

1. Comparing, Sorting and Ordering

↦ Children may have difficulty in recognizing positions such as left and right. Parents should give them more practice in various situations so that they can internalize the concept.

↦ Ordering is a higher level of comparing. Parents can let children arrange objects under various rules.

2. Numbers 1 to 10

↦ Through games and daily experiences, children can learn and understand the difference between cardinal numbers (1, 2, 3 ...) and ordinal numbers (1st, 2nd, 3rd ...).

Example 5 children are buying snacks. Mary is the first one in the line.

↦ Practising counting forward and backward helps children understand more about number sequencing.

↦ Simple words such as and/join (for addition), and take away/leave (for subtraction) can be used to guide children's calculation before they can use "+", "–" and "=" signs.

3. Addition and Subtraction

↦ To write vertical addition or subtraction, it is necessary to align all the numbers on the right-hand side.

Example Vertical addition :

$$\begin{array}{r} 3 \\ +\ 1 \\ \hline 4 \end{array}$$ ↙ align on the right-hand side

Vertical subtraction :

$$\begin{array}{r} 5 \\ -\ 3 \\ \hline 2 \end{array}$$ ↙ align on the right-hand side

Matching addition sentence:
$3 + 1 = 4$

Matching subtraction sentence:
$5 - 3 = 2$

4. Numbers 11 to 20

↦ Counting on (forward) helps to find the sum faster.

Example 7 plus 5 means counting 5 forward from 7, and the sum of $7 + 5$ is 12.

↦ Counting back (backward) helps to find the difference faster.

Example 13 minus 4 means counting 4 backward from 13, and the difference of $13 - 4$ is 9.

↔ Any number plus or minus 0 equals itself.

Examples $7 + 0 = 7$ $9 - 0 = 9$

↔ Using tens may also help to find the sum or difference faster.

Examples $7 + 5 = 7 + 3 + 2$ $(5 = 3 + 2)$ $13 - 4 = 10 + 3 - 4$ $(13 = 10 + 3)$
                      $= 10 + 2$ $= 10 - 4 + 3$ (order changed)
                      $= 12$ $= 6 + 3$
                                                                                      $= 9$

↔ Even if the order of addition changes, the answer remains the same.

Example $5 + 4 = 4 + 5 = 9$

5. Numbers 20 to 100

↔ It is easier for children to learn the numbers 20 to 100 by splitting them into two
stages: 20 to 50, and 50 to 100

↔ Counting in groups of ten leads to the recognition of ones and tens.

Example

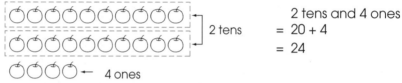

2 tens and 4 ones
$= 20 + 4$
$= 24$

↔ When comparing numbers, parents should remind children to compare the
tens digit first, and if they are the same, compare the ones.

Examples   1. Which one is greater, 25 or 51?
                  Compare the tens digit.

                        2⌐5
                        5⌐1
                        └ 5 is greater than 2

            51 is greater than 25.

            2. Which one is greater, 38 or 32?
                  Compare the tens digit.   Compare the ones digit.

                        3⌐8   3⌐8⌐
                        3⌐2   3⌐2⌐
                        └ same   └ 8 is greater than 2

            38 is greater than 32.

6. More about Addition and Subtraction

↔ Before doing addition and subtraction, parents should make sure that children
understand the meaning of place value. Children should understand that
the digits in a 2-digit number represent groups of tens and groups of ones
respectively.

Example   Sixty-five can be written as 65, six tens and five ones, and 60 + 5.

↔ To do vertical addition or subtraction:

1st   Align the numbers on the right-hand side.
2nd Add or subtract the ones.
3rd   Add or subtract the tens.

Example   16 + 23 =

<table>
<tr><td>1st</td><td>2nd</td><td>3rd</td></tr>
<tr><td>1 6
+ 2 3</td><td>1 6
+ 2 3
──
9</td><td>1 6
+ 2 3
──
3 9</td></tr>
</table>

↔ If the sum of the ones is 10, remind children to write 0 under the ones column, and bring 1 to the tens column.

Example

```
  1 3            1 3
+ 2 7          + 2 7
─────  ✗       ─────  ✓
    4            4 0
```

↔ If the difference of the ones is 0, remind children to write 0 under the ones column.

Example

```
  3 2            3 2
- 1 2          - 1 2
─────  ✗       ─────  ✓
    2            2 0
```

↔ If the difference of the tens is 0, there is no need to write 0 under the tens column.

Example

```
  3 8            3 8
- 3 0          - 3 0
─────  ✗       ─────  ✓
  0 8              8
```

7.   Measurement

↔ Parents should encourage children to describe dimensions with mathematical language, e.g. height, length, width etc., and use appropriate non-standard units such as erasers or books to measure different things. After that, parents can show them how to use standard units, e.g. centimetres, to do measurement.

↔ To measure the length of an object, remind children to align "0" to one end of the object and get the length of the object from the other end.

Example

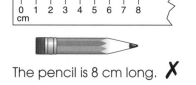

The pencil is 8 cm long. ✗

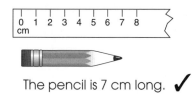

The pencil is 7 cm long. ✓

ISBN: 978-1-897164-11-2

8. Time

↔ Children learn how to read the analog clock and tell the time by the hour and half hour. As they may have difficulty telling the exact position of the hour hand, parents should provide more guidance and practice for them.

Example

half-past three ✗

The hour hand is halfway between 3 and 4.

half-past three ✓

9. Money

↔ Children learn to name coins up to $2 and state the value of pennies, nickels and dimes. Real coins can be used to play "buying things" with children to get them familiar with the value of each coin.

10. Shapes

↔ At this stage, children learn to recognize some 3-dimensional figures such as sphere, cylinder, cube and cone, and some 2-dimensional figures such as circle, triangle, square, and rectangle. Parents may let children use building blocks and construction sets to consolidate their concepts of 3-dimensional and 2-dimensional figures.

↔ Symmetrical figures may have more than 1 line of symmetry.

Example

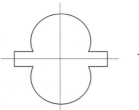

This symmetrical figure has 2 lines of symmetry.

11. Graphs

↔ Children need to know how to display and interpret data in a pictograph or solid column graph. Parents should encourage them to make comments about the graphs so that they can develop a better understanding of the data shown in the graphs.

1 Comparing Heights and Lengths

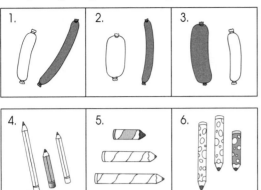

7– 12. (Suggested answers)

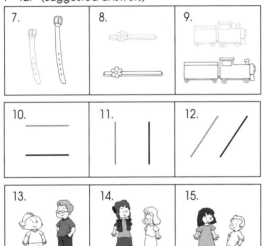

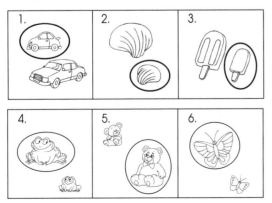

2 Comparing Sizes

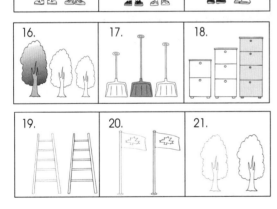

7 – 9. (Suggested answers)

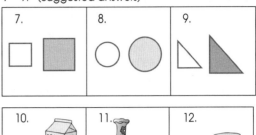

13 – 15. (Suggested answers)

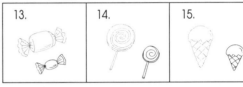

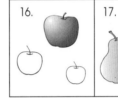 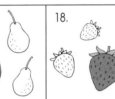

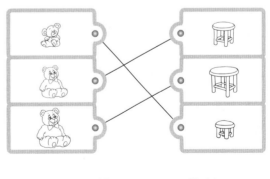

25 – 27.

28. smaller   29. bigger   30. bigger
31. bigger   32. smaller   33. bigger
34. smallest   35. biggest

3 Comparing Positions

1. under	2. on	3. right
4. left	5. right	6. behind
7. in front of	8. inside	9. outside
10. right	11. left	12. right
13. right	14. in front of	15. behind
16. behind	17. over	18. under
19. over	20. under	

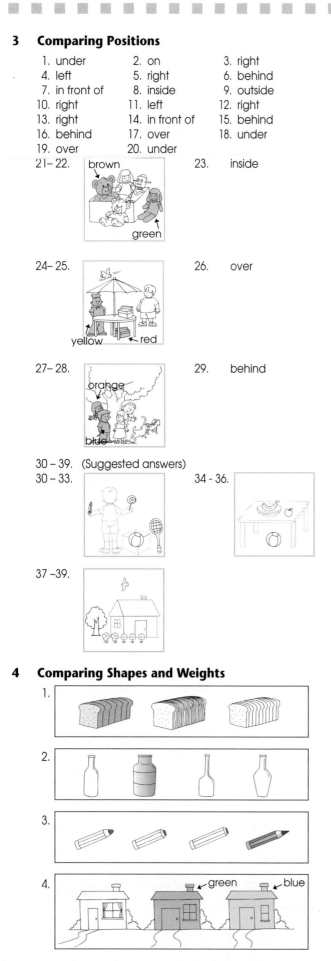

21–22.   brown / green

23.   inside

24–25.   yellow / red

26.   over

27–28.   orange / blue

29.   behind

30 – 39.   (Suggested answers)

30 – 33.

34 - 36.

37 –39.

4 Comparing Shapes and Weights

1.

2.

3.

4.   green / blue

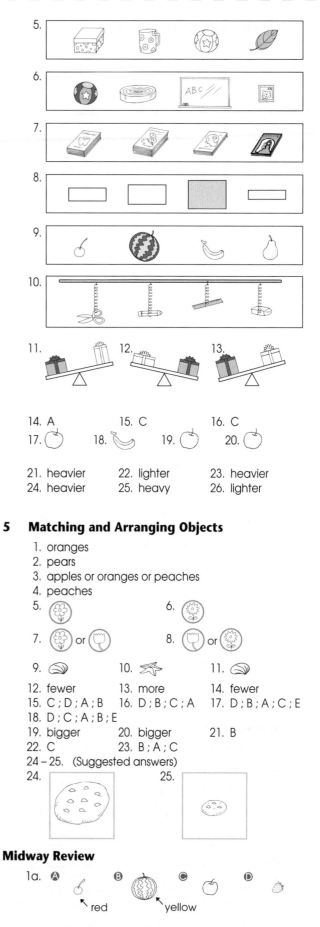

5.

6.

7.

8.

9.

10.

11.   12.   13.

14. A   15. C   16. C

17.   18.   19.   20.

21. heavier	22. lighter	23. heavier
24. heavier	25. heavy	26. lighter

5 Matching and Arranging Objects

1. oranges
2. pears
3. apples or oranges or peaches
4. peaches
5.   6.
7.   or   8.   or
9.   10.   11.

12. fewer	13. more	14. fewer
15. C ; D ; A ; B	16. D ; B ; C ; A	17. D ; B ; A ; C ; E
18. D ; C ; A ; B ; E		
19. bigger	20. bigger	21. B
22. C	23. B ; A ; C	

24 – 25.   (Suggested answers)

24.   25.

Midway Review

1a.   Ⓐ   Ⓑ   Ⓒ   Ⓓ

red   yellow

b. B ; C ; D ; A

ISBN: 978-1-897164-11-2

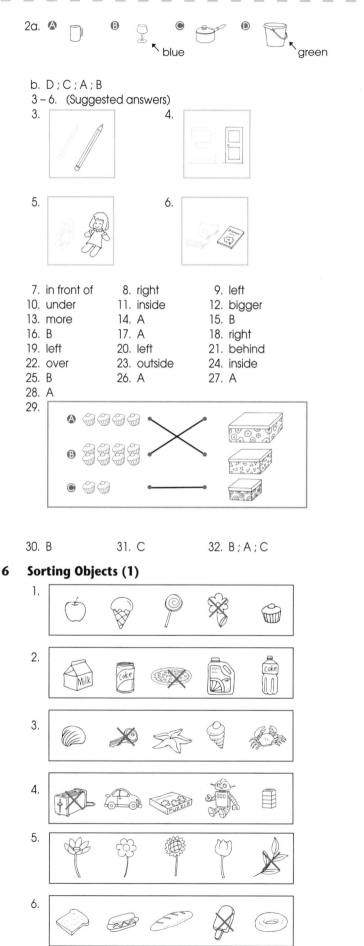

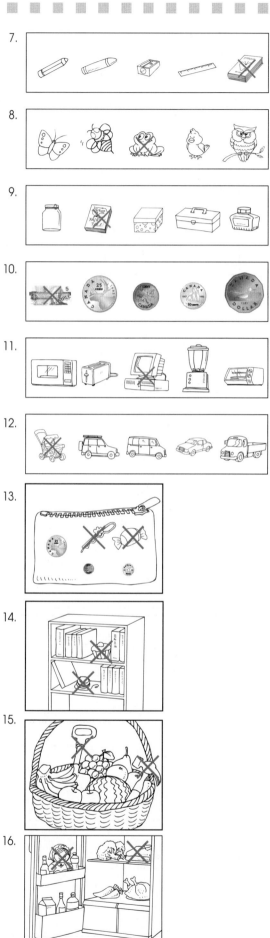

17.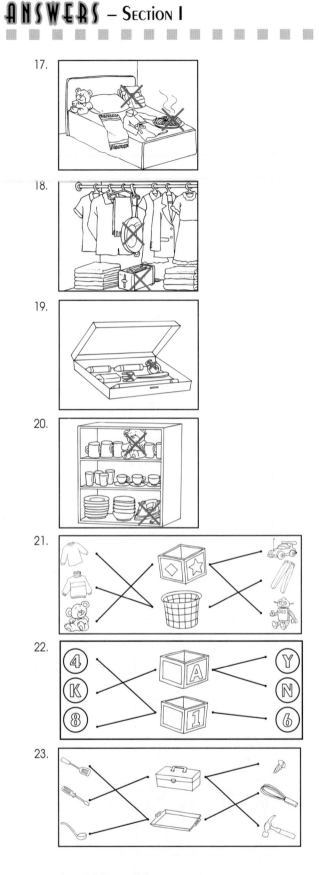

18.

19.

20.

21.

22.

23.

7 Sorting Objects (2)

1.

2.

3.

4.

5.

6.

7.

8.

9. can fly : B ; D   cannot fly : A ; C ; E
10. edible : A ; C ; D   not edible : B ; E
11. stationery : C ; D   not stationery : A ; B ; E
12. toys : B ; E   not toys : A ; C ; D
13. animals : B ; C ; E   plants : A ; D

14.

15.

16.
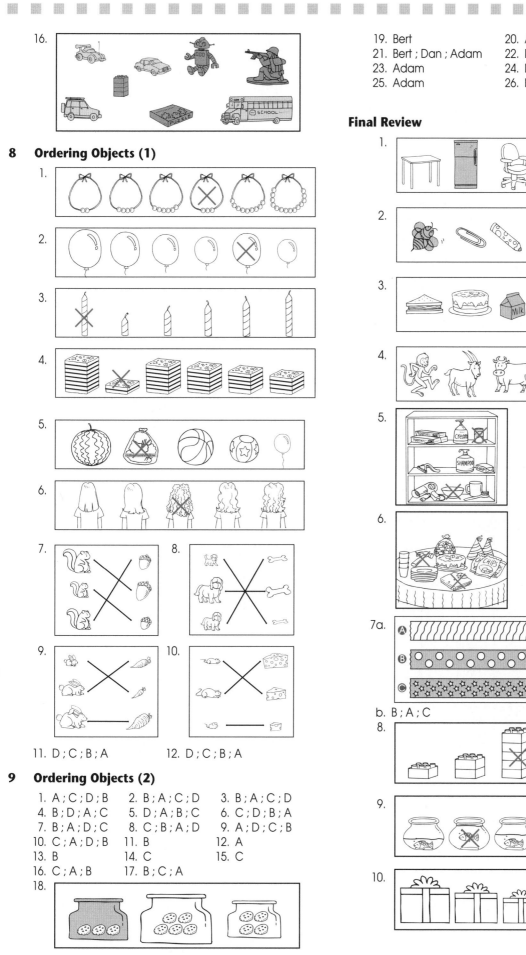

8 **Ordering Objects (1)**

1.

2.

3.

4.

5.

6.

7.   8.

9.   10.

11. D ; C ; B ; A   12. D ; C ; B ; A

9 **Ordering Objects (2)**

1. A ; C ; D ; B   2. B ; A ; C ; D   3. B ; A ; C ; D
4. B ; D ; A ; C   5. D ; A ; B ; C   6. C ; D ; B ; A
7. B ; A ; D ; C   8. C ; B ; A ; D   9. A ; D ; C ; B
10. C ; A ; D ; B   11. B   12. A
13. B   14. C   15. C
16. C ; A ; B   17. B ; C ; A
18.

19. Bert   20. Adam
21. Bert ; Dan ; Adam   22. Dan
23. Adam   24. Dan
25. Adam   26. Dan ; Bert ; Adam

Final Review

1.

2.

3.

4.

5.

6.

7a.

→blue

→yellow

b. B ; A ; C

8.

9.

10.

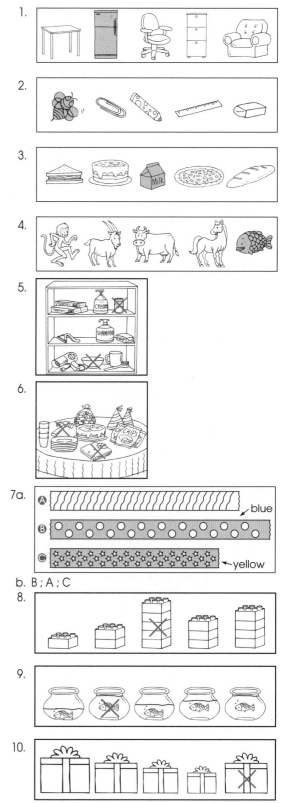

ISBN: 978-1-897164-11-2

11. B ; C ; A   12. A ; B ; C
13. A ; C ; B   14. C ; B ; A

15.

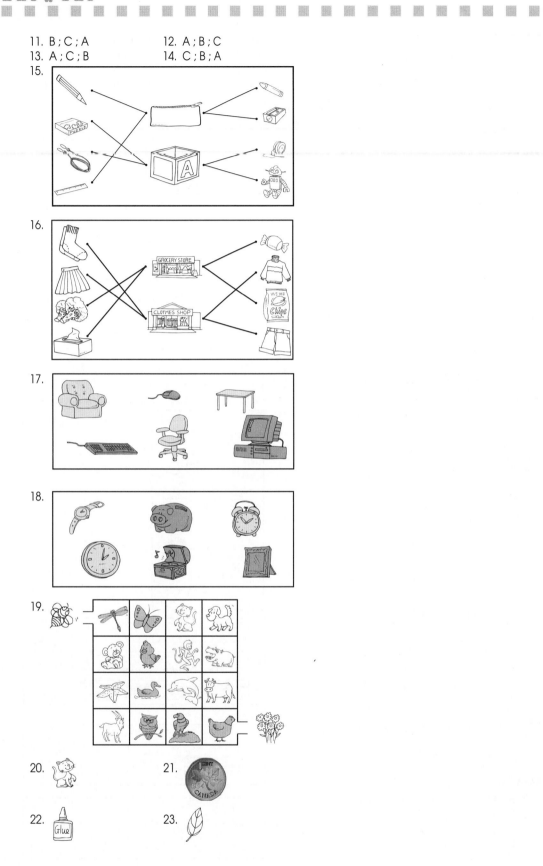

16.

17.

18.

19.

20.

21.

22.

23.

1 Addition and Subtraction of 1

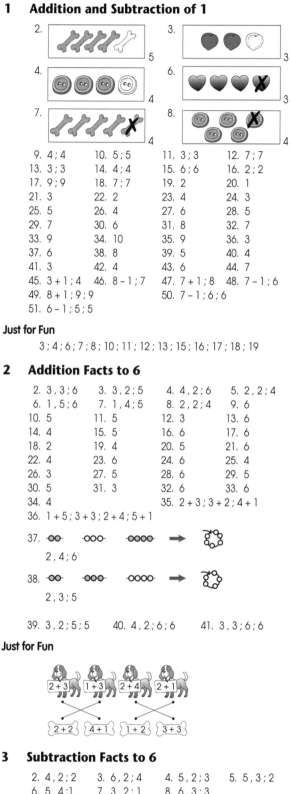

2. 5   3. 3   4. 4   6. 3   7. 4   8. 4

9. 4 ; 4   10. 5 ; 5   11. 3 ; 3   12. 7 ; 7
13. 3 ; 3   14. 4 ; 4   15. 6 ; 6   16. 2 ; 2
17. 9 ; 9   18. 7 ; 7   19. 2   20. 1
21. 3   22. 2   23. 4   24. 3
25. 5   26. 4   27. 6   28. 5
29. 7   30. 6   31. 8   32. 7
33. 9   34. 10   35. 9   36. 3
37. 6   38. 8   39. 5   40. 4
41. 3   42. 4   43. 6   44. 7
45. 3 + 1 ; 4   46. 8 – 1 ; 7   47. 7 + 1 ; 8   48. 7 – 1 ; 6
49. 8 + 1 ; 9 ; 9   50. 7 – 1 ; 6 ; 6
51. 6 – 1 ; 5 ; 5

Just for Fun

3 ; 4 ; 6 ; 7 ; 8 ; 10 ; 11 ; 12 ; 13 ; 15 ; 16 ; 17 ; 18 ; 19

2 Addition Facts to 6

2. 3, 3 ; 6   3. 3, 2 ; 5   4. 4, 2 ; 6   5. 2, 2 ; 4
6. 1, 5 ; 6   7. 1, 4 ; 5   8. 2, 2 ; 4   9. 6
10. 5   11. 5   12. 3   13. 6
14. 4   15. 5   16. 6   17. 6
18. 2   19. 4   20. 5   21. 6
22. 4   23. 6   24. 6   25. 4
26. 3   27. 5   28. 6   29. 5
30. 5   31. 3   32. 6   33. 6
34. 4   35. 2 + 3 ; 3 + 2 ; 4 + 1
36. 1 + 5 ; 3 + 3 ; 2 + 4 ; 5 + 1

37. ➔ 🍇
2, 4 ; 6

38. ➔ 🍇
2, 3 ; 5

39. 3, 2 ; 5 ; 5   40. 4, 2 ; 6 ; 6   41. 3, 3 ; 6 ; 6

Just for Fun

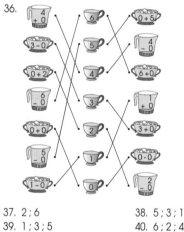

3 Subtraction Facts to 6

2. 4, 2 ; 2   3. 6, 2 ; 4   4. 5, 2 ; 3   5. 5, 3 ; 2
6. 5, 4 ; 1   7. 3, 2 ; 1   8. 6, 3 ; 3
9. 2   10. 5   11. 1   12. 1
13. 2   14. 1   15. 4   16. 3
17. 1   18. 2   19. 3   20. 3
21. 4   22. 2   23. 1   24. 2
25. 4   26. 2   27. 2   28. 2
29. 1   30. 3   31. 1   32. 3
33. 4   34. 1
35. 5 – 3 ; 4 – 2 ; 3 – 1   36. 5 – 4 ; 3 – 2 ; 6 – 5

37.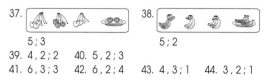
5 ; 3   38. 5 ; 2
39. 4, 2 ; 2   40. 5, 2 ; 3
41. 6, 3 ; 3   42. 6, 2 ; 4   43. 4, 3 ; 1   44. 3, 2 ; 1

Just for Fun

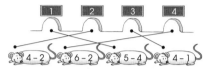

4 Addition and Subtraction of 0

1. 4   2. 0   3. 0   4. 3
5. 0   6. 4   7. 3   8. 5
9. 6   11. 6   12. 5   13. 5
14. 4   15. 4   16. 3   17. 3
18. 2   19. 2   20. 1   21. 1
22. 0   23. 0   24. 5   25. 4
26. 3   27. 1   28. 6   29. 3
30. 5   31. 6   32. 4   33. 2
34. 4   35. 2

36.
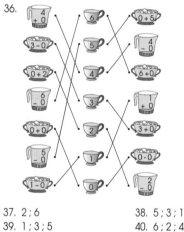

37. 2 ; 6   38. 5 ; 3 ; 1
39. 1 ; 3 ; 5   40. 6 ; 2 ; 4
41. 4 ; 4   42. 3 + 0 = 3 ; 3
43. 4 – 0 = 4 ; 4   44. 6 – 0 = 6 ; 6

Just for Fun

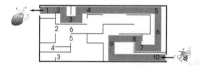

5 Addition and Subtraction Facts to 6

2. 6 – 1 ; 5   3. 3 + 3 ; 6   4. 4 – 2 ; 2
5. 5 – 2 ; 3   6. 2 + 3 ; 5
7. 1   8. 4   9. 4   10. 3
11. 6   12. 3   13. 6   14. 3
15. 0   16. 2   17. 2   18. 3
19. 4   20. 5   21. 5   22. 1
23. 4   24. 1   25. 5   26. 1
27. 1   28. 6   29. 2   30. 2
31. 2   32. 4   33. 6   34. 5
35. 3   36. 4   37. 6   38. 3
39. 3   40. 2   41. 6   42. 5
43. 3   44. 1   45. 2   46. 4
47. 2 ; 2   48. 4 + 2 = 6 ; 6
49. 3 + 3 = 6 ; 6   50. 6 – 4 = 2 ; 2
51. 5 – 2 = 3 ; 3   52. 5 – 1 = 4 ; 4

ANSWERS – SECTION II

Just For Fun

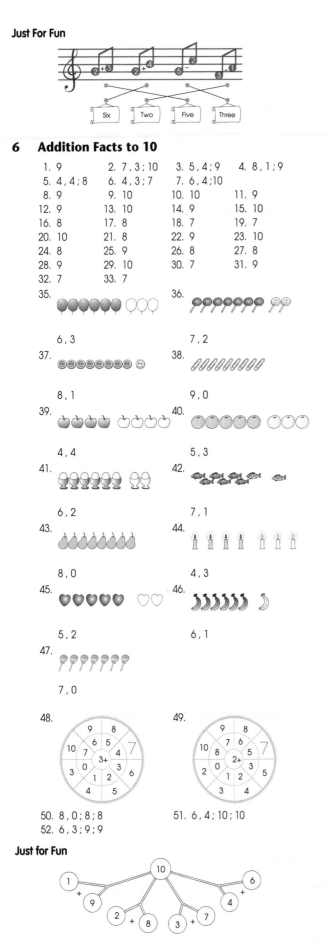

6　Addition Facts to 10

1. 9
2. 7 , 3 ; 10
3. 5 , 4 ; 9
4. 8 , 1 ; 9
5. 4 , 4 ; 8
6. 4 , 3 ; 7
7. 6 , 4 ;10
8. 9
9. 10
10. 10
11. 9
12. 9
13. 10
14. 9
15. 10
16. 8
17. 8
18. 7
19. 7
20. 10
21. 8
22. 9
23. 10
24. 8
25. 9
26. 8
27. 8
28. 9
29. 10
30. 7
31. 9
32. 7
33. 7

35.　6 , 3

36.　7 , 2

37.　8 , 1

38.　9 , 0

39.　4 , 4

40.　5 , 3

41.　6 , 2

42.　7 , 1

43.　8 , 0

44.　4 , 3

45.　5 , 2

46.　6 , 1

47.　7 , 0

48.

49.

50. 8 , 0 ; 8 ; 8
51. 6 , 4 ; 10 ; 10
52. 6 , 3 ; 9 ; 9

Just for Fun

7　Subtraction Facts to 10

1. 6
2. 10 , 2 ; 8
3. 9 , 4 ; 5
4. 8 , 2 ; 6
5. 8 , 4 ; 4
6. 7 , 3 ; 4
7. 8 , 6 ; 2
8. 6
9. 6
10. 6
11. 2
12. 5
13. 5
14. 5
15. 1
16. 1
17. 2
18. 2
19. 4
20. 4
21. 3
22. 3
23. 1
24. 2
25. 4
26. 1
27. 2
28. 3
29. 5
30. 8
31. 4
32. 10
33. 8

34. 10 – 5 = 5
35. 8 – 4 = 4
36. 10 – 2 = 8
37. 10 – 0 = 10
38. 7 – 6 = 1
39. 8 – 8 = 0
40. 9 – 6 = 3
41. 10 – 1 = 9
42. 7 – 5 = 2
43. 6 – 0 = 6
44. 9 – 2 = 7

10 – 0 = 10　Ⓗ
8 – 0 = 8　Ⓤ
9 – 4 = 5　Ⓘ
7 – 3 = 4　Ⓐ
8 – 5 = 3　Ⓢ
9 – 0 = 9　Ⓡ
8 – 7 = 1　Ⓛ
7 – 7 = 0　Ⓑ
8 – 2 = 6　Ⓣ
10 – 3 = 7　Ⓜ
10 – 8 = 2　Ⓞ

45. BRITISH COLUMBIA

46.

47.

48. 7 , 4 ; 3 ; 3
49. 8 , 3 ; 5 ; 5
50. 10 , 2 ; 8 ; 8

Just for Fun

8 　10 – 2 = 8 　6
9 　7 　6 – 3 = 3
6 – 5 = 1 　7 　1
9 – 5 = 4 　10 　6

8　Addition and Subtraction Facts to 10

1. 9
2. 4 + 2 + 1 ; 7
3. 9 – 2 ; 7
4. 9 – 3 ; 6
5. 2 + 4 + 4 ; 10
6. 4 + 3 ; 7
7. 7
8. 2
9. 6
10. 10
11. 9
12. 3
13. 2
14. 7
15. 10
16. 1
17. 7
18. 7
19. 9
20. 10
21. 8
22. 9
23. 9
24. 8
25. 1
26. 3
27. 2
28. 5
29. 7
30. 8
31. 10
32. 9
33. 4
34. 9
35. 3
36. 10
37. 5
38. 2
39. 10
40. 10
41. 6
42. 4
43. 9
44. 6
45. 8
46. 5
47. 5
48. 4
49. 10
50. 3
51. 7
52. 6 ; 6
53. 10

```
    6
+   4
   10
```

54. 9

```
    5
+   4
    9
```

ISBN: 978-1-897164-11-2

55. 3 9
    − 6
    3

56. 7 2
    4
    + 1
    7

Just for Fun

 3 ; 4

Midway Review

1. 9 − 3 ; 6 2. 5 + 3 + 1 ; 9 3. 6 + 4 ; 10
4. 5   5. 6   6. 2   7. 2
8. 7   9. 1   10. 6   11. 7
12. 9   13. 7   14. 9   15. 1
16. 3   17. 8   18. 2   19. 7
20. 4   21. 8
22.

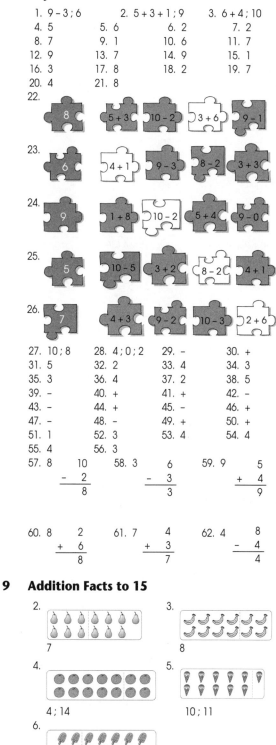

23.

24.

25.

26.

27. 10 ; 8 28. 4 ; 0 ; 2 29. − 30. +
31. 5   32. 2   33. 4   34. 3
35. 3   36. 4   37. 2   38. 5
39. −   40. +   41. +   42. −
43. −   44. +   45. −   46. +
47. −   48. −   49. +   50. +
51. 1   52. 3   53. 4   54. 4
55. 4   56. 3
57. 8 10 58. 3 6 59. 9 5
   − 2   − 3   + 4
    8   3   9

60. 8 2 61. 7 4 62. 4 8
   + 6   + 3   − 4
    8   7   4

9 Addition Facts to 15

2.

7

3.

8

4.

4 ; 14

5.

10 ; 11

6.

4 ; 13

7. 15 8. 13 9. 14 10. 15
11. 14 12. 12 13. 12 14. 13
15. 14 16. 11 17. 11 18. 11
19. 14 20. 15 21. 13 22. 15
23. 12 24. 11 25. 12 26. 14
27. 13 28. 14 29. 15 30. 15
31. 15 32. 14 33. 11 34. 6
35. 10 36. 5 37. 9 38. 4
39. 8 40. 3 41. 7 42. 2
43.

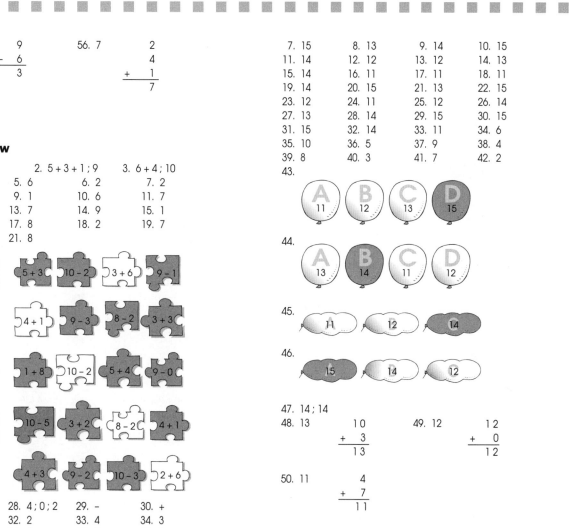

44.

45.

46.

47. 14 ; 14
48. 13 10 49. 12 12
   + 3   + 0
    13   12

50. 11 4
   + 7
    11

Just for Fun

 5 ; 1

10 Subtraction Facts to 15

1. 8
2.

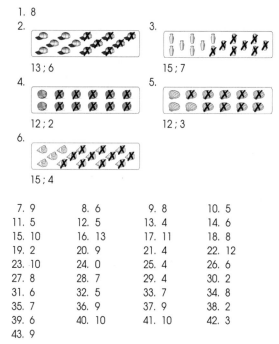

13 ; 6

3.

15 ; 7

4.

12 ; 2

5.

12 ; 3

6.

15 ; 4

7. 9   8. 6   9. 8   10. 5
11. 5 12. 5 13. 4 14. 6
15. 10 16. 13 17. 11 18. 8
19. 2 20. 9 21. 4 22. 12
23. 10 24. 0 25. 4 26. 6
27. 8 28. 7 29. 4 30. 2
31. 6 32. 5 33. 7 34. 8
35. 7 36. 9 37. 9 38. 2
39. 6 40. 10 41. 10 42. 3
43. 9

44. 6 ; 6

45. 5
```
    12
  -  7
     5
```

46. 8
```
    13
  -  5
     8
```

47. 9
```
    15
  -  6
     9
```

Just for Fun

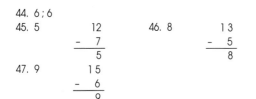

11 Addition and Subtraction Facts to 15

1. 9

3.
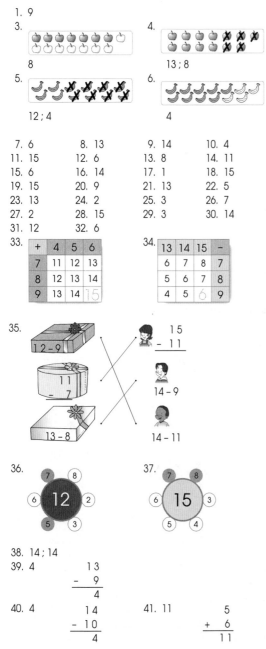
8

4.
13 ; 8

5.
12 ; 4

6.
4

7. 6	8. 13	9. 14	10. 4
11. 15	12. 6	13. 8	14. 11
15. 6	16. 14	17. 1	18. 15
19. 15	20. 9	21. 13	22. 5
23. 13	24. 2	25. 3	26. 7
27. 2	28. 15	29. 3	30. 14
31. 12	32. 6		

33.

+	4	5	6
7	11	12	13
8	12	13	14
9	13	14	15

34.

13	14	15	–
6	7	8	7
5	6	7	8
4	5	6	9

35.
12 - 9
11 - 7
13 - 8

15 - 11
14 - 9
14 - 11

36.
7 8
6 **12** 2
5 3

37.
7 8
6 **15** 3
5 4

38. 14 ; 14

39. 4
```
    13
  -  9
     4
```

40. 4
```
    14
  - 10
     4
```

41. 11
```
     5
  +  6
    11
```

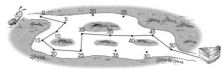

12 Addition Facts to 20

1. 9 , 8 ; 17	2. 14 , 5 ; 19	3. 11 , 6 ; 17
4. 15 , 3 ; 18	5. 13 , 7 ; 20	6. 10 , 6 ; 16
7. 20	8. 19	9. 19	10. 19
11. 19	12. 20	13. 19	14. 18
15. 17	16. 20	17. 17	18. 17
19. 17	20. 20	21. 19	22. 18
23. 20	24. 18	25. 16	26. 19
27. 17	28. 19	29. 20	30. 16
31. 20	32. 20		

33. 15 + 3 = 18   n   13 + 3 = 16
34. 10 + 6 = 16   k   12 + 2 = 14
35. 9 + 5 = 14   r   16 + 2 = 18
36. 11 + 6 = 17   h   16 + 4 = 20
37. 12 + 8 = 20   c   16 + 1 = 17
38. 13 + 2 = 15   e   15 + 4 = 19
39. 16 + 3 = 19   d   14 + 1 = 15
40. 11 + 1 = 12   a   6 + 5 = 11
41. 9 + 4 = 13   f   10 + 2 = 12
42. 7 + 4 = 11   i   6 + 7 = 13

43. handkerchief
44. 10 + 10 ; 20 ; 20
45. 12 + 6 ; 18 ; 18
46. 8 + 8 ; 16 ; 16
47. 9 + 10 ; 19 ; 19
48. 13 + 4 ; 17 ; 17

Just for Fun

13 Subtraction Facts to 20

1. 8	2. 18 , 9 ; 9	3. 17 , 6 ; 11
4. 19 , 7 ; 12	5. 20 , 10 ; 10	6. 19 , 9 ; 10
7. 11	8. 7	9. 9	10. 15
11. 9	12. 6	13. 12	14. 14
15. 2	16. 13	17. 18	18. 3
19. 14	20. 6	21. 16	22. 6
23. 10	24. 12	25. 15	26. 9
27. 7	28. 6	29. 3	30. 4
31. 14	32. 13	33. 6	34. 7
35. 11	36. 5	37. 5	38. 1
39. 2	40. 5	41. 2	42. 7
43. 9	44. 12		

45. 18 - 12 ; 6 ; 6
46. 17 - 9 ; 8 ; 8
47. 20 - 18 ; 2 ; 2
48. 16 - 5 ; 11 ; 11
49. 19 - 9 ; 10 ; 10

Just for Fun

18 - 4   12 - 8   16 - 11
19 - 5   17 - 4   20 - 6   14 - 10

14 Addition and Subtraction Facts to 20

3. 7 ; 19   4. 18 ; 13

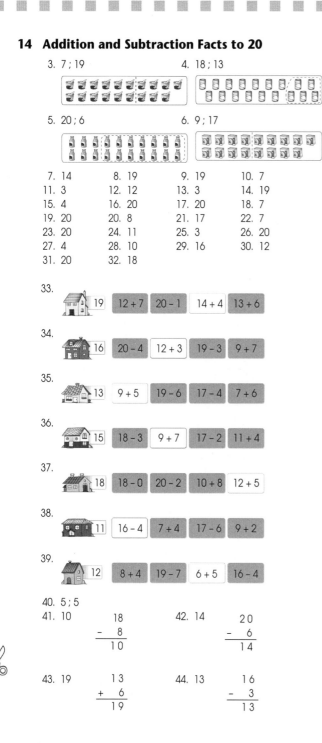

5. 20 ; 6   6. 9 ; 17

7. 14	8. 19	9. 19	10. 7
11. 3	12. 12	13. 3	14. 19
15. 4	16. 20	17. 20	18. 7
19. 20	20. 8	21. 17	22. 7
23. 20	24. 11	25. 3	26. 20
27. 4	28. 10	29. 16	30. 12
31. 20	32. 18		

33. 19 | 12 + 7 | 20 − 1 | 14 + 4 | 13 + 6 |

34. 16 | 20 − 4 | 12 + 3 | 19 − 3 | 9 + 7 |

35. 13 | 9 + 5 | 19 − 6 | 17 − 4 | 7 + 6 |

36. 15 | 18 − 3 | 9 + 7 | 17 − 2 | 11 + 4 |

37. 18 | 18 − 0 | 20 − 2 | 10 + 8 | 12 + 5 |

38. 11 | 16 − 4 | 7 + 4 | 17 − 6 | 9 + 2 |

39. 12 | 8 + 4 | 19 − 7 | 6 + 5 | 16 − 4 |

40. 5 ; 5

41. 10
```
  18
−  8
  10
```

42. 14
```
  20
−  6
  14
```

43. 19
```
  13
+  6
  19
```

44. 13
```
  16
−  3
  13
```

Just for Fun

65 ; 56 ; 48 ; 32 ; 29 ; 12 ; 7

15 More Addition and Subtraction

1a. 15	b. 16	c. 17	d. 18
e. 19			
2a. 17	b. 18	c. 19	d. 20
3a. 11	b. 12	c. 13	d. 14
4a. 9	b. 8	c. 7	d. 6
e. 5			
5a. 7	b. 8	c. 9	d. 10
e. 11			
6. 12			

7. 5 ; 15   8. 3 ; 13

9. 4 ; 14   10. 7 ; 17

11. 5 ; 15

12. 8

13. 2 ; 8   14. 3 ; 7

15. 4 ; 6   16. 3 ; 7

17. 2 ; 8

18. 14	19. 12	20. 18	21. 15
22. 16	23. 17	24. 19	25. 15

Just for Fun

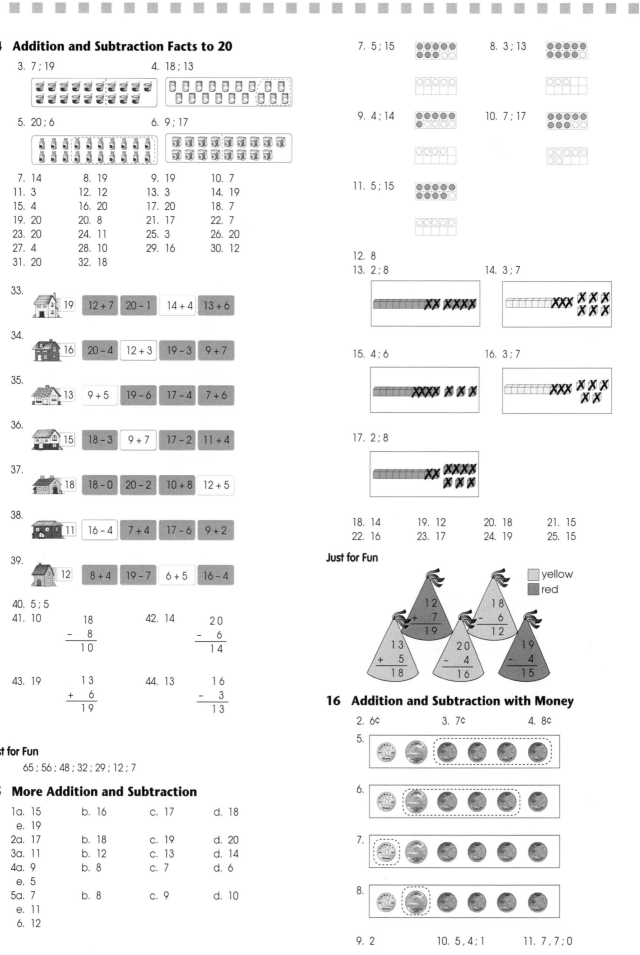

yellow
red

```
  12
+  7
  19
```
```
  18
−  6
  12
```
```
  13
+  5
  18
```
```
  20
−  4
  16
```
```
  19
−  4
  15
```

16 Addition and Subtraction with Money

2. 6¢   3. 7¢   4. 8¢

5.

6.

7.

8.

9. 2   10. 5, 4 ; 1   11. 7, 7 ; 0

12. 10 , 5 ; 5   13. 10 , 6 ; 4   14. 3
15. 10 , 6 ; 4   16. 6 , 4 ; 2   17. 7 , 2 ; 5
18. 5 , 5 ; 0   19. A   20. D
21. B , C   22. B , D   23. C , D
24. A , B

25.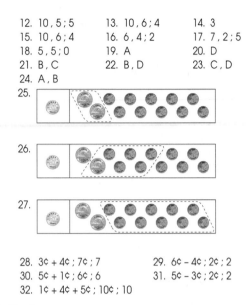

26.

27.

28. 3¢ + 4¢ ; 7¢ ; 7   29. 6¢ – 4¢ ; 2¢ ; 2
30. 5¢ + 1¢ ; 6¢ ; 6   31. 5¢ – 3¢ ; 2¢ ; 2
32. 1¢ + 4¢ + 5¢ ; 10¢ ; 10

Just for Fun

Final Review

1. 20   2. 11   3. 18   4. 15
5. 13   6. 16   7. 17   8. 10
9. 16   10. 10   11. 14   12. 19
13. 11 ; 8 ; 6 ; 9   14. 19 ; 18 ; 16 ; 20
15. 13 ; 10 ; 6 ; 12
16. 19   17. 13

18.
19.
20.
21.
22.
23.
24.
25.

18 - 2 = 16 N	17 - 2 = 15
10 + 4 = 14 A	7 + 4 = 11
8 + 7 = 15 D	9 + 7 = 16
17 - 6 = 11 O	19 - 5 = 14
20 - 7 = 13 U	16 - 4 = 12
5 + 12 = 17 I	5 + 8 = 13
19 - 7 = 12 S	12 + 6 = 18
9 + 9 = 18 R	20 - 3 = 17

26. DINOSAUR
27. +   28. –   29. –   30. +
31. +   32. –   33. +   34. +
35. –   36. +   37. –   38. –
39. 10   40. 5   41. 8   42. 2
43. 5   44. 1   45. 12   46. 3
47. 4th ; 1st ; 2nd ; 3rd
48a. 13   b. 14   c. 15
49a. 8   b. 9   c. 10
50. 3 ; 13   51. 3 ; 13

52. 3 ; 7   53. 4 ; 6

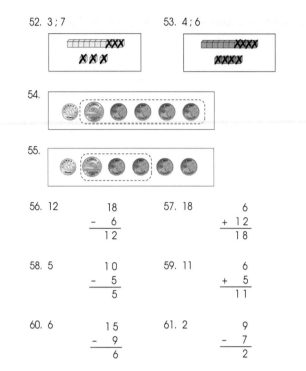

54.

55.

56. 12
$$\begin{array}{r} 18 \\ -\ 6 \\ \hline 12 \end{array}$$
57. 18
$$\begin{array}{r} 6 \\ +\ 12 \\ \hline 18 \end{array}$$

58. 5
$$\begin{array}{r} 10 \\ -\ 5 \\ \hline 5 \end{array}$$
59. 11
$$\begin{array}{r} 6 \\ +\ 5 \\ \hline 11 \end{array}$$

60. 6
$$\begin{array}{r} 15 \\ -\ 9 \\ \hline 6 \end{array}$$
61. 2
$$\begin{array}{r} 9 \\ -\ 7 \\ \hline 2 \end{array}$$

ISBN: 978-1-897164-11-2

Review

1. 8 ; eight
2. 1 ; one
3. 4 ; four
4. 5 ; five
5. Alex ; Paul
6. 5th ; 8th
7. 8
8. 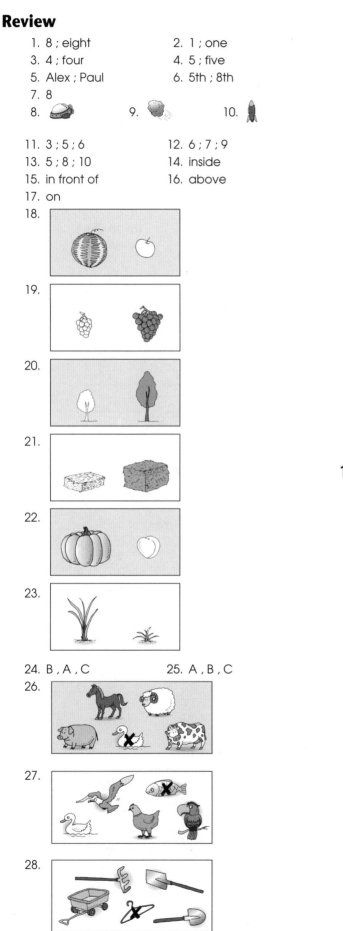 9. 10.

11. 3 ; 5 ; 6
12. 6 ; 7 ; 9
13. 5 ; 8 ; 10
14. inside
15. in front of
16. above
17. on

18.

19.

20.

21.

22.

23.

24. B , A , C
25. A , B , C

26.

27.

28.

29.

30.

31. green yellow red blue

32. red yellow green blue

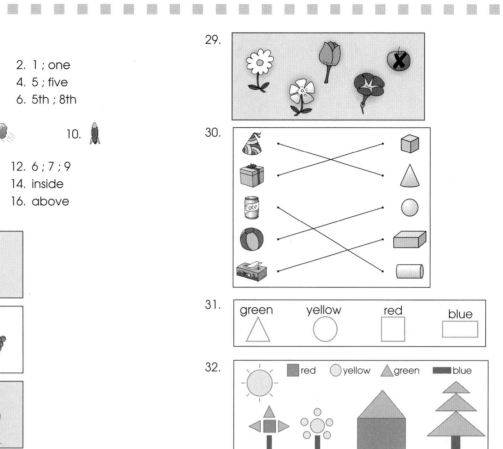

1 Numbers 1 - 20

1a. 16 ; ✔
b. 15
2a. 9
b. 11 ; ✔
3a. 13 ; ✔
b. 12
4a. 18 ; ✔
b. 17
5. 10
6. 12
7. 7
8. 8
9. 11
10. 8
11. Thirteen
12. eighteen
13. Eighteen
14. two
15. one

16.

17.

18.

19.

20.

21.

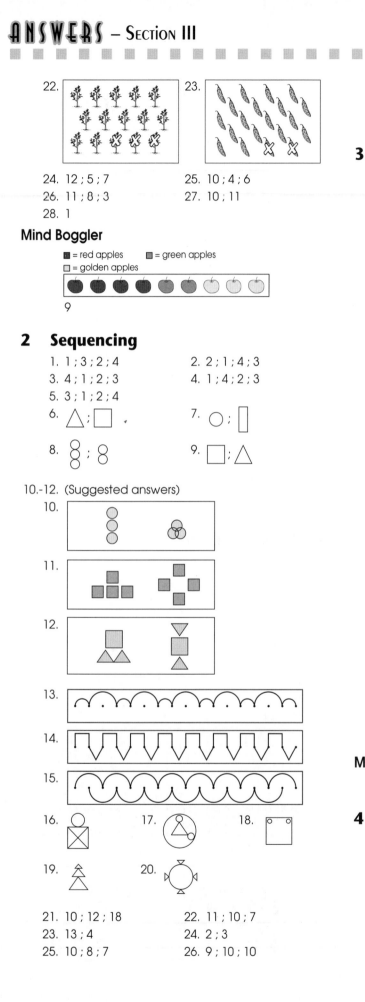

22.

23.

24. 12 ; 5 ; 7
25. 10 ; 4 ; 6
26. 11 ; 8 ; 3
27. 10 ; 11
28. 1

Mind Boggler

■ = red apples ■ = green apples
□ = golden apples

9

2 Sequencing

1. 1 ; 3 ; 2 ; 4
2. 2 ; 1 ; 4 ; 3
3. 4 ; 1 ; 2 ; 3
4. 1 ; 4 ; 2 ; 3
5. 3 ; 1 ; 2 ; 4
6. △ ; □
7. ○ ; ▯
8. ⊗ ; ○
9. □ ; △

10.-12. (Suggested answers)

10.

11.

12.

13.

14.

15.

16.

17.

18.

19.

20.

21. 10 ; 12 ; 18
22. 11 ; 10 ; 7
23. 13 ; 4
24. 2 ; 3
25. 10 ; 8 ; 7
26. 9 ; 10 ; 10

Mind Boggler

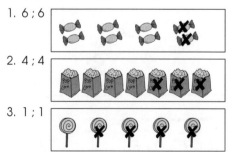

3 Addition

1. 7
2. 6
3. 8
4. 9
5. 8
6. 4
7. 6
8. 6
9. 8
10. 5
11. 9
12. 8
13. 7
14. 6
15. 10
16. 10
17. 10
18. 9
19. 8

20.

+	1	2	3	4	5
1	2	3	4	5	6
2	3	4	5	6	7
3	4	5	6	7	8
4	5	6	7	8	9
5	6	7	8	9	10

21.
$$\begin{array}{r} 2 \\ + 5 \\ \hline 7 \end{array}$$

22.
$$\begin{array}{r} 4 \\ + 3 \\ \hline 7 \end{array}$$

23.
$$\begin{array}{r} 5 \\ + 4 \\ \hline 9 \end{array}$$

24.
$$\begin{array}{r} 3 \\ + 3 \\ \hline 6 \end{array}$$

25.
$$\begin{array}{r} 2 \\ + 6 \\ \hline 8 \end{array}$$

26. 4 + 2 = 6
27. 3 + 1 = 4
28. 6 + 3 = 9
29. 7 + 2 = 9
30. 1 + 4 = 5
31. 5 + 5 = 10
32. 4 ; 3 ; 7
33. 5 ; 4 ; 9
34. 6 ; 4 ; 10

$$\begin{array}{r} 4 \\ + 3 \\ \hline 7 \end{array}$$
$$\begin{array}{r} 5 \\ + 4 \\ \hline 9 \end{array}$$
$$\begin{array}{r} 6 \\ + 4 \\ \hline 10 \end{array}$$

35. Ann
36. Andy

Mind Boggler

George

4 Subtraction

1. 6 ; 6

2. 4 ; 4

3. 1 ; 1

ISBN: 978-1-897164-11-2

4. 5 ; 5

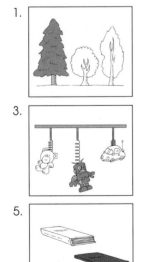

5. 8 ; 8

6. 3 ; 3

7.
$$\begin{array}{r} 8 \\ -\ 3 \\ \hline 5 \end{array}$$

8.
$$\begin{array}{r} 6 \\ -\ 5 \\ \hline 1 \end{array}$$

9.
$$\begin{array}{r} 7 \\ -\ 4 \\ \hline 3 \end{array}$$

10.
$$\begin{array}{r} 5 \\ -\ 2 \\ \hline 3 \end{array}$$

11.
$$\begin{array}{r} 4 \\ -\ 3 \\ \hline 1 \end{array}$$

12. 6 ; 4
13. 4 ; 5
14. 5
15. 3
16. 3
17. 2
18. 6
19. 1
20. 8
21. 2
22. 3
23. 7
24. 4
25. 4
26. 7 − 2 = 5
27. 6 − 2 = 4
28. 4 − 1 = 3
29. 7 − 6 = 1
30. 9 − 4 = 5
31. 3
32. 3
33. 7
34. 3
35. 2
36. 2
37. 6
38. 6

Mind Boggler

4

5 Measurement I

1.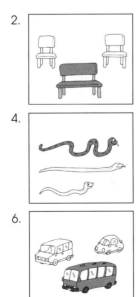
2.
3.
4.
5.
6.

7. 7 ; 4
8. 11 ; 6
9. 10 ; 6
10. 5 ; 3
11. 9 ; 5
12a. 3 ; 2
b. 7 ; 4
13. B
14. A
15. C
16.-18. (Individual answers)
19. (Suggested answers)
10 ; 6 ; 6 ; 9

Mind Boggler

12

6 Patterns

1. ✔
2. ✔
3. ✗
4. ✗
5. 3 ; ◆ ▲ ▲
6. 4 ; ★ ★ ♥ ♥
7. 3 ; ● ■ ●
8. 3 ; ▮ ▮ ▬
9. 4 ; ▲ ● ● ●
10. ○ × ○
11. **4 6 3**
12. **T P G**
13. ◯ ○ ∘
14. △ ▲ ▽

15.-18. (△ yellow ○ red □ blue ⬡ green ⬠ purple)

15. △ ○ ○ □ △ ○ ○ □
16. ⬠ ○ ⬡ ○ ⬠ ○ ⬡ ○
17. ⬠ □ □ △ ⬠ □ □ △
18. ⬡ ○ ⬠ □ ⬡ ○ ⬠ □

19a. 10 ; 9 ; 8 ; 7
b.
c. down ; 1
20a. 1 ; 2 ; 3 ; 4
b.
c. triangles ; 1
21. 6 ; 7 ; 8
22. 8 ; 7 ; 6

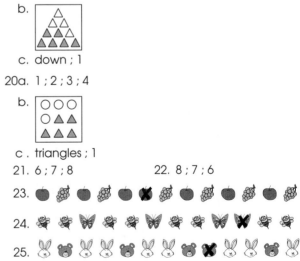

23.
24.
25.

26a.-c. ■ = green ■ = blue

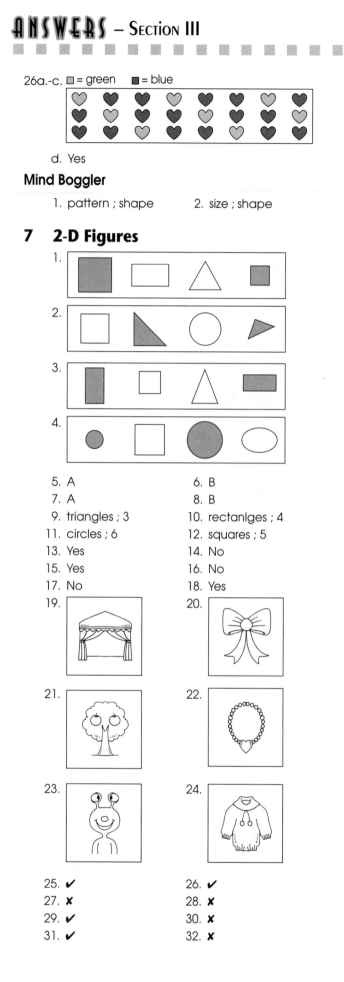

d. Yes

Mind Boggler

1. pattern ; shape   2. size ; shape

7   2-D Figures

1.

2.

3.

4.

5. A	6. B
7. A	8. B
9. triangles ; 3	10. rectanlges ; 4
11. circles ; 6	12. squares ; 5
13. Yes	14. No
15. Yes	16. No
17. No	18. Yes

19.   20.

21.   22.

23.   24.

25. ✔	26. ✔
27. ✗	28. ✗
29. ✔	30. ✗
31. ✔	32. ✗

33.

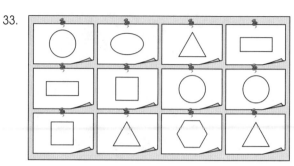

34. 3   35. 2

Mind Boggler

(Suggested answers)

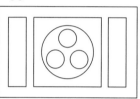

Progress Test

1a. 8	b. 5	c. 13	d. 3
2a. 6	b. 9	c. 15	d. 3
3. 12		4. 10	
5. fork		6. 2	
7. 1 ; 3 ; 2 ; 4		8. 4 ; 2 ; 1 ; 3	
9. 3 + 4 = 7		10. 6 + 3 = 9	
11. 8 – 5 = 3		12. 7 – 2 = 5	
13. 9		14. 3	
15. 4		16. 6	
17. 4		18. 9	
19. 4		20. 3	
21. 24		22. 20	
23. A		24. C	

25a. ⟨shapes⟩   b. triangles

26a. ⟨shapes⟩   b. squares

27a. ⟨shapes⟩   b. circles

28. 7 ; 2 ; 7 + 2 = 9 ; 9
29. 9 ; 9 – 7 = 2 ; 2
30. 4 ; 4 ; 4 + 4 = 8 ; 8
31. 10 ; 10 – 9 = 1 ; 1
32. 8 ; 8 – 5 = 3 ; 3

8   Numbers to 100

1. - 4. (Estimate: Individual answers)

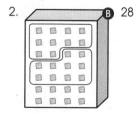

1. Ⓐ 41   2. Ⓑ 28

ISBN: 978-1-897164-11-2

3.  **C** 42
4. **D** 38

5. C
6. 1
7. 10
8. 40
9. Lucy
10. Janice
11. Alex
12. Lucy
13. Nancy
14. Lucy
15. Brenda
16. No
17. 42 ; 40 ; 35 ; 25 ; 19
18. 20 ; 41 ; 65 ; 70 ; 82
19a. 5 ; 7
b. 57
20a. 4 ; 9
b. 49
21a. 6 ; 4
b. 64
22. 36
23. 75
24. 64
25. 65

26.-28.

Mind Boggler

1. No
2. No
3. 10, 20, 30, 40, 50
4. 10, 20, 30, 40, 50

9   Addition and Subtraction

1. 14 ; 14
2. 6 + 7 = 13 ; 13
3. 8 + 4 = 12 ; 12
4. 5 + 8 = 13 ; 13
5. 6 + 9 = 15 ; 15
6. 8 + 8 = 16 ; 16
7. 5 ; 9 ; 9
8.

16 – 7 = 9 ; 9

9.

15 – 7 = 8 ; 8

10.

12 – 9 = 3 ; 3

11.

13 – 8 = 5 ; 5

12. 8
13. 17
14. 9
15. 15
16. 2
17. 13
18. 12
19. 7
20. 7
21. 7
22. 16
23. 11
24. 11
25. 7

26.

15 take away 8		12 – 7 = 5
12 take away 7		8 + 9 = 17
8 plus 9		7 + 7 = 14
7 plus 7		15 – 8 = 7
16 take away 8		16 – 8 = 8

27. 9 + 5 = 14 ; 14
$$\begin{array}{r} 9 \\ +\ 5 \\ \hline 14 \end{array}$$

28. 6 + 8 = 14 ; 14
$$\begin{array}{r} 6 \\ +\ 8 \\ \hline 14 \end{array}$$

29. 15 – 6 = 9 ; 9
$$\begin{array}{r} 15 \\ -\ 6 \\ \hline 9 \end{array}$$

30. 12 – 4 = 8 ; 8
$$\begin{array}{r} 12 \\ -\ 4 \\ \hline 8 \end{array}$$

Mind Boggler

3

10   Measurement II

1. B
2. B
3. A
4. A
5. morning
6. night
7. evening
8. afternoon
9. (Individual answers)
10. Friday
11. Saturday
12. Saturday
13. Monday
14. Thursday
15. Tuesday
16. 7
17. Friday
18. 2
19. 3
20. Wednesday
21. Tuesday
22. February
23. December

24. October
25. July
26. October
27. January
28. 12 ; 4
29. June
30. summer ; fall
31. Winter ; summer
32. June
33. Friday
34. Wednesday
35. May 12
36. May 15
37. 7 o'clock / 7:00
38. 9:30
39. 2 o'clock / 2:00
40. 12 o'clock / 12:00
41. 11:30
42. 8:30

43. 44. 45.

Mind Boggler

5:30

11 3-D Figures

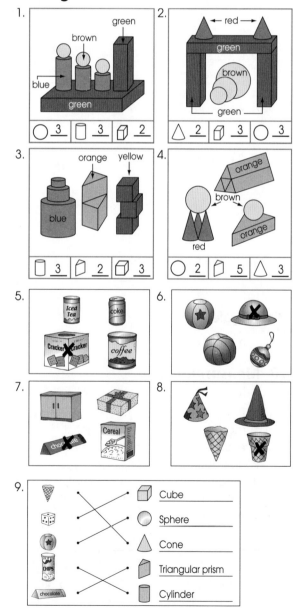

12 Money

1. 3 ; 2 ; 4 ; 2 ; 3 ; 2
2. 4 ; 3 ; 2 ; 3 ; 2 ; 2

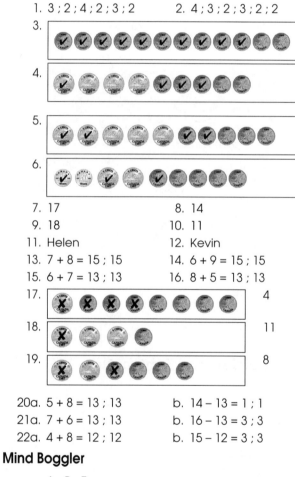

10a. Cylinder
b. Yes
c. Yes
d. Yes
11a. Cube
b. Yes
c. Yes
d. Yes
12a. Cone
b. Yes
c. No
d. Yes
13a. Sphere
b. Yes
c. No
d. Yes
14. B
15. B
16. A
17. C
18. Three
19. Three
20. Two
21. Two

Mind Boggler

1. Cylinder
2. Sphere

7. 17
8. 14
9. 18
10. 11
11. Helen
12. Kevin
13. 7 + 8 = 15 ; 15
14. 6 + 9 = 15 ; 15
15. 6 + 7 = 13 ; 13
16. 8 + 5 = 13 ; 13
17. 4
18. 11
19. 8

20a. 5 + 8 = 13 ; 13
b. 14 – 13 = 1 ; 1
21a. 7 + 6 = 13 ; 13
b. 16 – 13 = 3 ; 3
22a. 4 + 8 = 12 ; 12
b. 15 – 12 = 3 ; 3

Mind Boggler

A ; B ; E

13 Graphs

1. 6
2. 5
3. 4
4. 2
5. 21
6. 🐢
7. 🐱
8. 4
9. 6
10. 6
11. 3
12. 10

ISBN: 978-1-897164-11-2

13. 12   14. 22

15.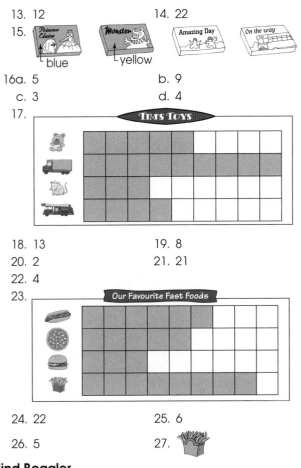

16a. 5   b. 9
 c. 3   d. 4

17.

18. 13   19. 8
20. 2   21. 21
22. 4
23.

24. 22   25. 6
26. 5   27.

Mind Boggler

1. 4
2. She should buy fries. A lot of students like fries.

14 Probability

1. Yes   2. No
3. Yes   4. No
5. No   6. Yes
7. Yes   8. No
9. No   10. Yes
11. Yes   12. No
13. Yes   14. Yes
15. No   16. A
17. C   18. C
19. A   20a. Often
 b. Sometimes   c. Never
21a. Never   b. Sometimes
 c. Often   22a. Sometimes
 b. Often   c. Never

Mind Boggler

The yellow balls are bigger than the red balls, so there is a greater chance to pick a yellow ball than a red ball.

Final Test

1a. rectangle   b. 44

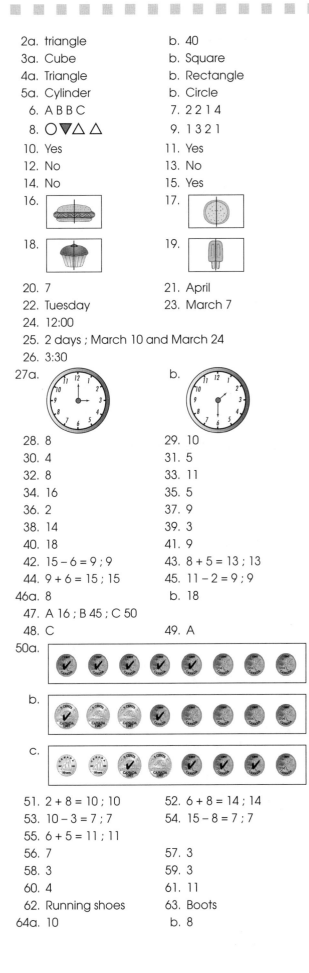

2a. triangle   b. 40
3a. Cube   b. Square
4a. Triangle   b. Rectangle
5a. Cylinder   b. Circle
 6. A B B C   7. 2 2 1 4
 8. ○ ▼ △ △   9. 1 3 2 1
10. Yes   11. Yes
12. No   13. No
14. No   15. Yes
16.   17.
18.   19.
20. 7   21. April
22. Tuesday   23. March 7
24. 12:00
25. 2 days ; March 10 and March 24
26. 3:30
27a.   b.
28. 8   29. 10
30. 4   31. 5
32. 8   33. 11
34. 16   35. 5
36. 2   37. 9
38. 14   39. 3
40. 18   41. 9
42. 15 − 6 = 9 ; 9   43. 8 + 5 = 13 ; 13
44. 9 + 6 = 15 ; 15   45. 11 − 2 = 9 ; 9
46a. 8   b. 18
47. A 16 ; B 45 ; C 50
48. C   49. A
50a.
 b.
 c.
51. 2 + 8 = 10 ; 10   52. 6 + 8 = 14 ; 14
53. 10 − 3 = 7 ; 7   54. 15 − 8 = 7 ; 7
55. 6 + 5 = 11 ; 11
56. 7   57. 3
58. 3   59. 3
60. 4   61. 11
62. Running shoes   63. Boots
64a. 10   b. 8

1 Numbers 1 to 10

1. 8	2. 7	3. Helen
4. 10	5. 6	6. 7
7. Dan	8. Rick	9. 8
10. 9	11. 7	12. 5
13. 8	14. 6	15. 6
16. 2	17. 8	18. Jamie
19. Barry		

2 Addition and Subtraction to 10

1. 3	2. 6	3. 9
4. 4	5. Carol ; Ann	6. 9
7. 10	8. 7	9. 6
10. 3	11. 5	12. 7
13. 3	14. 4	15. 3
16. 9	17. 3	18. 2
19. 9	20. 1	21. 6
22. 10	23. 7	24. 10
25. 2	26. 4	27. 3
28. 10	29. 6	30. 7
31. 2	32. 5	33. 2
34. 7	35. 2	36. 4
37. 7		

3 Addition and Subtraction to 20

1. 12	2. 16	3. 15
4. 9	5. 7	6. 13
7. 13	8. 11	9. 6
10. 8	11. 12	12. 14 ; 14

13. 20 ;
$$\begin{array}{r} 8 \\ + 12 \\ \hline 20 \end{array}$$
14. 6 ;
$$\begin{array}{r} 12 \\ - 6 \\ \hline 6 \end{array}$$

15. 4 ;
$$\begin{array}{r} 12 \\ - 8 \\ \hline 4 \end{array}$$
16. 7 ;
$$\begin{array}{r} 12 \\ - 5 \\ \hline 7 \end{array}$$

17. 18 ; 18
18. 11 – 7 = 4 ; 4
19. 17 – 5 = 12 ; 12
20. 12 – 5 = 7 ; 7
21. 13 + 7 = 20 ; 20
22. 13 – 7 = 6 ; 6
23. 3 + 11 = 14 ; 14
24. 11 – 3 = 8 ; 8
25. 6 + 6 + 6 = 18 ; 18
26. 20 – 18 = 2 ; 2
27. 12 – 4 = 8 ; 8
28. 12 + 5 = 17 ; 17

4 Shapes

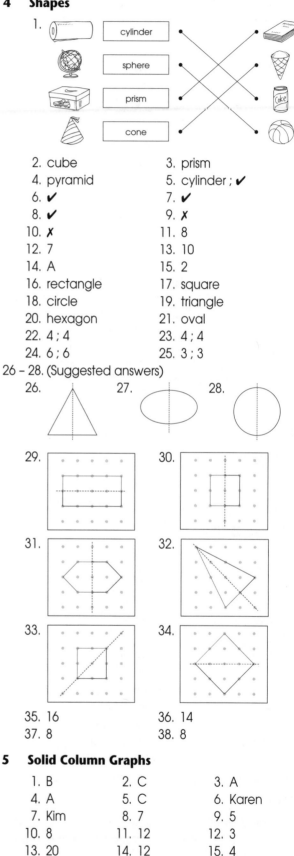

1.

2. cube	3. prism	
4. pyramid	5. cylinder ; ✔	
6. ✔	7. ✔	
8. ✔	9. ✗	
10. ✗	11. 8	
12. 7	13. 10	
14. A	15. 2	
16. rectangle	17. square	
18. circle	19. triangle	
20. hexagon	21. oval	
22. 4 ; 4	23. 4 ; 4	
24. 6 ; 6	25. 3 ; 3	

26 – 28. (Suggested answers)

26. 27. 28.

29. 30.

31. 32.

33. 34.

35. 16	36. 14
37. 8	38. 8

5 Solid Column Graphs

1. B	2. C	3. A
4. A	5. C	6. Karen
7. Kim	8. 7	9. 5
10. 8	11. 12	12. 3
13. 20	14. 12	15. 4
16. 1	17. 3	18. 7

ISBN: 978-1-897164-11-2

19.

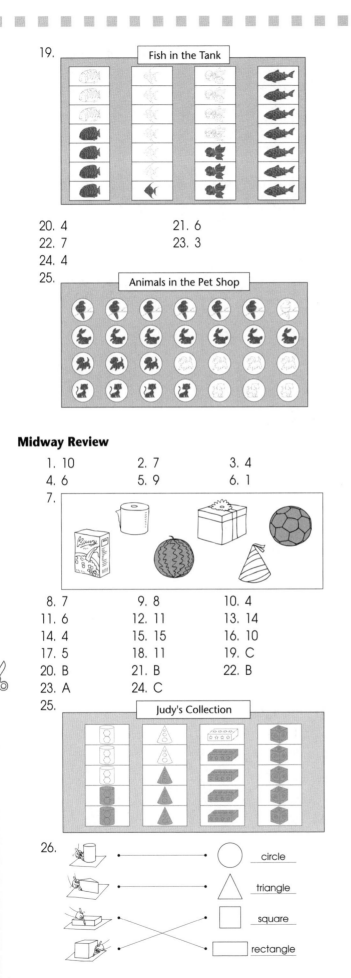

Fish in the Tank

20. 4   21. 6
22. 7   23. 3
24. 4
25.

Animals in the Pet Shop

Midway Review

1. 10   2. 7   3. 4
4. 6   5. 9   6. 1
7.

8. 7   9. 8   10. 4
11. 6   12. 11   13. 14
14. 4   15. 15   16. 10
17. 5   18. 11   19. C
20. B   21. B   22. B
23. A   24. C
25.

Judy's Collection

26.
- circle
- triangle
- square
- rectangle

27.

28.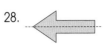

29.

6   Numbers 20 to 100

1. 34   2. 50
3. 46   4. 29
5. B   6. D
7. B ; C ; A ; D   8. 60
9. 36   10. 30
11. 45   12. 62
13. 38   14. Amy
15. Ivan   16. Amy ; Lily ; Ivan
17. 28   18. 67
19. Dan   20. Mike
21. Brenda   22. Brenda
23. Derek
24. Derek ; Mike ; Dan ; Brenda
25. 68 ; 53   26. 80 ; 77
27. Dan
28. 55 ; 56 ; 57 ; 58 ; 59 ; 60
29. 69 ; 68 ; 67 ; 66 ; 65 ; 64
30. 35 ; 40 ; 45 ; 50 ; 55 ; 60
31. 84 ; 86 ; 88 ; 90 ; 92 ; 94
32. Mary   33. William
34. 45

7   Addition and subtraction to 50

1. 12 ; 9   2. 15 ; 14
3. 12 + 15 = 27 ; 27   4. 9 + 14 = 23 ; 23
5. 12 + 9 = 21 ; 21   6. 15 + 14 = 29 ; 29
7. 21 + 29 = 50 ; 50   8. 17
9. 29   10. 17 + 29 = 46 ; 46
11. 29 – 17 = 12 ; 12   12. 17 + 15 = 32 ; 32
13. 29 + 15 = 44 ; 44   14. 29 – 16 = 13 ; 13
15. 15 + 17 = 32 ; 32   16. 11 + 14 = 25 ; 25
17. 18 + 19 = 37 ; 37   18. 37 – 25 = 12 ; 12
19. 15 + 11 + 18 = 44 ; 44
20. 17 + 14 +19 = 50 ; 50
21. 21 – 17 = 4 ; 4   22. 24 – 18 = 6 ; 6
23. 28 – 19 = 9 ; 9   24. 21 + 24 = 45 ; 45
25. 21 + 28 = 49 ; 49   26. 18 + 19 = 37 ; 37

8   Addition and Subtraction to 100

1. 41   2. 25   3. 33
4. 41 + 33 = 74 ; 74

$$\begin{array}{r} 4\,1 \\ +\ 3\,3 \\ \hline 7\,4 \end{array}$$

ISBN: 978-1-897164-11-2

5. 33 – 25 = 8 ; 8
$$\begin{array}{r} 33 \\ -\ 25 \\ \hline 8 \end{array}$$

6. 41 + 25 = 66 ; 66
$$\begin{array}{r} 41 \\ +\ 25 \\ \hline 66 \end{array}$$

7. 41 – 25 = 16 ; 16
$$\begin{array}{r} 41 \\ -\ 25 \\ \hline 16 \end{array}$$

8. 60 – 33 = 27 ; 27
$$\begin{array}{r} 60 \\ -\ 33 \\ \hline 27 \end{array}$$

9. 41 – 35 = 6 ; 6
$$\begin{array}{r} 41 \\ -\ 35 \\ \hline 6 \end{array}$$

10. 41 + 25 + 33 = 99 ; 99
$$\begin{array}{r} 41 \\ 25 \\ +\ 33 \\ \hline 99 \end{array}$$

11. Fred   12. Roy   13. Fred

14. 37 + 16 + 15 = 68 ; 68
15. 29 + 28 + 16 = 73 ; 73
16. 27 + 23 + 49 = 99 ; 99
17. 37 + 29 + 27 = 93 ; 93
18. 16 + 28 + 23 = 67 ; 67
19. 15 + 16 + 49 = 80 ; 80
20. 16 + 15 = 31 ; 31
21. 37 – 12 = 25 ; 25
22. 29 + 12 = 41 ; 41
23. 23 + 18 = 41 ; 41
24. 49 – 16 = 33 ; 33
25. 27 – 13 = 14 ; 14

9 Money

1. 42   2. 23
3. 31   4. 39
5. 3   6. Chocolate bar
7. Juicy Gum
8. 65 ; 65   9. 70 ;
$$\begin{array}{r} 31 \\ +\ 39 \\ \hline 70 \end{array}$$

10. 19 ;
$$\begin{array}{r} 50 \\ -\ 31 \\ \hline 19 \end{array}$$
11. 16 ;
$$\begin{array}{r} 39 \\ -\ 23 \\ \hline 16 \end{array}$$

12. 84 ;
$$\begin{array}{r} 42 \\ +\ 42 \\ \hline 84 \end{array}$$
13. 24 ;
$$\begin{array}{r} 31 \\ -\ 7 \\ \hline 24 \end{array}$$

14. 5 ;
$$\begin{array}{r} 23 \\ -\ 18 \\ \hline 5 \end{array}$$

15. Chocolate bar ;
$$\begin{array}{r} 24 \\ +\ 18 \\ \hline 42 \end{array}$$

16. 54 ; 81   17. 18¢ ; 36¢ ; 54¢
18. 24¢ ; 48¢ ; 72¢ 19. 27 + 18 = 45 ; 45
20. 18 + 24 = 42 ; 42 21. 50 – 27 = 23 ; 23
22. 50 – 24 = 26 ; 26
23.

24. 35 – 27 = 8 ; 8
25.

26. 27 + 36 = 63 ; 63
27.

28. 18 + 48 = 66 ; 66
29.

10 Measurement

1. 4   2. 5
3. 3   4. 6
5. D ; B ; A ; C   6. 2
7. 3   8. A ; B ; C
9.   10. One o'clock

11.

12. After   13. Early
14. 5 ; 4   15. 6 ; 2
16. 20   17. 12

11 Pictographs

1. B   2. C   3. B
4. A   5. A   6. C
7. B   8. Paula   9. Anita
10. Britt   11. 11   12. 10
13. 4   14. 3   15. 2
16. 21   17. 7   18. No

ISBN: 978-1-897164-11-2

19.

20. 8   21. 6
22. 13   23. 8
24. 13
25.

26.

27. 3   28. 21
29. 9

12 Probability

1. A   2. A   3. B
4. A   5. A   6. B
7. A   8. B   9. C
10. B
11a. C   b. B   c. A

Final Review

1. 26   2. 22
3. 26 + 22 = 48 ; 48   26
                         + 22
                         ——
                          48
4. 26 − 22 = 4 ; 4   26
                         − 22
                         ——
                           4
5. 26 + 5 = 31 ; 31   26
                         + 5
                         ——
                          31
6. 22 − 7 = 15 ; 15   22
                         − 7
                         ——
                          15
7. 7   8. 8
9. 56   10. 32
11. 9   12. Two o'clock
13. Half-past three
14. B   15. A
16. A   17. C
18. [1]   19. [2]
20. [1]

21.

22.

23. 6   24. 5
25. 2   26. 4
27. 32 + 16 + 9 = 57 ; 57
28. 14 + 28 + 13 = 55 ; 55
29. 32 − 14 = 18 ; 18
30. 28 − 16 = 12 ; 12
31. 9 + 13 = 22 ; 22
32. 16 + 28 = 44 ; 44
33. 32 − 13 = 19 ; 19

ISBN: 978-1-897164-11-2

ISBN: 978-1-897164-11-2